Who Speaks For The Child

The Child
The Problems of Proxy Consent

THE HASTINGS CENTER SERIES IN ETHICS

A Continuation Order Plan is available for this series. A continuation order will bring delivery of each new volume immediately upon publication. Volumes are billed only upon actual shipment. For further information please contact the publisher.

Who Speaks For The Child
The Problems of Proxy Consent

Edited by

WILLARD GAYLIN

The Hastings Center
Institute of Society, Ethics and the Life Sciences
Hastings-on-Hudson, New York

and

RUTH MACKLIN

Albert Einstein College of Medicine
Bronx, New York

PLENUM PRESS • NEW YORK AND LONDON

ISBN 0-306-40860-0

© 1982 The Hastings Center
Institute of Society, Ethics and the Life Sciences
360 Broadway
Hastings-on-Hudson, New York 10706

Plenum Press is a
Division of Plenum Publishing Corporation
233 Spring Street, New York, N.Y. 10013

Contributors

PETER G. BROWN is the founder and Director of the Center for Philosophy and Public Policy. His publications include *Human Rights and U.S. Foreign Policy* (Lexington Mass.: Lexington Books, 1979), co-edited with Douglas MacLean; *Food Policy: The Responsibility of the United States in the Life and Death Choices* (New York: The Free Press, 1977), co-edited with Henry Shue; "Ethics and Policy Research," *Policy Analysis* 2:2 (Spring, 1976); and "Assessing Officials: The Methods" in *Public Duties: The Moral Obligations of Government Officials,* edited by Joel Fleishman and Mark Moore (Cambridge: Harvard University Press, in press). He is also the editor of the Rowman & Littlefield Series, Maryland Studies in Public Philosophy.

ALEXANDER MORGAN CAPRON is Professor of Law and Professor of Human Genetics at the University of Pennsylvania. After graduating from Swarthmore College and Yale Law School, where he served as Note and Comment Editor of the *Yale Law Journal,* Professor Capron clerked for Chief Judge David L. Bazelon of the U.S. Court of Appeals for the District of Columbia. He is a Fellow and former member of the Board of the Institute of Society,

Ethics and the Life Sciences, and a member of the Institute of Medicine. Professor Capron's principal teaching and research interests are torts, the professions, and the social and legal aspects of medicine and science. He now lives in Washington, with his wife and six-year-old son, while on leave as the Executive Director of the President's Commission for the Study of Ethical Problems in Medicine and Biomedical and Behavioral Research.

GERALD DWORKIN is Professor of Philosophy at the University of Illinois, Chicago. His main interests are in moral, political and legal philosophy. He is an Associate Editor of *Ethics* and was Luce Senior Visiting Scholar at The Hastings Center for 1980–1981.

WILLARD GAYLIN, M.D. (Western Reserve University, 1951; Columbia Psychoanalytic School) is Clinical Professor of Psychiatry at Columbia University College of Physicians and Surgeons; co-founder and President since its inception of The Hastings Center (Institute of Society, Ethics and the Life Sciences) and co-director of its Behavioral Studies Research Group. He is author/editor of nine books, among the most recent: *Caring* (New York: Knopf, 1976); *Doing Good: The Limits of Benevolence*, with I. Glasser, S. Marcus, and D. Rothman (New York: Pantheon, 1978); *Feelings: Our Vital Signs* (New York: Harper & Row, 1979, and Ballantine, paperback, 1980); and *Mental Retardation and Sterilization: A Problem of Competency and Paternalism*, co-edited with R. Macklin, (New York: Plenum Press, 1981). He has published more than fifty articles in technical and professional journals as well as more general magazines.

JOSEPH GOLDSTEIN is Sterling Professor of Law at the Yale University Law School and Child Study Center. A political scientist, lawyer, and psychoanalyst, he is the author of many books, including *The Government of a British Trade*

Union, (New York: The Free Press, 1953); *The Family and the Law* (with Jay Katz) (New York: The Free Press, 1965); *Beyond the Best Interests of the Child* (both with Anna Freud and Albert J. Solnit) (New York: The Free Press, 1980). He holds degrees from Dartmouth College, The London School of Economics, and Yale Law School, and is a graduate (career research) of The Western New England Psychoanalytic Institute.

RUTH MACKLIN, Ph.D., is in the Department of Community Health at Albert Einstein College of Medicine. At the time the project from which this book emerged was carried out, Macklin was co-director, with Willard Gaylin, of the Behavioral Studies Research Group at The Hastings Center. She has contributed articles to professional journals in philosophy, law, psychiatry, and medical ethics. She is one of the editors of *Moral Problems in Medicine* (Englewood Cliffs, N.J.: Prentice-Hall, 1976), a widely used text in medical ethics, and co-editor, with Willard Gaylin, of *Mental Retardation and Sterilization: A Problem of Competency and Paternalism* (New York: Plenum Press, 1981). Her book, *Man, Mind, and Morality: The Ethics of Behavior Control,* was published by Prentice-Hall in 1982.

MARGARET O'BRIEN STEINFELS is a writer, editor, and social historian who is particularly interested in the history of the family and child-rearing practices and contemporary policy problems in those areas. She is the author of *Who's Minding the Children: The History and Politics of Day Care in America* (New York: Simon & Schuster, 1973), as well as many articles on foster care, adoption, newborn care, adolescent pregnancies, and child care. She served as editor of the *Hastings Center Report* (1976–1980), was a social science editor at Basic Books (1980–1981), and is now business manager at *Christianity and Crisis.*

Preface

This book is the product of a two-year project[1] conducted by
The Hastings Center. The Behavioral Studies Research
Group—an ongoing, interdisciplinary working group composed of philosophers, psychiatrists, psychologists, social scientists and lawyers—met several times over the course of the
two years with special consultants with expertise in the fields
of autonomy, consent, and the special notion of the child-
parent relationship. At those meetings participants gave informal presentations, which were followed by group discussion, which then led to final presentations incorporating the
criticisms and suggestions from the many disciplines. This
volume is the result of these deliberations.

The design and methodology of this project are characteristic of the research conducted at The Hastings Center,

[1]The project, entitled "Ethical Implications of Behavior Control," was supported by the EVIST Program of the National Science Foundation under
Grant No. OSS74-12745, and by the National Endowment for the Human-
ities. Any opinions, findings, conclusions, or recommendations expressed
herein are those of the authors and do not necessarily reflect the views of
the funding agencies.

which concerns itself with ethical and policy problems arising out of the field of medical technology and new developments in the social sciences.

WILLARD GAYLIN
RUTH MACKLIN

Contents

III   THE VALUES AT STAKE

Part I

The Issues

Who Speaks for the Child?

WILLARD GAYLIN

In 1975, profound and complicated moral and philosophical issues, which had been the private agony of physicians, philosophers, and lawyers, and which had been slowly and steadily infiltrating the public conscience and the public media, became, finally, headline news. It was the plight of Karen Ann Quinlan, a severely brain-damaged, deteriorating young girl, being maintained (or at least believed to be so at the time)[1] by artificial life-supporting mechanisms that captured the public's attention.

[1]Among the many paradoxes and ironies of the case was that after the decision was made to remove the artificial life-supporting systems and to permit Karen Ann Quinlan to die, the patient stubbornly refused to do so, proving the system an unnecessary artifact and the case, indeed, moot.

WILLARD GAYLIN • The Hastings Center, Hastings-on-Hudson, New York 10706.

It was not that Karen Ann Quinlan's medical situation was unique—such issues had been faced over and over again in a multitude of hospitals. Anonymous physicians have traditionally made such life-and-death decisions under the protection and privacy of their professional role—with or without the consultation of the grieving parents. What made this case unique was that the Quinlans decided to thrust the issue into the public sphere by demanding legal authority to do what they wished to do.

The case received an astounding amount of attention, and most of it for the wrong reasons. It deserves even more attention—for the right ones. Countless articles filled the daily papers about the definition of death—which was, of course, not at issue at all. By no existing definition was Karen Quinlan dead. What was at issue was an interrelated set of questions about authority and autonomy: the rights of the individual, or the family, versus the power of the state; the nature of decision making and the values of society, all of which may be joined together under the confusing and inadequate heading "proxy consent." It is to this issue of proxy consent that this book is addressed, an issue many of us believe to be one of a half dozen most crucial moral problems emerging from the biological revolution.

In almost all moral and legal codes certain rights are vested absolutely in the autonomous human being. A person, simply by nature of being a person, is granted a range of privileges and immunities. These rights may be abridged at times, as, for example, when the rights of the individual jeopardize the security of the group, or when the rights of one individual conflict with the rights of another. But even when infringing on these rights, we recognize them as such; they are the privileges of personhood existing beyond property or thing.

The right of the competent adult to accept or refuse medical treatment is a fundamental one. In the words of Justice Schroeder, "Anglo-American law starts with the premise of thoroughgoing self-determination. It follows that each man is considered to be the master of his own body and may, if he be of sound mind, expressly prohibit the performance of life-saving surgery or other medical treatment."[2]

But even if we accept the absolute commitment to autonomy in this area, the problem is complicated by the fact that precisely at the point when a decision is most crucial, the individual is likely to be incapable of speaking for himself. He may vigorously refuse treatment to his last moments of communication, but once he slips into unconsciousness his decision-making privileges pass from his control.

When autonomous rights cannot be claimed by the individual—whether because he is in a state of unconsciousness, or because competence has not yet fully developed, as in a child, or because competence is in question because of mental retardation or mental illness—we have tended to delegate this power to the family of the individual. The authority vested in the "next of kin" is testament to the high value our society places on the structure of the family. Occasionally, however, the value we place on the family is brought into conflict with other highly valued things. Our society places a high value on human life, and we tend to be repelled by the thought of granting *any* third party, even a parent, the power of life and death.

When we deal with such cases—the child, the mental patient, the comatose—these are no clear legal guidelines, except at the most extreme limits. Where children are concerned, the courts have been more than ready to protect what has been seen as the transcendent right to life. When parents have attempted to refuse lifesaving measures, the courts have intruded into traditional family rights by naming a guardian. It is irrelevant that the parents may be Jehovah's Witnesses, who by the logic of their convictions *should* willingly sacrifice an ephemeral and transient existence on earth for the "eternal preservation of the soul." Society has decided that the refusal is unreasonable.

[2]Justice Schroeder, Nathanson v. Kline 186 Kan. 350 P. 2d 1093 (1960).

In this context, Robert Veatch's designations "reasonable" and "unreasonable" are probably more appropriate terms than that other test of treatment—ordinary and extraordinary. A respirator may be reasonable for a polio victim but unreasonable for someone in irreversible coma. An artificial portable heart transplant may become a reasonable procedure for a healthy young person but unreasonable for a senile patient with pains of terminal cancer. It will, in either case, *at first*, always be an extraordinary procedure even when most reasonable. The test of reasonability can only be made within a matrix of concerns that include consideration of the rights of the individual, the quality of life that will be sustained, and the values of both the individual and the society that define that quality.

The case of the comatose patient, although a dramatic example that forces the issue into public awareness, is only one example—and surely not the most important—of proxy consent. Before beginning to analyze the various components of this complex problem, it is important to realize the scope of the problem and to visualize the areas in which proxy consent will occur as a central issue.

We have already listed the first category—that group of people permanently comatose and incapable of expressing their wishes, and who have thereby irrevocably lost all capacity to regulate or direct their lives. The questions about the rightness of the decisions, the identity of the decision maker, and the quality of controls are all modified by the fact of a totally helpless and uncommunicative individual *who will remain so for the rest of his life*. But there is a spectrum of cases extending on from this extreme condition.

Closely related physically to this condition, but at the opposite end of the spectrum in a moral and legal sense, is the individual who is in a *temporary* state of unconsciousness. Although he, too, is totally excluded from the decision-making processes of his life, the reversibility dramatically alters our perception. "Temporary," a vague and open-ended concept, introduces a broad spectrum of problems conditional to the *time* of limitation. The problem will be resolved differently in a state that lasts one hour and in one that lasts a week, or one that is open-ended into the years. But even the time of incapacity will have a varying significance, depending on the urgency and dangerousness of the condition, and the nature and costs (in all senses of that word) of the treatment.

If the time factor significantly alters our moral judgments about appropriate decision making, so, too, does the degree of incapacitation. Here, too, there is a continuum of small, relatively insignificant steps from autonomy to parentalism, from freedom to control. The problem becomes more treacherous, and the solutions more speculative, as the degree of impairment becomes progressively less.

Obviously, there are people who are not unconscious but whom we would not want to have managing their affairs. One class of individuals who have traditionally been labeled incompetent, even though the levels of consciousness and of communication are intact, are those whose judgment is seen as insufficient—where we calculate that to allow them to represent themselves would not serve their own best interests. This classification would include the mentally retarded child, the mentally retarded adult, the senile and senescent, the organically psychotic and the functionally psychotic. Again, it must be remembered that each condition, in its difference from the other, dictates different standards of evaluation that may in turn demand different solutions to serve the same ends. This brier patch of variables, uncertainties, undefinable distinctions, contradictions of rights, and competitions of values is where we must go to formulate our moral solutions.

The most intriguing and the most difficult of slippery slopes in which we will have to take a stand will involve the largest population for whom we traditionally assign proxies—healthy "children." Here we are dealing with a population that is not impaired, but instead is in a transient phase of normal development awaiting only the passing of time for the inheritance of their legal (if not actual) maturity. It is with this group that we anticipate the most difficulty. When is a child a child? And when ought the child be a child? The case law, in handling these questions in a willy-nilly fashion, has brought itself to a point of humiliation in more than one state. For example, in New York State, a seventeen-year-old has no right to donate a sample of her urine for experimental purposes without her parents' consent, but a child has a perfect right to contract for an abortion at age eleven without parental consent. It would seem, then, that in New York State at least, the capacity to become pregnant defines legal maturity. The capacity to impregnate—in a classic of sexism—is not so honored. But the law, even for the pregnant girl, seems to be offering a unilateral autonomy. She is "free" to elect to have an abortion, independent of her parents' concerns—but it has not been established that she is legally free to bear the child against her parents' wishes.

The problem of proxy consent, therefore, not only involves deciding who speaks for the helpless, but the added burden of defining who *is* helpless, or more precisely, who is incompetent to decide. To understand fully the nature of the problem, it will be best to examine the components on which the issues are to be constructed. The proxy consent problem rests on a number of principles, a number of concepts, without which it has no real validity.

THE CONCEPT OF AUTONOMY

Human beings are sui generis. Man represents an incredible gap in "the great chain of life," a discontinuity that is not measurable in the traditional incremental changes from the lower species of animals to the highest. We are as unlike the ordinary creatures of the earth as God, if he exists, must be unlike us. We are a splendid and peculiar discontinuity.

Among the many ways in which we qualitatively and quantitatively differ from our inferior relatives is the degree in which we are freed from a fixed instinctual development. I am not arguing total freedom—it would be a strange ar-

gument coming from someone raised in a psychological tradition rooted in determinism—but there is no question that
man's "intelligence" is the complement to his freedom from
instinctual fix. We rarely talk about biological determinism in
Homo sapiens—we are more likely to refer to genetic "direc-
tive" as though God or nature, while dictating to other species, only dares advise or direct man. The "incredible intelligence" demonstrated by the beaver in building his dam or
the spider his web is, of course, precisely the opposite of
intelligence. It is as fixed and determined as the response of
a plant to light, and can as easily be fooled. The ingeniousness
of these instinctive designs may appear as "brilliant" solutions
to difficult environmental problems, but instincts involve no
thinking—let alone good thinking. The unthinking quality is
reflected in the incapacity to adjust to even trivial change. In
the vast majority of their activities the lower creatures have
no choice and therefore no intelligence, and are therefore
nonautonomous.

To the degree that man is seen to have choice, he is seen
as being autonomous. Obviously, without real choice the concept of consent, and therefore proxy consent, is meaningless.
We are assumed to have a capacity for decision making.

> Human beings are commonly spoken of as autonomous crea-
> tures. We have suggested that their autonomy consists in their
> ability to choose whether to act or refrain and to choose whether
> to think in a certain way insofar as thinking is acting; in their
> freedom from obligation within certain spheres of life; and in
> their moral individuality.[3]

To put it another way, "autonomy may be conceived as the
contradictory of control."[4]

A new challenge to the concept of autonomy has come
from the field of psychoanalysis. Sigmund Freud in his evo-
lution of the unconscious has told the modern intellectual

---

[3]R. S. Downie and Elizabeth Telfer, "Autonomy," *Philosophy* 46 (1971): 301.
[4]Felix Oppenheim, *Dimensions of Freedom* (New York: St. Martin's Press, 1961),
p. 110.

community that man is less rational than he would like to consider himself and that, indeed, his current behavior is not free. It is more often dictated by unconscious emotions than by rational choice. Beyond that, Freud has raised questions about the very nature of rational choice. In seeing behavior in a developmental context; seeing it in a dynamic form, that is, each piece of behavior is a result of forces and counter-forces; and in seeing behavior as motivated, that is, theologically directed toward the future and causally related to the past, he has raised certain obstacles to the concept of free choice and autonomy. Indeed, in a research meeting here at the Center it was surprising to find unanimity among five members of a research group (always a rare phenomenon) in approving a definition of autonomy as the *"feeling"* of freedom rather than the fact of it. This group, at least, was prepared to allow autonomy to be an illusional system. Less psychoanalytically oriented groups are not. Even within the psychoanalytic community there has been great distress over the freedom–determinism problem. The philosopher's comfort in the distinction between necessary and sufficient causes has never sufficiently impressed the psychoanalyst. Generally, the psychoanalyst has operated under a peculiar compromise: although he personally believes in autonomy, free will, and the free act, it is difficult to incorporate this belief into psychoanalytic theory. Often, he accepts the illusion of free choice as an essential ingredient and an important determinant in future behavior. Robert Knight, summarizing the argument of the psychoanalytic community, allows that what the healthy person possesses is

> the subjective sense of complete freedom of choice. . . . This subjective experience, however, is subjective in a special sense, not in the one which equates "subjective" with "spurious." The behavior of a well-integrated civilized person can be objectively assessed as "free." Observers see that such a person makes egosyntonic choices, that his motives are "good," and that he is able to carry out what he wills to do.[5]

---

[5]Robert Knight, "Determinism, Freedom, and Psychotherapy," *Psychiatry* 9 (1946): 251ff.

Knight then goes on to acknowledge that there are experiences of freedom that are illusions and that are subjective and in that sense, spurious. He uses as examples "the sense of freedom in children or immature adults which occurs with the removal of external pressure,"[6] or "the release from inner checks and restraints that occurs in mania [and] likewise conveys a sense of complete freedom."[7] He then goes on to define complete freedom:

> The genuine freedom which is a mark of mental health in emotional maturity is best expressed by the following quotation, whose authorship I do not know: "That man is free who is conscious of being the author of the law that he obeys." This definition includes both the sense of freedom and the sense of inner compulsion which we have designated as inseparable subjective feelings in matters of real importance in life. It also includes the concept of integration of the personality, that is, the individual's energies and impulses are subject to conscious control but are capable of satisfying discharge according to standards which the ego accepts. . . .[8]

Because it was the consensus of our group that the concept of autonomy is not essential to the issue of proxy consent, a more detailed discussion of autonomy was not included in this book. Nevertheless (to paraphrase Gerald Dworkin's argument on why consent is an important notion in proxy consent), I would say that the concept of autonomy is an essential—if undiscussed—notion for our purpose. Proxy consent only arises when one is dealing with an autonomous creature. It is the basic assumption on which the concept of consent must be built.

AUTONOMOUS RIGHTS

Autonomous rights refer to the acknowledged sense that "every human being of adult years and sound mind has

[6]Ibid.
[7]Ibid.
[8]Ibid.

a right to determine what shall be done with his own body."[9]

The term "autonomous rights" also was disturbing to many of our group. It is, indeed, troublesome. Some saw it as redundant; some saw it as a nonsequitur. "What is a non-autonomous right?" one of our group asked; "Are you not simply talking about self-determination?" another asked, and if so, "Why not use the simpler terminology?"

I agree with both criticisms—yet I stubbornly insist on retaining the term because of its importance in the current language of rights, and in the current vogue for using that language to define the moral contract between the individual and the social institutions.

What we really mean when we talk of autonomous rights is not the right *to* something, but the right to be free from something.

> The makers of the Constitution sought to protect Americans in their beliefs, their emotions, and their sensations. They conferred, as against the Government, the right to be let alone—the most comprehensive of rights and the right most valued by civilized men.[10]

There are certain rights vested in us as acknowledgment of our status as autonomous human beings, and in accordance with the principles of a democratic society that recognizes self-determination as a legitimate entity in that society.

The principle of autonomous rights implies the right to decide for ourselves, to be at least in part the authors of our future. It stakes out certain areas in which it says the state may not intrude—unless it can prove an overwhelming interest. Autonomous rights, therefore, define an area in which a general agreement, political in nature, has been established. In this area, at least, an individual may act as an arbitrary decision maker. It is my decision what I shall wear, how I

---

[9]Schloendorf v. Society of the New York Hospital, 211 NY 125 129, 105 NE 92, 93 (1914).
[10]Brandeis dissent in Olmstead v. United States.

shall cut my hair, what I shall eat, whom I shall marry, whether I shall marry, and so on.

The borders of this area are worthy of attention. It is my right to decide what I shall wear, unless I decide to wear nothing and to appear so in the public space. Then I may intrude on more basic rights accepted by society. Similarly, it is my right to raise my children as I will, provided I do so within the broad value system of our society.

In the same way that a right to vote, or a right to medical care, or a right to freedom of assembly means that the state must establish such conditions that I am granted the *opportunity* to exercise those rights, there are certain areas in which I have a right to nonintrusion, to self-determination, and the state must agree not to interfere (always excepting when its interests are threatened). It is this sphere that has been designated the area of autonomous rights.

THE CONCEPT OF CONSENT

Consent is another concept closely linked to (1) the fact that one is an autonomous creature, and (2) the state's acknowledgment of our privilege to behave autonomously in certain areas. If you have rights over yourself, your body, your property, and your future, those who would engage in alterations or intrusions in those areas must have your permission, that is, your consent. It is these first three linked concepts that Dworkin deals with in his chapter.

The problem of consent can be approached in terms of justification for consent but also in terms of validation. Dworkin deals essentially with historical and philosophical justifications. He does not, however, take up the equally important question of how one knows *when* consent has been given. That is a whole area covered in the law under the general heading "voluntariness," and it is a crucial question that must reluctantly be sidestepped in this particular book. Volumes have been written, and volumes remain to be written, on the question of a voluntary action. What is voluntary is obviously tied to how one defines freedom and intention. For this volume we will assume that there must be some criteria by which consent will be determined—without articulating the criteria ourselves.

Briefly, however, one must acknowledge that for something to be consented to, it must fulfill minimal standards. It must be *freely* consented to, that is, not coerced. The coercion issue is another issue that, ideally, might be considered here but, alas, cannot. In addition to being free from coercion, to be truly voluntary would at least require that consent also be free from deception and manipulation. We do not ascribe voluntariness to uninformed consent if the individual was deceived or, indeed, in certain cases simply denied knowledge of the implications of the actions to which he was consenting.

All of these limitations on the voluntary nature of consent are by implication crucial to the problems with which we are dealing, but are not central to them. Since we are not dealing with direct consent of an individual, but the delegation of that to someone else, the issues of his voluntariness are bypassed. That there may be questions about the voluntariness of the consenting surrogate or proxy is another matter. Surely the proxy, particularly in the example to which we are attending (the parent in relationship to his own child), can be in an extraordinarily sensitive position and vulnerable to the same kinds of coercive and manipulative maneuvers as if he were consenting to his own procedure.

COMPETENCE

If autonomy is the cornerstone on which the structure of proxy consent is built, competence is the framework. If we acknowledge the principle of autonomy and the rights to exercise one's judgment in prescribed areas free of societal interference, what is still essential for the proper exercising of these rights is the adjudged *competence* to do so. This issue has been focal in the problem with children. Obviously, a normal child of a certain age can tell his wishes; but is he "competent" to know what is in his best interests? Is he trustworthy; is he capable of being vested with power over his own future?

The law, it seems to me, has always been most sensitive to the needs of the individual where money is concerned. Here the minor is clearly protected against abuse or exploitation, including self-abuse. He may be forbidden to enter certain contracts, and he may not control his fortune or his estates. The obvious purpose is to protect the child from damaging the adult he is eventually to become.

But in all areas it is incredible how often children are completely foreclosed from life-binding decisions—even when such decisions might be easily deferred until the age of their competence. The law—as it must and ought—in most areas defines competence in a totally arbitrary way, that is, according to a fixed age. It is easy to deride such arbitrariness, but in the issues that arise in bioethics we have all long learned that arbitrary lines *must* be drawn, along a continuum. At any point at which one draws the line there will be positions just proximal to the line, so close and so indistinguishable that one will be subject to ridicule. The intelligent man has a choice of sitting back and never doing anything, or risking the cheap shots of the uninformed.

In recent years we have begun to recognize the relevant relationship between the ascribing of competence and the nature of the decision that is to be made. For example, in the case of the mentally ill we recognize that they may be incompetent to handle certain complex financial decisions yet still competent to decide certain issues of lifestyle. Sometimes we become ridiculous because of the disordered and happenstance way in which case law will order these definitions. What is emerging, however, is a progressive concept of limited and variable competence in which we ascribe autonomous rights in certain areas at certain ages while restricting such rights in others. Certainly one of the purposes in preparing this research, and presenting it in this form, is to begin the process of line drawing, in order to establish some principles of variable competence on which to build a system. It was our feeling that until someone bit the bullet and made a stand, regardless of how arbitrary, the issue would be lost in theoretical complexities. By defining our position, we allow the next group to dismiss what is superficial in our presentation, and to hone first crude definitions into a more sophisticated product of their own.

SURROGATION OF AUTHORITY VERSUS FAMILY AUTONOMY

However difficult, there will be conditions where we will decide that someone is *not* competent to exercise his rights of self-determination. Similarly, we will inevitably decide that there is some age and some condition when even the reasonable child ought not be invested with the authority he will eventually acquire with age. We then are faced with the question of how and where to delegate that authority. To whom do we surrogate the responsibility? Who is to represent the interests of the child? Who is to be the decision maker? Traditionally, we have turned to the family and family members. We have selected the "next of kin." There has been a natural assumption that the family is the safest repository for these rights, that there is a primary congruence of interests between parent and child. It is obvious that here, too, there are difficulties. A different relationship (and therefore different correlation of interests) exists between a mother and a healthy two-year-old child, a mother and a mentally retarded child who has been institutionalized all his life, a brother and a comatose man, or a son-in-law and heir and a wealthy, senile eighty-year-old woman. Our task is easier in the context of this book, because we have used the paradigm of the healthy child and parent. It should be kept in mind, however, that when we extend our arguments beyond this category into the others, the easy assumption of identity of interests cannot necessarily be made.

Even, however, when dealing with parent and child one is aware of failures in the assumption of protective, paternalistic concern. One need only think of the battered child to recognize the limitations of trust, even in the parental relationship. Because of this awareness of limitation, because of the many cases where the family has failed the individual, there have been more and more arguments made by those who defend the "rights of the unborn," the "rights of the infant," the "rights of the mentally ill," or the "rights of the retarded"—arguments asking for some intervention and/or supervision of the family structure. Since no one can know the will of the unborn or infant (and often of the retarded or severely ill), all of these movements tend in actuality to be advocating some limiting factor to the assignment or delegation of proxy (i.e., the privileges of decision making) to the family. All of these rights spokesmen are asking that we restrict the hitherto almost complete dominion of the family, and redistribute some of its powers to agencies of the state. That, after all, was the fundamental issue in the Quinlan case.

In the end I expect that, with all its faults, we must be slow to abridge the power of the family. In a pluralistic society it is inevitable, and probably wise, that parents and guardians should continue to make choices for their offspring or charges. They are the child's primary teachers of values, and so it is fitting that as guardians of those values they should also be responsible for determining whether medical treatment, for example, is reasonable or not. We must continue to presume that parents are acting in the best interests of their children, until proved otherwise. We must ask ourselves who—*in general*—best represents the will of him who cannot speak for himself: the family, or the courts. We are free, however, to demand that parents use some criteria of "best interest" for their child, and that they exercise their awesome responsibility in the service of their wards.

In lifesaving matters, society has decided that the refusal of treatment is unreasonable. Despite such decisions, generally the family has been valued highly and granted great autonomy, as well as authority over the health of the child. The courts have permitted parents the privilege of refusing profound medical treatments, even when to do so severely handicaps the child.

There is the extraordinary case of a child severely deformed by harelip and cleft palate denied corrective surgery by a father who believed in "mental" healing. By the time the case reached the courts, the boy was nineteen years old and had converted to his father's position. The courts ruled that since he had suffered that long, the two years remaining until his majority did not warrant state intrusion. The reversals and dissents in this case show the particular agonies of the court with such delicately balanced (short of life-and-death) issues.[11] We usually deny the claims of family only when the claims are on life itself—although that is now changing.

The question of surrogation of authority involves the question of whether, in certain specific areas, the rights of the family ought to be abridged, and if so, how. Should the power be assigned to the courts to decide on a case-by-case basis, and thereby build a maze of precedents? Should it be assigned to the legislatures, so that the boundaries of parental authority can be established in law? To delegated ombudsmen? To a committee of moral judges? To a *pro bono publico* children's defense committee? The solutions are not easy to come by. But what remains is the recognition that the place of the family is as critical as the tensions between the individual and his society. It is a three-pronged dynamism.

The central historical role of the family should not be ignored, though to this point it has been. We attack the family with peril; what is to replace it? The dangers of a parentalistic state may be worse.

---

[11]*In re* Seiferth, 127 N.Y.S. 2d rev'd., 284 App. Div. 221, 137 N.Y.S. 2d 35 (1955).

In addition, attacking the authority of the family in one area may diminish its cohesive force in areas required by society. There are dangers, as well as safeguards, in attempting to legislate and litigate all moral decisions. The nature of the family as an institution in our society must be reevaluated and must be one factor in a complex set of variables that plague decision making in the area of proxy consent.

THE NATURE OF REPRESENTATION

Each alternative solution to the problem of who is the proxy will force another series of questions. Having decided who should represent the individual, we come to the thorny question of the nature of representation. What does it mean to represent someone? Too often here we have glibly assumed knowledge, but the classic argument persists on whether representation ought to be visualized in a Burkean sense of doing that which we assume best for the individual or in a Millean sense of doing that which we assume the individual would have done for himself had he had the opportunity. It is a critical moral decision that must be made. It may indeed be one of the distinguishing factors among the variable categories of incompetence.

One of the great values of studying competence in the limited context of the child is to begin to clarify the distinctions between two categories that have been prematurely lumped together. Surely, one distinction between the child and the senile adult, both of whom may have the identical incapacity of wisdom or judgment, is the knowledge that the adult is in a regressive state whereas the child is in a state of improvement.

In addition, there are obligations of a different nature, shaped by the different stages of life. To the old man we have a responsibility to the life that he has led, to what he was. That wasted creature, senile and unconscious though he is, is still the repository of the memories, achievements, and relationships of a lifetime. In the same way that the mortal remains of a human being are different from the decaying remnants of last night's dinner, the senile elderly are the shadow representatives of the virile people they once were. In honor of their past it may be just and wise to extend rights to them beyond our logical sense of their capacity to exercise them to their best interest. We must be stingy in abrogating their rights out of respect not for what they are capable of now doing, but for what they once were.

In contrast, with children the awareness of what they are to become may operate in both directions: we may deprive them of rights against their parents even at a time of rationality when we sense that deferral does them no harm, and with the assurance that they will enter an age when they can seize those rights themselves; or we may protect them from harmful decisions of the parents with the sure knowledge that only a temporary period is necessary before the child becomes an adult and can exercise his own options, weighing his own opinions as to the risk he is willing to entail for the benefit that would ensue. But in deciding when to intrude for the preservation of the child's potential autonomy, whose values do we use in rating risk or gain? Do we act parentalistically or interpretively (i.e., according to what is "good" for them by our standards, or by theirs)? The question has validity whether the surrogate is a judge or a father.

Some attention must be paid to the various forms of representation and to the moral defense of each. For my part, I have no problem with the issue; I am prepared to argue for a Millean approach with the aging as I am dogmatically Burkean with the child. But then again, I do not share with most of my colleagues the current disenchantment with paternalism.

PATERNALISM

I think it is fair to say that there has been in modern America a steady retreat from the concepts of paternalism habilitative model we have been able to abuse the prisoners without disabusing our conscience.

It is ironic to see the extension into medicine proper of this distrust of paternalism and indeed of the whole patient–doctor gestalt. Where once we excused the behavior of the patient (the sick role grants exculpability), we are now prepared to demand responsibilities in order to enhance independence. Thomas Szasz has indicated that, even in the delusional state induced by an overdose of drugs, he would hold a person to the responsibility of law. He would allow, beyond that, the destructive act to take place (suicide, homicide, what have you) rather than interfere in a preventive and paternalistic way. Those who defend the rights of the mentally retarded are willing—at least they now say—to allow culpability and increased risk to increase the autonomy of their charges. That they speak so paternalistically about their charges, with such authority and such assurance that they represent them is, of course, another story.

Ivan Illich would say that it is not only the myth of *mental* illness from which we must free ourselves, but the myth of *all* illness, and he has managed to convince a decent percentage of otherwise rational people that sickness is the product, rather than the occupation, of the medical profession. In a period in which there is a press for individual rights and a rising mistrust of authority in general, all benevolence is suspect and all morality is cast in the language of rights. But here we are not dealing with the mentally ill, the prisoner, the mentally retarded, the senile, or the unconscious; we are dealing with the child. The most rigid antipaternalists may want to restrict the definition of "child" to its extreme (under seven, five, two-and-a-half years). But inevitably we will end up with *some* population who are to be considered "children," and as such may be assumed to be childish. Here such parentalism is not only necessary, but desirable. To be a parent, one must obviously behave parentalistically. To be parental to a child does not imply the condescension or presumption that it does with the adult. The parent is an authentic instrument of parentalism with a minor child.

that once were traditionally respected and valued. Even w
there have been defenses of paternalism (e.g., T. L. B
champ, Joel Feinberg, Gerald Dworkin),[12] these have b
written as minority reports against the prevailing trend. 7
are countervailing in their tone, which by its implications
confirms the antipaternalistic movement. No better exam
of the antipaternalistic feeling of our time are available
those arising from the field of mental health. The entire
ical model and the expansion of the reach of medicine
been questioned in such areas as the treatment of the mer
ill, the protection of the mentally retarded, and the like
movement toward deinstitutionalization of the menta
and the retarded, and the attack on models of rehabili
in prison as well as in the institutions of health are evi
of disillusionment with the *results* of paternalism, if r
intentions.

It might be well at this point to define paternalism
Dworkin's definition seems as good as any that have pre
it. It is "the interference with a person's liberty of
justified by reasons referring exclusively to the welfare,
happiness, needs, interests or values of the person
coerced." Within the field of medicine, coercion has
had a respectability that it did not have in other place
one of the objections to the extension of the medical
into other areas is that the readiness to abandon on
authority, which may have been justified in a medical
will tend to be less justified in less benign areas. Th
surely the case in prisons where under the medical m
became more punitive than a frankly punitive mode
probably have been. In another context I have poir
that medicine is allowed to be "bitter"; inflicted pai
cruel if it is treatment instead of punishment. Unde

[12]As, for example, in Gerald Dworkin, "Paternalism," *The Monist* 5
1972): 65; T. L. Beauchamp, "Paternalism and Bio-Behavioral C
Contemporary Issues in Bioethics, ed. T. L. Beauchamp and LeR
(Encino, Calif.: Dickerson, 1978); or Joel Feinberg, *Doing and*
Essays in the Theory of Responsibility (Princeton: Princeton Unive
1970).

We may, at the same time, wish to examine whether there are not absolute judgments as to the quality of parental care and to list certain absolute limits that define whether the role of parent is being fulfilled. If that is not the case, certainly at the point of saving life or providing relief from extraordinary abuse, then we have the option of intervention. Here, the state must appropriate the parental authority. Here, the state must abrogate not just the rights of individual autonomy, but the domain of "family" autonomy.

INDIVIDUALISM

The dedication to individualism, which was so particularly characteristic of nineteenth-century America, was to achieve even further idealization in the twentieth century. Here we see the ripening of the concept of individualism, and perhaps with that ripening we are coming to grips with its limitations. For man is not, technically speaking, an individual creature; he is an obligate social animal. His social structure is a part of his biology, and as necessary a part of his functioning as the air and water and nutrients on which he is dependent for life. A distinguished biologist, Adolph Portmann, cautioned us, "We are a social animal not by election, but by nature." Because of our extraordinarily prolonged dependence period we could not even survive as a species or develop as a type were there not a social structure to support us, and when we are stripped, by accident or bad design of social institutions, of human contact in the early days of our existence, we will perish, or what is specifically human about us will be seriously damaged or destroyed. Although it would be extending my argument too far to say that Homo sapiens is a colonial animal, like coral, it is equally wrong to conceive of man as a true individual like an amoeba. He rests somewhere in between. We must recognize his dependence, even for his rights as an individual, on the social structure. We therefore cannot press too far for individual rights without ultimately, and ironically, destroying the individual. In the pursuit of individualism we must never forget the fact that there is no such thing as an individual human being outside the nexus of his social environment. As G. H. Meade put it, "human nature is something social through and through and always presupposes the truly social individual." Indeed, any psychological or philosophical treatment of human nature involves the assumption that the individual depends on an organized social community, and derives his human nature from the social interactions and relationships with that community as a whole, and with the other individual members of it. Therefore we must recognize the rights to limit our autonomy not just in terms of direct threat to the state, but beyond that to values and institutions that are essential to the development of the individual and individualism.

The obligation to live in groups renders the destruction of social living a most dangerous phenomenon. The unconscionable use of the words "law and order" as a euphemism for racism was a singular factor in making intellectuals recoil from a serious consideration of the importance of that issue. But law and order are both essential for group living, and group living is a requirement of our species if we are to sustain that specific blessed nature that defines our species. The degradation of the public space, therefore, is a profound and threatening problem in our society, and it may be that *true autonomy* will require a limit to individual rights in order to protect the milieu in which alone the concept "individual" has any psychological meaning. As I have stated before, the individual is only a euphemism, an attractive and artificial designation, a false definition necessary to facilitate the reasoning that illuminates the truth. Even were we to adopt the most individualistic of philosophies, were we to define justice in terms of the maximizing of autonomy in the Millean sense of absolute autonomy, up to a point of restriction of autonomy of the other, we would still have to recognize that the destruction of the public space may ultimately restrict *individual* freedom as much as other limitations that seem to pertain more directly and dramatically to autonomous rights.

If we accept the rights to limit autonomy for survival of the state, and we say that certain values are necessary to define the quality of state that is worthy of being saved, we may find that we must limit individualism for this broader moral purpose.

HIERARCHY OF VALUES

It is part of the problem of being a partisan that we tend to see all issues in terms of the deficiency we are trying to correct. If a four-legged chair is missing its left rear leg, we can argue that the entire stability of the chair depends on the presence or absence of that leg. Although literally true, that claim overvalues the leg and creates a false notion of reality. Were *that* leg present and any of the other three missing, their advocates could equally and incorrectly press the primary, essential importance of their supporting structure. The answer is that we must not overvalue that which is deficient in our society. It is no solution to the instability of the chair to replace the right rear leg by chopping off the left front leg.

Rights advocates can live with a pure conscience if they keep their focus narrow, but rights talk only becomes significant when we see a conflict of rights, both of which we respect. In the area of proxy consent we are faced with a hierarchy of conflicting values, the gratification of some of which is often only at the expense of others: the rights of the child versus the rights of the family; the right to privacy versus the right to safety; the right to autonomy versus the right to health. Obviously, the problems become compounded in a heterogeneous society like ours. We then have to moderate between the values *in* a society versus the values *of* society. Even if we value heterogeneity over homogeneity, minority rights will still have to be balanced against certain other moral priorities.

Certain principles, of course, may be respected even to the risk of societal survival and individual life; others are not.

We find, for example, that in war we permit ourselves the taking of innocent lives if it is necessary to preserve the state. We would not, on the other hand, sacrifice an innocent to save a particular group, even though mathematics might so indicate.

There is no issue that presents as anguished a conflict as that of proxy consent. If we examine those values that have a high priority in our present culture, certainly we would list life itself; the family; health (and here I am using it as at its most constrictive level); and somewhere down the line but certainly high on the list, certain aspects of autonomy, dignity, and privacy. The problems of proxy consent in terms of the child ask us to balance these respected rights against each other. There is no conclusion in any area that cannot lead to distress. There is no conclusion that is *worthy* of adopting that *will* not lead to distress. Any position in a complex area such as this one that does not produce anxiety is probably too simple to be argued, too unworthy to be held. Similarly, conclusions must always be tentative, of a time, and receptive to immediate modification and constant reexamination.

We offer here, therefore, only unhappy compromises and transient solutions.

CHAPTER 2

Competence

No Longer All or None

WILLARD GAYLIN

FROM ARBITRARY TO VARIABLE COMPETENCE

On the day before one's eighteenth birthday (twenty-first in some states), an individual under law traditionally existed as an essentially disenfranchised member of the state. He lived according to laws set by others, governed by leaders in whose selection he had no part, and with little or no control over his estates and fortune. One day later, that same individual was miraculously transformed. He was welcomed into the decision-making apparatus of his country. No longer would "they" decide his future; today he was a man!

We have accepted this arbitrariness of law, this miraculous transformation (in comparison with which the sluggish conversion of a tadpole into a frog loses all mystery) with an insouciance usually reserved for inevitable natural events.

WILLARD GAYLIN ● The Hastings Center, Hastings-on-Hudson, New York 10706.

The arbitrariness of "all or none" in the allocation of the right to vote, and particularly in the area of economic rights, was not only accepted, but accepted with gratitude. It was accepted with the full knowledge of its arbitrariness! It is patent that one eighteen-year-old differs from another. Nevertheless, we ignored these distinctions in levels of intelligence, wisdom, impulsiveness, maturity, emotional stability, and balance of selfishness and greed, or of conscience or public service—all those aspects that could distinguish one eighteen-year-old from another, all the considerations that might be "scientifically" established by individual determination of maturity. We ignored them for the convenience and the incorruptibility of the standard age—a specific time and a specific date.

What was balanced was the value, on the one hand, of a fixed definition for competence (eighteen years of age), with full awareness that in the "real" world there would be marked variability in true competence—against the greater accuracy of judging each individual, with the unwieldiness, subjectivity, and unlimited potential for corruptibility of such judgment. We all know when an individual is eighteen; we do not know when an individual is mature. It is for such reasons that lawyers generally are more comfortable with arbitrary (i.e., age) definitions completely independent of such considerations and measurements that might be available to test "actual" competence. Increasingly, however, the insistence on a fixed age of competence is being undermined. Not just because case law is operating on an ad hoc basis to destroy that position, but also because the conditions of the new technology (e.g., safe abortion techniques) and the new decisions they require, and the temper of the times militate against it.

To the argument that one cannot determine maturity, the answer was presented that, to an extent, we always automatically had. The decision to use eighteen years instead of eighteen months was, after all, not an arbitrary one. There was the implicit recognition that the eighteen-year-old possessed attributes and capacities not yet developed in the eigh-

teen-month-old. There is obviously an easy distinction between an eighteen-year-old and an eighteen-month-old.
There are, as well, distinctions between an eighteen-year-old
and a fourteen-year-old, but here the distinguishing factors
are much less evident.

However, even if one concurs that an arbitrary age determinant might in the long run be more secure from abuse,
or more "just," the current pressures from society at large,
particularly in the areas of medical research and treatment,
are demanding a variability in our assignment of autonomous
rights and forcing a concept of variable competence.

Some of the reasons that were suggested in the first chapter are worth reexamining. We live in a society that has ele-
vated individual rights beyond any example, with the possible
exception of our own country in the late nineteenth century.
We are emotionally committed to autonomy, and we assume
the state somehow survives despite our emphasis on liberty
and the rights of individual decision making. This concern
for the individual (as against the state) has carried us to the
protection of individuals' autonomy even when we recognize
the limitations of the self-serving nature of the decision.

Currently we are going beyond even that; we are raising
the individual and his rights to a higher position of power in
relationship to other institutions of social life that traditionally
had been perceived as benevolent, and therefore less threatening to autonomy than the state. The power of the individual
in relationship to the caring professions—and the rights of
self-determination in medical treatment—has certainly been
extended. In addition, we are now questioning the power of
the individual within (and against) the family, even when the
individual is *legally* still a child.

Concern about the disenfranchised and the disadvan-
taged in our country has led to an increase in the casting of
moral arguments in terms of the language of rights. Many
moral issues, particularly those of social justice, have been
advanced by the arguments of individual rights. On the other
hand, many issues resist this approach; we are only just be-

ginning to see a return to respectability of the concept of "responsibility." Having won certain battles in our courts now, such as the right to abortion, we see how limited the legal definition of the right is when not reinforced by other forms of moral argument. To read Edmund Burke in his essays on "The Relationship of the British Government to the American Colonies" and "The Principle of Taxation" is to anticipate some of the problems we are currently facing. Burke begs Parliament to forget the argument of rights and to think in terms of responsibility, decency, and relationship.

But responsibility, obligation, and duty imply to too many (unfortunately) a paternalism that has been in disrepute in our modern, liberal time. No better spokesman for this distress exists than that quintessential liberal humanist, Lionel Trilling. "Some paradox of our nature leads us," he wrote, "when once we have made our fellow man the object of our enlightened interest, to go on to make him the object of our pity, then of our wisdom, ultimately of our coercion."[1]

This belief in the ultimate corruptibility of power—even when in the hands of the benevolent institutions of our society—has led to such extreme arguments as Thomas Szasz's defense of the rights of suicide for even an individual who is temporarily delusional because of toxicity; or pressing the rights of the mentally retarded even to the point of permitting physical parenthood when actual childrearing is impossible.

It is to prevent the corruption of benevolence, "the most ironic and tragic that man knows,"[2] as Trilling put it, that has led us to mistrust all paternalism and demand its exclusion from our social system.

But there is one place where paternalism cannot be abandoned, and that is in the relationship of parent to child. Here

---

[1]Lionel Trilling, *The Liberal Imagination: Essays on Literature and Society* (Garden City, N.Y.: Doubleday Anchor Books), p. 215.
[2]Ibid.

an abandonment of parental authority would be an act of immorality, as well as a failure in nurturing. The good parent does not just nurture to a point of maturation: he is expected to inhibit self-destructive impulses; he is expected to substitute his superior judgment for the short vision of the child; he is expected to use education, persuasion, seduction, and even force and coercion when necessary in the service of producing a healthy and independent adult.

The mistrust of paternalism has not, however, stopped at the borders of the family. As a result, the expanding claims of individual rights are now in conflict with two other ideals that have also traditionally been highly valued: one is the principle of parental authority, that is, the acceptance of paternalism at least within the family; the second, the concept of family autonomy, that is, that just as there are certain rights vested in the individual (as against the state), there have been traditional powers vested in the family that have been deemed independent of state interest. Obviously, at its limits—as in enforced blood transfusions for Jehovah's Witnesses' children—we have consistently been prepared to invade family autonomy. But in the very nature of the invasion and in the use of the courts to sanction it, it has been implicitly recognized that, for the most part, the decision-making apparatus must abide with the family. Only in *extremis* do we intrude. Now, however, we are intruding more and more as we expand our concepts of rights of self-determination even for those of limited competence. One thinks of the right of the twelve-year-old girl to an abortion without the knowledge or consent of her parents.

The problem then remains to define some of the conditions that limit competence; and to demarcate some of the border areas where those limitations may not be so great as had once been thought, and where we may begin to allow the individual of limited competence a role in the decision-making process concerning important elements of his life and future.

LIMITING CONDITIONS TO COMPETENCE

"Competent," at its most basic level, means "capable." "Competence" as used in this chapter, however, refers to the legal acknowledgment by the state of one's capability, by the granting of autonomous rights. First, it might help to examine conditions that limit "actual" competence. We shall examine the conditions that limit our capability to take charge of our life—to make the decisions that are normally considered our decisions to make. The limiting conditions may be divided into the following categories: (a) limits of consciousness; (b) limits of intelligence; (c) limits of rationality; (d) limits of perception; (e) limits of experience; and (f) limits of age.

Limits of Consciousness

As with most questions that relate to mental functioning, the normal limits of consciousness occur along a spectrum from the extremes. One obvious extreme, and in that sense perhaps the easiest case, is the unconscious patient, who is obviously not competent to exercise his right to self-determination. The fact that he is an intact perceptual being—only in a transient state of incapacity—is beside the point. During the state of unconsciousness there is absolutely no way for him to communicate what his desires might be, and he is thus totally incompetent. The unconscious patient, therefore, represents one extreme; the opposite is presumably some as yet unexemplified perfectly rational, mature, independent adult with sound mind and sound body. Even at the extreme of unconsciousness, however, there are limiting conditions that ought to alter our attitudes.

The rules for usurping a person's autonomous rights will vary depending on the length of time we anticipate he will remain unconscious. But even a transient state of unconsciousness may still demand the usurpation of the right to decision making if the individual faces imminent death or serious, permanent damage.

With the permanently unconscious we feel free to intervene for minor decisions, because we are obliged to make *all* decisions. With the temporarily unconscious we may even take risks, close to the point of survival, to avoid decision, with the acknowledgment that only a matter of hours (or minutes) may free the individual to participate in the decision making himself. Therefore, even with a seemingly easy case of the unconscious individual there is a spectrum of judgment and doubt.

Limits of Intelligence

When we move away from absolute incommunicability as represented by the unconscious person, we enter into that more complex spectrum of issues that plague the competent-incompetent polarity. At its most extreme, the severely retarded person, though conscious, is demonstrably not competent by nature of his limited intelligence to make important decisions. At that level of retardation speech is, of course, not present, but his limitation is not just one of communication, which would link him to the unconscious person, but instead his inability to assess or determine his own best interests. Even were he capable of communicating by grunting or nodding, most of us would not honor his decision not to take a health-preserving medication.

As we move up the spectrum of retardation, we will again come to a border area where the intelligence of the retarded will need to be weighed against the seriousness of the decision and multiple other variables involving dignity, social well-being, and the like, complicating our decision in awarding autonomy.

Limits of Rationality

If the severely retarded person is not competent, neither is the audacious, bright, perky toddler. He is not competent either because he has not reached the age of communication or, having reached that age, his perception of his world and his place in it or his grasp of the problems and their implications is too limited. Or, simply because he still lacks the moral and psychological development. This entire classification could be broken down into a number of specific variables, but many of them can be lumped together under the heading of rationality—our suspicion of the reasonableness of his decisions. Here, our doubts arise not because he is not intelligent—there is no greater learner than the three- or four-year-old, as any parent who has tried to compete in language learning with his prepubescent child will know—but because we recognize that there are many more components to reason than simple ability to learn.

Limits of Knowledge and Perception

Examples from the field of mental health are particularly well suited to exploring the relation between the concepts of rationality and perception. But here, too, it may be better to step back from a category as controversial as mental health, and first consider a physical example. If a blind man is about to walk into a busy thoroughfare without knowing it, he may be hit by an object he does not perceive or, indeed, see. In this case we are free to knock him down, without being accused of an assault. We recognize that the limits of his perception modify the nature of his behavior so as to seriously bring into question whether his behavior is serving his purposes. When the blind man chooses to cross the street, we may morally forcibly prevent him when we see an oncoming truck. We have a right to nullify his decision because we recognize that the end of his behavior is to get to the other side of the street, not to be squashed under the wheels of a truck. We recognize that his decision making is inhibited by limits of perception.

There are emotional conditions that limit one's "perceptions" as severely as sensory deficiencies. The phobic over-reacts to certain harmless things because of the symbolic value he endows them with, and can be made literally to jump out of a window to protect himself from what realistically is no threat to his survival.

Our reasonably objective evaluation of the leap from the window as a greater threat to his existence than the mouse that entered the room—coupled with our knowledge or assumption that the individual is attempting to avoid danger—would justify our "restricting his liberty" by barring him from the window, at least until the terrifying mouse can be eliminated.

Another limit of perception involves areas in which the absence of factual knowledge raises questions about whether the person's behavior coincides with our presumption of his purpose. Those ignorant of explosives or firearms should be protected from their limits of knowledge, which border on limits of perception. It is easy to see that with this fourth category we are now entering areas more and more controversial, with a wider spread and a greater potential for corruptibility.

Limits of Experience

It was William James who wisely distinguished between knowledge of something and knowing about something. Surely, part of what goes into our abridgment of the child's autonomy is the recognition that although he might be conscious, intelligent, rational, and probably quite perceptive, the nature of his experience has distorted his capacity for sound judgment. An adolescent might well value ambulation over life. Does an adolescent really acknowledge his own death? (Does anyone?) To ask a twelve-year-old for permission to amputate a leg to save his life is prematurely to impose judgments on the value of life that demand more "living" (i.e., more knowledge of life) than can be condensed into twelve years. A mere examination of the precipitating factors in suicide attempts of adolescents indicates the degree to which factors that will seem trivial in later life can tip the balance for a teen-ager: the failure to be elected to public office in a high school, being dropped from an athletic team, a low SAT score, a disappointment in a love affair. I am not so naïve as to suggest that these are the "causes" of the suicide attempt, but they are indeed seen by the adolescent as a burden that makes life unbearable and the future not worth waiting for. Most adults, in reconstructing their adolescence, are horrified by the scale of values and the degree to which they suffered because of what is retrospectively recognized as an immature distortion of priorities.

It will be argued that experience and maturity vary with normal adults, which of course they do, and I am not prepared to say that we must give a test of experience to each adult. We can, however, depend—as we do in all rule setting—on a statistical average that justifies the rule. Generally, one sees "maturity" increasing with age, at least to a limited point.

Limits of Age

Here we have returned to the comfortable and arbitrary ground of the original rule of competence. Age, in many ways, is seen as the summation of intelligence, rationality, perception, and experience. We assume a coming together and a maturation of these faculties at a certain time when we, the society, are willing to take the risk of allowing the child into the moral community and the world's political decision making. In the past, we had been prepared to say that statistically the balance tips for freedom and away from paternalism at such-and-such age. Our current dissatisfaction with a specific arbitrary test of competence is related to the complexity of the decisions we now face, and the profound consequences of many of them. It is for this reason that we must begin the examination of the evidence of competence to establish a variable grid.

Within each category (diminished intelligence, diminished consciousness, etc.) there will be a problem of relative competence, and we will have a dilemma along each locus.

In this volume we concern ourselves with the problem of defining competence in the normal, healthy child. It seems to me a particularly agonizing problem. On the other hand, the whole area of variable competence is so fraught with painful decisions that I suspect we will each tend to see whatever problem we are dealing with as the insoluble one. We are in that difficult area of defining: What is a child, and when does he leave childhood? By one definition, children are seen

> finally [to] pass to the level of autonomy when they appreciate that rules are alterable, that they can be criticized and should be accepted or rejected on a basis of reciprocity and fairness. The emergence of rational reflections about rules . . . central to the Kantian conception of autonomy, is the main feature of the final level of moral development.[3]

On the other hand, the age of autonomy would never be achieved if we were to follow the judgment of Judge S. Lee Vavuris, who in April 1977, in a case involving five adult members, ages 21 to 26, of the church of the Reverend Sun Myung Moon, awarded these "children" to their parents under a conservatorship law usually reserved for senile adults who are incompetent.

> We are talking about the essence of civilization—mother, father, and children. There is nothing like it. I know of no greater love than parents' for their children, and I'm sure they would not submit their children to harm. The child is the child, even though a parent may be ninety and the child, sixty.[4]

It is part of the complication of the English language that with all its richness (three times as many words as German or French) we seem to use only one basic word, "child," to denote both the progeny and the young. It may be a reflection of the fact that we tend to respond to *our* children always as

---

[3]R. S. Peters, in R. F. Dearden, ed. *Education and the Development of Reason* (London: Routledge & Kegan Paul, 1972), p. 130.
[4]Les Ledbetter, "Parents Win Custody of 5 Members of Moon's Church," *New York Times*, 25 March 1977, pp. 1–9.

though they *were* children (incomplete and dependent). But surely, even Judge Vavuris would not have us bind the twenty-year-old, let alone the sixty-year-old, to complete economic and sociological dependence on his parents.

> The search for a single test of competency is a search for a Holy Grail. Unless it is recognized that there is no magical definition of competency to make decisions about treatment, the search for an acceptable test will never end. Getting the words just right is only part of the problem. In practice, judgments of competency go beyond semantics or straightforward applications of legal rules; such judgments reflect social considerations and societal biases as much as they reflect matters of law and medicine.[5]

If that is true for competence—it is exquisitely so when we begin to adjust definitions of competence to accommodate special cases—when we move from an absolute to a variable concept of competence.

VARIABLE COMPETENCE

What is necessary at this point, then, is the establishment of a grid—crude though it may be—that sets some limits and identifies some principles on which we can begin to fill in the specifics of variable competence. This task ought to be done before we are forced to conclude, let us say, that at age eleven a child should have the right to decide to have an abortion or indeed to carry to term without parental guidance or permission; or that a thirteen-year-old will be free to consent to sex, as has recently been proposed in New Jersey. At this stage what is most urgently needed is an outline of principles, which others may modify according to their value systems and in terms of the specific situations of different cases. It should be explicitly understood from the start that this first

---

[5]L. H. Roth, A. Meisel, and C. W. Lidz, "Tests of Competency to Consent to Treatment," *American Journal of Psychiatry* 134 (1977): 283.

attempt will be admittedly crude. It is hoped that the argument here will start a process that can lead to a refinement of the ideas presented.

The question that is being asked, then, is: On what basis shall we decide that an individual is competent to make decisions about his life?

In its peculiar way, the law does not view competence as indigenous to the person, but instead as something with which one is vested by society. It is a judgment of maturity. At 13, the Jewish child shall be permitted to be a full participant in the house of God. In some states of our country a child does not become an adult, in terms of the privilege of determining his representatives in government, until 18—in others, at 21. At 16, many states allow a woman the right to determine whether she shall have sexual intercourse; in other states, under 16, her agreement has no standing in law. Even were she to seduce a "mature" (over 16) man, *he* will be guilty of the charge of statutory rape. And so it goes. At age 14, at age 15, at age 18, at age 21 (there are certain trusts and estates that can limit control until ages 35, 45, and 60), the law will arbitrarily invest a person with competence to make his own decisions.

How should we judge? How can we bring some order, some sensibleness to the chaotic and contradictory code that emerges when these decisions are left to case law? It is a complex problem in all of our categories, but it is particularly complex with a developing child who is progressively accumulating maturity, and with his counterpart, the senescent adult who is gradually losing his powers of judgment and entering into that state unattractively and imprecisely labeled "second childhood." (Would that it were!)

To simplify matters in this thicket of variables, we have decided to focus in this book on "medical" procedures, recognizing that even the definition of what is, or is not, a medical procedure is an arbitrary and elusive one. Nevertheless, the examples here will primarily be medical; the subject, determination of age of competence.

Before reducing the data to a grid, it is best to understand the way the terms will be used. There are at least five major variables.

Risk

"Risk" as it is used here means risk to the individual involved. That is, not to the family, not to the society; but to the subject of the decision to be made.

Gain

Similarly, "gain" is in the exclusive context of the individual himself. I am well aware that in both these categories the decision of what is high-risk or high-gain is itself dependent on individual values. For the most part, therefore, I shall try to give examples that fall within the *general* standards of society. For example, I shall place an extraordinarily high value on survival. This emphasis will, of course, do disservice to those religious groups who view life on earth as an ephemeral and unimportant transition point to an eternal and better life somewhere else. But since we are dealing with policy, not theology, it seems best to adopt the standard of our culture—wrongly or rightly—that life on earth is a central value, rarely transcended by others.

Risk–Gain Ratio

It will soon be seen that in a peculiar way, the very definition of risk and gain will be altered when they are viewed as a ratio rather than independently.

Social Benefits or Costs

In the most individualistic of societies, we must still be aware that we are all part of a complex whole, and that there will inevitably be times when transcendent rights of the society will force a limitation of individual rights. Biologists from Aristotle on down had been reminding us, even when the philosophers or social scientists had forgotten, that man is a social animal by design, not by choice, and that even his *individual* needs require respect for the community on which he is dependent. A commitment to individual liberty is meaningless if the social matrix that supports all freedom is allowed to be destroyed. We are living through a time that has seen a dangerous deterioration of the public space, necessitating a painful reassessment of the limits of individualism.

The Nature of the Decision

It is evident that even such specifics as "risk," "gain," and "social benefits" begin to have different definitions and meanings, dependent on the decision to be made. I am limiting my examples to medical ones. But those who would extend this grid beyond that area will immediately recognize that there are assumptions arising out of the medical model that are quite different from those that would surface with an economic, sociological, or pedagogic frame of reference. For example, one need only think about our abhorrence of pain inflicted for political purposes, which is defined as torture, and the legitimacy of pain inflicted for medical purposes. This distinction is not simply one between individual and state purposes. Even when only the individual and his family are involved, we draw crucial distinctions. We will allow painful methods to be inflicted on a child if it is necessary for ambulation. Yet I suspect we would not allow whipping or other painful methods to be used if such were necessary for a child to learn to read, or simply to learn. It is not, I submit, because reading is less important than ambulation, but instead that under the medical model, we are protected by the assumption (often false) that only the good of the individual is concerned, whereas with the pedagogic model, we are frightened that we may slip from serving the individual's needs into serving society, at which point the pain would be morally unacceptable. At any rate, it is a fact that the nature of the case will shift our relative values on the grid.

Other terms that will be used as variables are "generous" and "limited." Since I have defined competence as that which we (the state) are conferring on and endow the individual with, "generous" means that we should indeed be liberal in our allowance, even at times beyond our logical definition of "true" competence. When I say "generous," then, I mean we should be relatively free in granting the right of autonomy to the human being involved. When I say "limited," I mean we should be careful in our readiness to certify competence. "Generous" and "limited," therefore, refer to the attitude of the state in granting competence.

Here again, another set of variables must be introduced, and that is whether what is being granted is the right to elect to do something, or the right to refuse. As we get to the specific examples, it will be seen that often the state's generosity in certifying competence will be polar in these conditions. Where we are generous in granting a right to refuse, we will often limit the right to volunteer.

And finally, since we are using the medical model, it is important to understand the meaning of therapeutic and nontherapeutic experimentation or procedure. A therapeutic procedure is one that is done "as therapy." It is a treatment for the individual, and is presumed to serve his purposes and welfare, even if it is still "experimental"—meaning that whether it will benefit him more than it harms him is still not established. A therapeutic experiment involves the use of a procedure that is not yet proved to work but is used in this specific case to test its efficacy on the condition of the individual. To give someone penicillin for his pneumonia today is a therapeutic procedure; to have given someone with pneumonia penicillin in the early days before the risks and benefits of the drug were established would have been an experimental procedure, but a *therapeutic experiment*. To give someone penicillin who did *not* have pneumonia to test the effects of the drug on a healthy physiological system is a *nontherapeutic experiment*.

And finally, whenever we are involved with certifying the competence of a child, the assumption will be that when certified noncompetent, the decision making rests with the family out of respect for family autonomy. However, since we are aware that the family is not a totally trustworthy instrument, but only the safest of instruments, we acknowledge the rights of society to intervene in family autonomy when it is felt that it violates its primary charge to sustain, nurture, and protect the individual. The intrusion on family autonomy will be cast in terms of the state's right to intervene. Let us now, finally, look at our four major categories.

Category 1: High Risk/Low Gain

The obvious example for this category is the classic yellow-fever experiment where Walter Reed and his colleagues risked their lives to serve society at large. Despite the fact that they need not have been exposed to yellow fever, they ran the risk of the experimental procedure. Many more examples can be anticipated. Herpes virus has been implicated as a possible source of cervical cancer. Suppose a live-virus vaccination has been developed and is now in stage 3 testing. The marketing drug company is looking for healthy volunteers on whom to test the vaccine. Because the potential subject does *not* have the disease, the gain is low and the risk is high—since the subject has a chance of developing a herpes infection or a herpes-caused cervical cancer. Common sense indicates that a young child ought not be permitted to volunteer for such hazards before an age of understanding. Her right to refuse should be highly respected. Therefore, in this case, it would seem that our equation should be: autonomous right to volunteer—limited; autonomous right to refuse—generous.

When the prospective volunteer is a child, we are faced with the secondary question of whether the state has a right to intervene when consent or refusal is given by a surrogate, for example, a parent. Obviously, in cases where there is no social value, the state never has a right to intervene, but the two examples given above are both examples of high social value. The principle here at its extreme seems simple: on a high risk/low gain nontherapeutic procedure (the risk of a child to serve others is a prototypic example), the state has the right to intervene to forbid the procedure, and has extremely limited rights to intervene demanding the procedure.

Category 2: Low Risk/High Gain

The classic example here is the Jehovah's Witnesses problem involving an authorized blood transfusion (a limited-risk procedure) in order to save a life (a high gain). Here, obviously, in granting the autonomous right to elect the procedure, we should be generous; the autonomous right to refuse should be limited. Even a young child would seem competent to decide to save his life when there is no risk to him involved. Similarly, we must wait until the absolute date of maturity (beyond that, some would argue) to allow someone to refuse such a procedure. Therefore, autonomous right to elect—generous; autonomous right to refuse—limited.

The state's position here is an interesting one. For although no social purpose might be served directly, as in the two cases above, there is a social commitment to the high value on life. Here one would expect state intervention. The state, therefore, should overcome the presumption of family autonomy in such cases. Indeed, such was the decision of Judge Murphy for the Superior Court for the District of Columbia *In re Pogue*.[6] Judge Murphy intervened and overruled the parents, allowing a blood transfusion for an otherwise healthy newborn baby who would have died without the transfusion.

This case is of particular interest because at the same time the judge recognized the rights of the *mother* to refuse a blood transfusion for herself, even if refusing to intervene meant

[6] "In re: Pogue," *Washington Post,* 14 November 1974, C. at 1, col. 1 (No. M-18-74, Super Ct., D.C., 11 November 1974).

her death. In the case of the infant, over the objections of the adult parents' wishes, the judge as a surrogate decided to protect the child's right to live to the age of majority, when he would be entitled to make such life-and-death decisions for himself. In so doing, the judge implicitly found the mother temporarily *incompetent* to decide for the child, while at the very same time he acknowledged her *competence* by declining to use the mother's refusal of blood, despite its obvious danger, as a basis for declaring her incompetent.

There is an interesting subdivision of this category where we tend to modify our attitudes about the relative respect we give to family autonomy. At the extremes of life, when we are dealing with a fetus or a senescent old man, we tend to *increase* the degree of family autonomy, that is, decrease the state's right to intervene. Most people are prepared to accept a difference between a first-trimester fetus and a child, and the law has already acknowledged that much. We will allow the fetus to be destroyed by parental authority. Some would even argue the case for nontherapeutic experimentation on the about-to-be-destroyed fetus.[7] It may well be that at the ends of life the state should also place a lesser value on the comatose old man irreversibly deteriorating into death, and allow a greater degree of family autonomy in weighing the potential value of the experimental procedure for society as a whole against the specific value of the life at risk. Here the arguments are complex, and the slope particularly slippery.

Category 3: High Risk/High Gain

Here the prime examples are cases where the risk is life and the gain is life. A child has a severe cardiac impairment and needs an experimental operative procedure to correct it; the child's life is at risk because of the cardiac insufficiency, and yet the high mortality rate of the operation is also an

---

[7]Willard Gaylin and Marc Lappé, "Fetal Politics," *Atlantic Monthly*, May, 1975, pp. 66–71.

awesome risk. It seems clear here that since both the risk and the benefit involve that which is valued highly by the state, that is, life, the rights of the state are canceled by the balance, and the state ought to abandon its power of intervention. When we talk, then, about certifying competence here, we are talking about balancing the right of the child as a decision maker as against the right of the parent.

Should the child have any say in such decisions? I think we have been remiss in the past in totally ignoring the child, and I would press for some moderately generous certification of competence both for the right to refuse and the right to elect. In a state where the age of competence is eighteen, it seems inconceivable that a decision to operate on a sixteen-year-old can now be made independent of his feelings or judgments. I am prepared here to be moderately generous in the application of competence. Even when we are aware of loving parents, something is wrong if the individual whose life is at risk is totally on the sidelines in such a decision. Participation need not mean complete autonomy. In either case, we must decide how much participation, and at what age. To exclude the child completely, to acknowledge no autonomy and no competence, seems most unreasonable.

High risk/high gain, however, need not mean simply life versus life; it can mean life versus days of work, life versus ambulation, and so on. Here too I would press for a moderately generous lowering of the age of competence. Consider an operative procedure that would remove an individual from a state of permanent invalidism but that represented a significant risk to his life. Here too common sense would demand some consideration of the individual judgment of the person to whom the risk or gain is most germane.

It becomes clear that as one moves farther and farther away from lifesaving, the pressure to include the individual in the decision making becomes less. With work and ambulation, it will often be the case that were his parents to refuse the operation, the patient could reverse them when he reaches the age of maturity. On the other hand, there will be examples where the operative procedure must be done at a certain age or it cannot be done at all. In those cases I would insist that we be generous in allowing the child the role as a competent judge of the future life he is about to lead.

Category 4: Low Risk/Low Gain

Here we must subidivde into two categories, depending on whether the experimentation or procedure is (a) of low social value, or (b) of high social value. Let us first consider category 4a, where there is low risk, low gain, and low social value. In this case, as there is low social value, there is an automatic assumption that the state has little or no right to intervene, particularly since the child is not at risk. Once again, if we allow the child competence, the autonomy we are granting is specifically in relationship to the parent. Here, in seeking an example, I am obliged to leave the medical arena, because there is no medical experimentation that is proposed that is not at least thought to have some social value—if only in the mind of the experimenter. Let us therefore take the example of a movie screening. The producer has completed a picture for children; he wants to test audience reaction. There is little to be gained by the child, little to be risked. The automatic right to refuse (vs. the parents), it seems to me, should be extremely limited. Some might argue that, since no risks are involved whether the parent volunteers the child or not, a child at a very early age ought to be able to decide that he simply "doesn't want to"; and similarly, an automatic right to volunteer should also be generous—a child ought to be able to make such decisions at a very young age. I take the contrary position—not because I think a child should not be free to make these decisions, but because in this case, out of respect for family integrity as distinguished from family autonomy, I would not want to make it a *right*. Even though I would hope that sensible parents would allow the child to make such decisions, I would not want to elevate such an issue to a point of *rights*. It seems to me we ought not encourage family discord over trivial matters.

Category 4b, low risk/low gain with a high social value, seems to me a case where the state has a strong right to intervene.

If a parent has no sense of moral obligation to the community at large, it may be to the good of the child as well as the community for the state to instruct the parent as well as the child as to social responsibility. An example might be an epidemiologic study that would collect urine as it is transmitted through the urinals in school. There would be no particular exposure of the child; the child, indeed, would be unaware that he was part of an experimentation. The risk to him, therefore, is zero. On the other hand, the epidemiologic purposes could be significant. If we were looking for baselines of certain trace elements excreted through the urine to determine the impact of environmental pollution, these are the kind of data we would need, and the child might someday benefit. But even if there were a case where no possible gain to the child would accrue, I would allow state intervention. Refusal of permission for such an experimental involvement would be trivial, arbitrary, and ungenerous. There are limits to family autonomy. Here the autonomous right of the individual to refuse would be extremely limited, and the autonomous right to volunteer extremely generous.

This category introduces another violation of a principle dearly held by many. I myself, for years, felt that nontherapeutic experimentation ought never be allowed via *proxy* consent. It was one of the few basic principles that it seemed could be established in an unconditional way. My reasoning was that although it is a noble and generous act for someone to offer himself at risk for the good of the community or of science, it is somewhat less generous, noble, or courageous for one person to offer another person. I was forced to make one exception to that rule when I began to examine the problem of fetal experimentation.[8] But another example offered me anecdotally by a friend further shook my confidence in the inviolability of this principle.

He described a scene in an office where he had taken his nine- or ten-year-old son for a physical examination. The doctor, after having completed the examination, turned to the child and in a formal manner asked for permission to take a small sample of blood for an epidemiologic research that he was doing on a major disease of childhood. As the father related the story, the doctor in a somewhat precious way explained to the child that this procedure was not a part of his examination but would help some "other little boys." The boy asked the doctor, "Will it hurt?" The doctor answered, "A little—like a pinprick." The boy said, "I don't want it," whereupon the father said to his son, "Listen, young man, you just get your hand up on that table and let the doctor take the blood."

The boy, recognizing the note of authority in his father's voice, immediately complied, whereupon the doctor, forgetting the formalism of his original consent proceedings, gladly took the sample.

In explaining the event to me, the father said that it was not just an expression of authoritarianism, or paternalism if you will, but of his moral obligation to teach his child that there are certain things one does, even if it causes a small amount of pain, to the service or benefit of others. "This is my child. I was less concerned with the research involved than with the kind of boy that I was raising. I'll be damned if I was going to allow my child, because of some idiotic concept of children's rights, to assume that he was entitled to be a selfish, narcissistic little bastard."

Paternalism by a parent in relationship to a young child is not, this father would contend, patronizing or "paternalistic." The instillation of a set of values is the moral respon-

[8]Ibid.

sibility of a parent, and the failure to do so is a grievous abdication of responsibility. I tend to agree with the father, and although my approach might have been different, each parent has the right to his own style within the limits of decency. I accept this category as another one where proxy consent may be suitable in a nontherapeutic experimentation. The benefit to this child at this time is zero (i.e., it is a nontherapeutic procedure), but the cost is very low and the social gain may be very high. In such cases a parent may "volunteer" his child for a nontherapeutic experiment.

All of these principles can now be summarized in a two-part table: one column of Table 1 indicates family autonomy, and will set the limits for state intervention and for intrapersonal decision making; the second column indicates the state's readiness to certify competence (grant legal autonomy) at variable ages.

Table 1 is a primitive grid, composed of a structured set of crude, tentative principles, on which we can begin to locate the specific case—rather than simply depending on an individual, situational approach, which inevitably leads to the inequities inherent in any ad hoc system.

Even with these tentative principles, certain complications are already apparent. I have alluded (in Category 2) to one of them, that is, the tendency to extrapolate assumptions and recommendations for the end of life (the elderly dying) from conclusions drawn at the beginnings of life (the damaged newborn). Much mischief has been created by equating the moral decisions about lifesaving and the termination of treatments at these two extremes. There are very few generalizations that hold one to the other.

Even in the intervals in between, we are aware that the age of the individual alters our attitudes not just about the capacity for autonomy, but also about the relative importance of the area of decision making. For example, suppose we face a problem of whether to grant permission to withdraw from a lifesaving treatment such as a dialysis machine. If the legal age of maturity in the state is eighteen, I for one would want

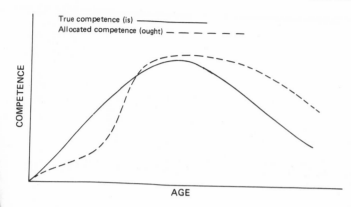

Legend:
True competence (is) ——————
Allocated competence (ought) — — — —

COMPETENCE (y-axis)

AGE (x-axis)

Figure 1

…e knowledge that he will shortly achieve an age in which
…will automatically be awarded him, and that this short delay
…ll do little harm to his self-image or the values of our society.
…ropose that we compensate this young person for this
…privation by granting him, in his senescence, a more liberal
…cation of autonomy (a more generous judgment of com-
…ence) than he deserves.

…What I offer, then, is simply one example of a form of
…e analysis—a mechanism of negotiation, analysis, and
…ration—that will be necessary to establish some sound
…rpinnings to a concept as complex as variable compe-

Table 1. Summary Table Variable Competence

Category	Family Autonomy	Rules certifying competence for individual autonomy
1. High risk/low gain. Example given. Life-risking, nontherapeutic experiment.	State has right to intervene (forbidding).	Autonomous right to refuse: generous Autonomous right to elect: limited
2. Low risk/high gain. Example: blood transfusion to save life.	State has right to intervene (demanding).	Autonomous right to refuse: limited Autonomous right to elect: generous
3. High risk/high gain. Examples given. Life vs. life; life vs. work; life vs. ambulation.	State has no right to intervene.	Autonomous right to refuse: moderately generous Autonomous right to elect: moderately generous (Here vs. parents, since state has no authority)
4a. Low risk/low gain, low social value. Example: movie screening.	State has no right to intervene.	Autonomous right vs. parents to refuse: extremely limited Autonomous right vs. parents to elect: extremely limited
4b. Low risk/low gain, high social value. Example: urinalysis for epidemiologic purposes.	State has right to intervene.	Autonomous right vs. state to refuse: extremely limited Autonomous right vs. state to volunteer: generous

to be extremely ungenerous in lowering that age of permission to discontinue treatment. Even acknowledging the fact that the sixteen-year-old—by almost every set of variables—is close to maturity, one recognizes that a certain level of *consciousness* is different at that age from what may exist at thirty, let alone fifty. By "consciousness" I mean a sense not just of one's own identity, but of one's own purposes; the relationship of the sense of self to the environment—and beyond the immediate environment to a concept of one's future. The mere appreciation of time varies between the fifteen-year-old to whom the three months before his graduation seems like an eternity, and the sixty-five-year-old whose forty years of productive work seem like a single yesterday. From a distance, we can know that two years is not that great a time to wait before allowing a sixteen-year-old to sacrifice a potential thirty to fifty more years of living.

Can this decision be defended on logical grounds? I doubt it. It is, by every definition, paternalistic. But it seems to me the state might well want to be paternalistic at this point when what is at risk is a future life of unknown and unlimited potential. I grant that at eighteen the same bias might still be there, but one presumes that age brings a certain solidification of values, and eighteen may be two years more balanced a time than sixteen.

Similarly, we may be aware that a 72-year-old-man on the same dialysis machine may have, over the years, suffered arteriosclerotic deterioration and brain damage of a sort that clearly indicates, by objective and measurable criteria, that he is no longer the rational human being he once was. If we compare the 16-year-old and the 72-year-old in an adversarial position in a court of law, I have no doubt that the 16-year-old would win hands down against all variables introduced as determinants of competence. Nevertheless, I would allow the 72-year-old to be "deemed competent," even when he is beyond the limits of certain objective criteria of competence, that is, when there are beginning signs of impairment of memory, judgment, and the like.

What I am suggesting, therefore, is that as in many moral issues, there is not a direct correlation betwe and "ought." We may deprive the younger person of privileges of autonomy out of respect for the person become, and out of fear that his own vision of this f be too limited to allow even himself a proper res value. With the older person, on the other han honor a lifetime of feelings, achievement, exp lating, and simply being; we must measure his against the residuals of his past; and we must r to protect his own dignity, which is in such older age. The old man is often less concern tential for the future than with the preserv the future he is sacrificing may be only a sh and deterioration. With the adolescent, we concerned about where he is going, an where he came from. A person is, after a is, but also what he was.

Thus it seems to me that even w solutely judging "true" competence (w there would be psychological, social allocating competence independent are certain illusions that ought to be for the simple biological life cycle. I would propose that even as we knowledge about moral decision tinction between "true" compete edgment of competence. In oth parison in Figure 1 between c be, and competence as it oug

I offer this as an examp and to point the way in wh moral judgments indepenc In my system, I am more th of the child beyond my int I am prepared to allow l loss of pride, that com

th
it
wi
I
de
allo
Pete

valu
arbit
unde
tence

Part II

Legal Considerations

CHAPTER 3

The Competence of Children as Self- Deciders in Biomedical Interventions

ALEXANDER MORGAN CAPRON

When a person is competent, a physician or other provider of medical care must obtain the person's informed consent before performing any procedure.[1] Failure to obtain consent is a tort: if effective consent has not been secured the bodily

---

[1]*See generally* W. PROSSER, LAW OF TORTS 105–109 (4th ed. 1971); Capron, *Informed Consent in Catastrophic Disease Research and Treatment*, 123 U. PA. L. REV. 340 (1974).

ALEXANDER MORGAN CAPRON ● University of Pennsylvania Law School, Philadelphia, Pennsylvania 19104.

intrusion is a battery, or the failure to secure it may be deemed professional negligence, resulting in either case in liability for damages even if the procedure has been carried out non-negligently.[2] Not all patients are competent to consent to medical treatment for themselves, however. This fact raises two issues of particular concern in examining medical therapy and experimentation with children: When is a person competent, and who may authorize an intervention when the patient is incompetent? The first issue is treated in this chapter and the second in the following one.

VANTAGE POINT

There are two ways in which the first issue might be addressed. One could begin by establishing an objective rule of competence for everyone from which one would deviate on a case-by-case basis for reasons particular to the individual being considered; or one could rely on a subjective determination about each person's competence. Under the former approach the question becomes, What are adequate reasons for suspending self-choice?; under the latter, On what grounds should a person's choices about him or herself be honored?

The law has traditionally followed the former approach as regards persons who have attained their majority. The origin of the legal rules setting the age of majority—typically, at 21 years of age—are obscured in antiquity. Although they may have arisen more as a reflection of the physical development and training needed by young men to engage in armed combat,[3] they seem also to recognize the mental and emotional maturity and personal independence appropriate to an autonomous individual. From the Middle Ages through

---

[2]Hively v. Higgs, 120 Or. 588, 253 P. 363 (1927); Shulman v. Lerner, 2 Mich. App. 705, 141 N.W.2d 348 (1966).

[3]See generally G. ANNAS, L. GLANTZ & B. KATZ, INFORMED CONSENT TO HUMAN EXPERIMENTATION: THE SUBJECT'S DILEMMA 64–67 (1978).

the nineteenth century, the age of decisional authority was gradually increased by statutory and common law. Although the age was not uniform for all purposes—for example, women could marry without parental consent at 16 years under the Marriage Act of 1753, whereas men could do so only on turning 21—the general point for termination of legal infancy became 21 years.

In recent years, most jurisdictions in the United States have by statute lowered the age of majority to eighteen years. On passing that date a person enters legal adulthood and is presumed to be competent. This presumption, which operates throughout all phases of a person's life as well as in the medical sphere, may be rebutted by proof of mental incapacity, such as insanity[4] or intoxication,[5] or severe physical disability, such as unconsciousness.[6]

The competence of persons below the age of majority has not been viewed from the same vantage point, however. For minors the alternative approach—Why honor self-choice in this case?—is employed. The standards by which this question is answered vary with the choices being made. Thus there is no single thread running through the legal rules that have emerged on the competence of minors. Instead, these rules are idiosyncratic and seem to be consistent, if at all, only in each connecting with a particular purpose for which competence needs to be measured. In deciding about minors' capacity to purchase goods and services, convey property, bring legal proceedings, or secure medical care the courts and legislatures have created many "exceptions" to the general rule of minors' incapacity, some of which are explored in this chapter. As with the basic determination that competence for minors should be approached from the negative vantage (denying self-choice except in particular cases), the guiding

[4]Farber v. Olkon, 40 Cal.2d 503, 254 P.2d 520 (1953); Pratt v. Davis, 224 Ill. 300, 79 N.E. 502 (1906); Bolton v. Stewart, 191 S.W.2d 798 (Tex. Civ. App. 1945).
[5]Hollerud v. Malamis, 20 Mich. App. 748, 174 N.W.2d 626 (1970).
[6]Schloendorff v. Society of N.Y. Hosp., 211 N.Y. 125, 105 N.E.92 (1914); Mohr v. Williams 95 Minn. 261, 263, 1021 N.W. 12, 13 (1905).

principle of most of these exceptions seems to be convenience of administration or other benefits to society, rather than a recognition of any right of minors to self-determination.

In its approach to the competence of minors the law reflects the same ambivalence that characterizes our societal attitude toward all matters of self-choice.[7] At work are the competing drives to protect physical well-being (which may manifest itself in refusing to allow procedures deemed not to be in a patient's "best interests") and to protect the patient's status as a human being with the power of self-determination (which may result in permitting an apparently harmful procedure that is desired by the individual). Of course, the sacrifice of the latter value does not always guarantee that the former will be achieved. The denial of decisional power to minors may, for example, have served as much to protect parental control over children's property as to safeguard children from their own follies. If a minor could not enter into a binding contract he could not convert any of his family's property to his own use nor dissipate any of his own earnings, to the receipt of which his father was entitled at common law.[8] Feudal law gave lords even greater powers over their minor tenants. "Although the minor [was] protected from squandering his inheritance, it [was] a rather expensive means of protection."[9]

Thus there is good reason to question the rosy view of Blackstone that though minors "have various privileges, and various disabilities, . . . their very disabilities are privileges."[10] Not only are minors exposed to the possibility of harm or exploitation at their guardians' hands, but the very loss of self-determination is itself a harm—a less palpable hurt

---

[7]J. Katz, *Informed Consent: A Fairy Tale? Law's Vision*, 39 U. PITT. L. REV. 137 (1977).

[8]Edge, *Voidability of Minors' Contracts: A Feudal Doctrine in a Modern Economy*, 1 GA. L. REV. 205, 220 (1967).

[9]G. ANNAS, L. GLANTZ & B. KATZ, INFORMED CONSENT TO HUMAN EXPERIMENTATION: THE SUBJECT'S DILEMMA 65 (1978).

[10]W. BLACKSTONE, COMMENTARIES *464.

Table 1. Summary Table Variable Competence

Category	Family Autonomy	Rules certifying competence for individual autonomy
1. High risk/low gain. Example given. Life-risking, nontherapeutic experiment.	State has right to intervene (forbidding).	Autonomous right to refuse: generous Autonomous right to elect: limited
2. Low risk/high gain. Example: blood transfusion to save life.	State has right to intervene (demanding).	Autonomous right to refuse: limited Autonomous right to elect: generous
3. High risk/high gain. Examples given. Life vs. life; life vs. work; life vs. ambulation.	State has no right to intervene.	Autonomous right to refuse: moderately generous Autonomous right to elect: moderately generous (Here vs. parents, since state has no authority)
4a. Low risk/low gain, low social value. Example: movie screening.	State has no right to intervene.	Autonomous right vs. parents to refuse: extremely limited Autonomous right vs. parents to elect: extremely limited
4b. Low risk/low gain, high social value. Example: urinalysis for epidemiologic purposes.	State has right to intervene.	Autonomous right vs. state to refuse: extremely limited Autonomous right vs. state to volunteer: generous

to be extremely ungenerous in lowering that age of permission to discontinue treatment. Even acknowledging the fact that the sixteen-year-old—by almost every set of variables—is close to maturity, one recognizes that a certain level of *consciousness* is different at that age from what may exist at thirty, let alone fifty. By "consciousness" I mean a sense not just of one's own identity, but of one's own purposes; the relationship of the sense of self to the environment—and beyond the immediate environment to a concept of one's future. The mere appreciation of time varies between the fifteen-year-old to whom the three months before his graduation seems like an eternity, and the sixty-five-year-old whose forty years of productive work seem like a single yesterday. From a distance, we can know that two years is not that great a time to wait before allowing a sixteen-year-old to sacrifice a potential thirty to fifty more years of living.

Can this decision be defended on logical grounds? I doubt it. It is, by every definition, paternalistic. But it seems to me the state might well want to be paternalistic at this point when what is at risk is a future life of unknown and unlimited potential. I grant that at eighteen the same bias might still be there, but one presumes that age brings a certain solidification of values, and eighteen may be two years more balanced a time than sixteen.

Similarly, we may be aware that a 72-year-old-man on the same dialysis machine may have, over the years, suffered arteriosclerotic deterioration and brain damage of a sort that clearly indicates, by objective and measurable criteria, that he is no longer the rational human being he once was. If we compare the 16-year-old and the 72-year-old in an adversarial position in a court of law, I have no doubt that the 16-year-old would win hands down against all variables introduced as determinants of competence. Nevertheless, I would allow the 72-year-old to be "deemed competent," even when he is beyond the limits of certain objective criteria of competence, that is, when there are beginning signs of impairment of memory, judgment, and the like.

What I am suggesting, therefore, is that as in many other moral issues, there is not a direct correlation between "is" and "ought." We may deprive the younger person of certain privileges of autonomy out of respect for the person he might become, and out of fear that his own vision of this future may be too limited to allow even himself a proper respect for its value. With the older person, on the other hand, we must honor a lifetime of feelings, achievement, experiencing, relating, and simply being; we must measure his limited future against the residuals of his past; and we must respect his right to protect his own dignity, which is in such short supply in older age. The old man is often less concerned with his potential for the future than with the preservation of his past; the future he is sacrificing may be only a short period of pain and deterioration. With the adolescent, we have a right to be concerned about where he is going, and with the elderly, where he came from. A person is, after all, not only what he is, but also what he was.

Thus it seems to me that even were we capable of absolutely judging "true" competence (which we will never be), there would be psychological, social, and moral reasons for allocating competence independent of the actual fact. There are certain illusions that ought to be maintained out of respect for the simple biological life cycle. In my scheme, therefore, I would propose that even as we begin to accumulate more knowledge about moral decision making, we maintain a distinction between "true" competence and the state's acknowledgment of competence. In other words, I propose the comparison in Figure 1 between competence as it might indeed be, and competence as it ought to be allocated.

I offer this as an example of my personal value system and to point the way in which others might wish to modify moral judgments independent of the facts of development. In my system, I am more than prepared to limit the autonomy of the child beyond my intellectual recognition of its presence. I am prepared to allow him to suffer the humiliation, or the loss of pride, that comes with limited autonomy, secure in

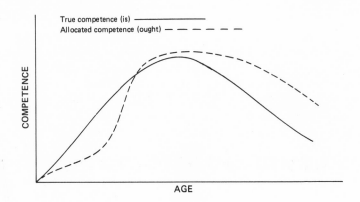

Figure 1

the knowledge that he will shortly achieve an age in which it will automatically be awarded him, and that this short delay will do little harm to his self-image or the values of our society. I propose that we compensate this young person for this deprivation by granting him, in his senescence, a more liberal allocation of autonomy (a more generous judgment of competence) than he deserves.

What I offer, then, is simply one example of a form of value analysis—a mechanism of negotiation, analysis, and arbitration—that will be necessary to establish some sound underpinnings to a concept as complex as variable competence.

perhaps than the ones to which minors might expose themselves "by their own improvident acts,"[11] but no less (and probably more) significant. The vantage from which the law views minors—that of presumed incompetence rather than competence—has costs for society as well as for minors. These costs include a shortage of treatment available to minors for conditions such as venereal disease, pregnancy, and drug abuse, as well as the recurrent withholding, while awaiting parental consent, of important but nonemergent medical treatment for juvenile injuries.[12] It is in part out of recognition of these costs that the law has come to acknowledge the competence of minors to decide or participate in decisions about various matters; indeed, the value of self-determination could be argued to weigh more heavily the more important the decision. Moreover, American judicial opinions and statutes have expanded children's self-choice, suggesting a change in vantage point that has already come about in the attitudes of other legal systems.

THREE NON–"EXCEPTIONS"

To apply the legal presumption of children's incompetence in practice it is not enough to determine whether a child's actual age is below a particular jurisdiction's age of majority. For the law has come to recognize at least a handful of exceptions to the general rule of minors' decisional incompetence; indeed it is hard to speak of "the rule" without

---

[11]*Id.* In modern law the notion that children are shielded from the consequences of their own "acts" is partially inaccurate. Minors' contracts may be voidable, but the minors will be judged by an adult standard of care in torts cases arising from their *acts*, at least while pursuing adult activities. Thus both as plaintiffs and defendants they may be greatly harmed by their improvident acts. *See, e.g.,* Daniels v. Evans, 107 N.H. 407, 224 A.2d 63 (1966).

[12]*See generally* Pilpel, *Minors' Rights to Medical Care,* 36 ALBANY L. REV. 462 (1972).

speaking of these limitations in the same breath as part of the legal standard of competence itself.

At the outset, however, one should note that three rules traditionally denominated "exceptions" by courts and commentators[13] are not really exceptions to the general law of minors' incompetence to consent to medical care. Instead, they permit treatment without valid consent by legally authorized persons. The most common is the "emergency exception," found generally in the case law and by statute as well in twenty-seven states.[14] The degree of urgency and danger that must be shown to overcome liability for proceeding without consent varies among American jurisdictions.

In its strictest form, the judicially created emergency rule permits treatment in cases where consent cannot be obtained quickly and delay will create a substantial risk to the life of the patient. In *Luka v. Lowrie*,[15] a 1912 Michigan case, a doctor was found not liable for failure to obtain consent of a fifteen-year-old boy's parents before amputating the boy's foot. Before the operation, the surgeon consulted with four doctors who agreed with him that an immediate amputation of the foot, which had been crushed by a locomotive, was necessary for the boy's survival. Because this emergency endangered life if not treated immediately and the time needed to reach the parents made it "impractical" to obtain their consent, the court held that as a matter of law, consent was not needed.

The Oklahoma courts reached a different outcome in 1936 in *Rogers v. Sells*,[16] where a fourteen-year-old boy's foot was amputated without the consent of his parents after an automobile accident. In this case, however, the emergency nature

---

[13]*See* Bennett, *Allocation of Child Medical Care Decision-Making Authority: A Suggested Interest Analysis*, 62 VA. L. REV. 285 (1976); Dunn, *The Availability of Abortion, Sterilization and Other Medical Treatment for Minor Patients*, 44 U.M.K.C. L. REV. 1 (1975); Wilkens, *Childrens' Rights: Removing the Parental Consent Barrier to Medical Treatment of Minors*, 31 ARIZ. ST. L. J. 31 (1975).

[14]*See* Appendix at 95–114.

[15]171 Mich. 122, 136 N.W. 1106 (1912).

[16]178 Okla. 103, 61 P.2d 1018 (1936).

of the injury was vigorously disputed. No X rays were taken, nor was there evidence that the operation could not have been safely delayed. Indeed, experts testified that the operation might not have been necessary. The court accepted the jury's determination that the doctor had failed to meet the burden of proving an emergency existed.

A year earlier a more expansive common law definition of emergency had been enunciated by a New York court in *Sullivan v. Montgomery*.[17] In refusing to find liability for a doctor's failure to obtain consent from the parents of a twenty-year-old baseball player before setting the youth's broken ankle, the court said:

> [T]he better reasoning supports the proposition that, if a physician or surgeon is confronted with an emergency which endangers the life or health of the patient, or that suffering or pain may be alleviated, it is his duty to do that which the occasion demands within the usual and customary practice among physicians and surgeons in the same locality.[18]

Most of the fifteen states that have enacted emergency statutes aimed specifically at minors require the physician to balance the feasibility of obtaining consent against the risks caused by the attendant delay.[19] The stricter rule formulated by most courts along *Luka* lines, however, has been incorporated in statutory law in a few states that permit emergency care without parental consent only when the physician (or other provider of medical care) believes the delay associated with obtaining consent will result in death or serious, irreparable harm.[20] Other states have followed the more liberal New York definition and allow minors to receive medical care without parental consent when delay in the initiation of care "would endanger *the health* of the minor."[21]

[17]155 Misc. 448, 279 N.Y.S. 575 (City Ct. of N.Y., Bronx Cty., 1935).

[18]*Id.* at 449, 279 N.Y.S. at 577.

[19]*See, e.g.*, ARIZ. REV. STAT. §44-133 (1967).

[20]*See, e.g.*, N. D. CENT. CODE §14-10-17.1 (Supp. 1977), where consent of parent or guardian is not needed only when a "life threatening situation" exists.

[21]FLA. STAT. ANN. §458.21(1) (West Supp. 1980) (emphasis added).

It is a mistake to treat the case law and statutes permitting emergency medical care for minors as establishing an "exception" to the general rule that minors are incompetent. The same rule applies to adults in emergencies. Thus the rule does not address the issue of competence; instead, presuming incompetence, it permits urgently needed care to be given without the consent of the adult patient (for him or herself) or the adult guardian (for a minor). The emergency rule is sometimes cited as an example of "implied consent," a denomination that reveals the same imprecision as terming it an "exception" to the rules about minors' incompetence to consent. The physical or mental incapacity of a patient to participate in emergency medical decisions does not *imply* anything about the patient's willingness to undergo treatment, but instead permits those rendering care to *infer* that this patient, like most people, would want such care to be given as is needed to preserve his or her life and health.[22]

A broadening of the emergency doctrine is found in the "physician-judgment" statutes enacted in seven states.[23] Under these statutes the condition requiring treatment need not be emergent. Instead, if in the professional's judgment an attempt to secure parental consent would increase the risk to the minor's health, then such consent is not required.

The third spurious "exception," termed the "best-interests" exception, is most often invoked when parents refuse to consent to a relatively simple procedure and failure to give treatment will result in substantial risk of death or permanent impairment of health. *In re Clark*[24] was such a case. There the

---

[22]*But see, e.g.*, R.I. GEN. LAWS §23-51-1 (Supp. 1980).

[23]ALA. CODE tit. 22, §8-3 (1975); KY. REV. STAT. §214-185 (1977); MD. ANN. CODE art. 43, §135(3) (Supp. 1980); MONT. REV. CODES ANN. §69-6104(2) (1977); OKLA. STAT. ANN. tit. 63 §2602(a)(6) (Supp. 1978); PA. STAT. ANN. tit. 35, §10104 (Purdon 1977); S.C. CODE §44-45-20 (1976). Two other states have what might best be termed "conditional minor" statutes that permit a minor to consent if he or she will be in serious danger unless health care is provided. ALASKA STAT. §09.65.100(2) (Supp. 1980); NEV. REV. STAT. §129.030(1)(d) (1978).

[24]21 Ohio Op.2d 86, 185 N.E.2d 128 (C.P. Lucas Cty. 1962).

court permitted blood transfusions for a badly burned boy despite the opposition of his parents, who were Jehovah's Witnesses. Because they involve limitations on parents' authority and not modifications of the general rule of children's incompetence to choose medical care for themselves prior to reaching the age of majority, these cases are more fully examined in the next chapter.

THE TRUE EXCEPTIONS

Emancipation

Under the common law, contracts made by minors are voidable.[25] Since the power to avoid a contract cannot be relinquished until the minor has reached majority, the contract is binding only after the minor has reached his majority and ratified it.[26] There are exceptions to this rule based on the subject matter of the contract: minors are liable for payment for necessaries provided to them, including medical treatment.[27]

The first true exception to the rule of minors' legal incompetence came into play in litigation commenced by people wishing to hold minors to their contracts. A minor who was "emancipated" from the control of his or her parents, it was argued, ought to be able to enter into contracts without seeking parental approval. Emancipation has traditionally been seen as a release from the restraints of minority and a grant of the privileges and responsibilities of majority, by and with the consent of the minor's parents.[28] This consent may be

---

[25]2 S. WILLISTON, CONTRACTS §226 (3d ed. W. Jaeger 1959).

[26]*Id.* at 239.

[27]Bancredit v. Bethea, 65 N.J. Super. 538, 168 A.2d 250 (1961).

[28]Hensley v. Hilton, 191 Ind. 309, 131 N.E. 38 (1921); Bates v. Bates, 62 Misc.2d 498, 310 N.Y.S.2d 26 (1970). *See generally* Katz, Schroeder & Sidman, *Emancipating Our Children: Coming of Legal Age in America*, 7 FAM. L. Q. 211 (1973).

given expressly, by written[29] or oral agreement.[30] If such an agreement is found, it will be given great weight.

The conduct of parents and child provides an alternative basis for a finding of emancipation. A child's actions are important evidence in determining whether he or she is emancipated not because they reflect the child's maturity, but as evidence of the parents' attitudes and conduct toward the child. That a child entirely supports him or herself may be sufficient evidence that the child is emancipated, but that is so because it is evidence of the parents' consent to the emancipation through the omission of their duties to the child.[31]

Specific conduct by the parties, though essential evidence in determining emancipation, is controlling only in two instances, marriage[32] and military service.[33] These absolute indicators of emancipation developed for two reasons. First, both result in major changes in the life of the minor; particularly when in the service, it would be impractical if not impossible to treat the minor as unemancipated. Second, parental consent is often required before a minor can marry or join the military. Thus the parent is really expressly emancipating the minor by giving that consent.[34] Of course that is only partially true for marriage since the statutory age for marriage without parental consent is below the age of majority in some jurisdictions, and a legal marriage by a minor is sufficient by itself for a finding of emancipation whether or not there was parental consent.[35]

[29]Matter of Stillman, 60 Misc.2d 819, 304 N.Y.S.2d 20 (1970).

[30]Carricato v. Carricato, 384 S.W.2d 85 (Ky. Ct. App. 1964).

[31]Detwiler v. Detwiler, 162 Pa. Super. 383, 57 A.2d 426 (1948); Bates v. Bates, 62 Misc.2d 498, 310 N.Y.S.2d 26 (1976).

[32]Allen v. Arthur, 139 Ind. 460, 220 N.E.2d 658 (1968); Smith v. Seibly, 72 Wash.2d 16, 431P.2d 719 (1967); Bach v. Long Island Jewish Hosp., 49 Misc.2d 207, 267 N.Y.S.2d 289 (Sup. Ct. 1966). *But see, e.g., In re* Palumbo, 172 Misc. 55, 14 N.Y.S.2d 329 (1939).

[33]*See, e.g., In re* Grimley, 137 U.S. 147 (1890); Iroquois Iron Co. v. Industrial Comm., 294 Ill. 106, 128 N.E. 289 (1920); Baker v. Baker, 41 Vt.55 (1867).

[34]*See* note 31 *supra.*

[35]Smith v. Seilby, 72 Wash.2d 16, 431 P.2d 719 (1967).

A minor may be deemed emancipated without marrying or enlisting. Such a determination will be made only through an examination of the surrounding circumstances such as the living situation and relationship of the parents and child in question. In *Cohen v. Delaware, Lackawanna, and Western Railroad*[36] the court found that an eighteen-year-old who had left home with his mother's consent, moved to another state, found a job, and provided entirely for his own support, including education, was emancipated. The boy did live with his aunt, but there was no evidence that she exercised control over him. In several cases minors have been found to be emancipated, even if living at home with their parents, as long as they have been working and paying for their own support, including room and board.[37] The minor's residence and payment for that residence are thus important factors, although in one case a minor living at home was found to be emancipated on evidence that she was supporting herself *except* for room and board.[38] The minor's employment, if any, and retention of wages, responsibility for debts, and ownership of property will also be considered. Owning a car, for instance, may be evidence of emancipation.[39] Two other factors that have been cited by courts are the dependence of the minor for tax purposes[40] and the disciplinary control of the parents over the minor.[41]

Judicial recognition of emancipation can come in the form of a decree, declaring the emancipation, or through litigation in which emancipation of the minor is an issue. The latter is much more common. For example, emancipation is important in medical litigation as a defense to a suit for damages for failure to obtain parental consent to a procedure. If the minor

[36]150 Misc. 450, 269 N.Y.S. 667 (1934).
[37]*See, e.g.,* Wurth v. Wurth, 322 S.W.2d 745 (Mo., 1959); Giovagnioli v. Fort Orange Constr. Co., 148 App. Div. 489, 133 N.Y.S. 92 (1911).
[38]Wood v. Wood, 135 Conn. 280, 63 A.2d 586 (1948).
[39]Parker v. Parker, 230 S.C. 28, 94 S.E.2d 12 (1956).
[40]Wadoz v. United Nat'l Indem. Co., 274 Wis. 383, 80 N.W.2d 262 (1957).
[41]Gillikin v. Burbage, 263 N.C. 317, 139 S.E.2d 753 (1965).

consented to the procedure and if the minor is emancipated, parental consent is not required. In an action for either a decree or damages, the emancipation of the child is never presumed: the burden of proof in establishing emancipation is on the person asserting such a claim.[42]

There are few cases involving consent to medical procedures by minors where the case law on emancipation has been determinative.[43] More than half the states, however, have enacted emancipation statutes that give minors who have exhibited certain types of conduct the right to make decisions about medical treatment. Relevant factors are similar to those in the case law: age, marital status, parenthood or pregnancy, residency, and financial independence.[44]

Under either statutory or common law, emancipation is the result of engaging in certain recognizable types of conduct that evidence a split between the minor and his parents. When that separation is sufficiently large and when the parents, by action or omission, are found to have consented to it, the minor will be deemed emancipated and recognized as having the power of self-determination in medical matters.

Partial Emancipation

Not all judicial decrees of emancipation result in the total termination of mutual rights and obligations of parent and child.[45] A child may be able to assert rights normally incident to total emancipation (e.g., health care choice) while the parents maintain control of the family for all other purposes and the minor continues to be "protected" by all his legal disa-

[42]See Allen v. Arthur, 139 Ind. App. 460, 220 N.E.2d 658 (1966).
[43]Wilkens, *Childrens' Rights: Removing the Parental Consent Barrier to Medical Treatment of Minors*, 31 ARIZ. ST. L. J. 31 (1975).
[44]See Appendix, Table A-1, column III, at 95.
[45]Porter v. Powell, 79 Iowa 151, 44 N.W. 295 (1890).

bilities. Alternatively, a child might be able to exercise all rights for a limited period of time.[46]

The Mature-Minor "Exception"

Another exception to the rule that a minor is incompetent to consent for medical treatment is termed the "mature-minor rule." Stated generally, this exception provides that a minor may give effective consent for the purpose of receiving medical treatment if he or she understands the nature and purposes of the proposed treatment. This rule comes closer than emancipation to recognizing minors as individual human beings with an interest in self-determination that should enter into consideration in any proceedings in which they are involved.

The importance a minor's level of comprehension could have in determining whether an effective consent to medical care has been rendered was first recognized in a 1906 decision, *Bakker v. Welsh*.[47] There, a physician was sued after his seventeen-year-old patient died while under anesthesia for an operation to remove a tumor from the boy's ear. The plaintiff-father based his claim on the physician's failure to obtain parental consent. The court recognized not only that the father had been apprised of the general course of the treatment but also that the minor patient had "almost grown into manhood." The lack of consent was held not to result in any liability.

The formal requirement of parental consent was dispensed with by the Kansas Supreme Court in *Younts v. St. Francis Hospital & School of Nursing, Inc.*[48] A seventeen-year-old girl was visiting her divorced mother in the hospital when

---

[46]Vaupel v. Bellach, 261 Iowa 376, 154 N.W.2d 149 (1967); *See generally* Katz, Schroeder & Sidman, *Emancipating Our Children: Coming of Legal Age in America*, 7 FAM. L. Q. 211, 215 (1973).

[47]144 Mich. 632, 108 N.W. 94 (1906).

[48]205 Kan. 292, 469 P.2d 330 (1970).

her finger was injured by a closing door. Based on the inability of her mother to consent (she was unconscious at the time) and the nonserious nature of the injury, the court found that the minor's consent to first aid and a skin graft was effective and that no action for failure to obtain parental consent could be maintained against the treating physician. The factual situation in *Younts* thus reflects the narrowing of the "mature-minor rule" that has typically occurred in judicial decisions emphasizing the impracticability of obtaining parental consent (analogous to the "emergency exception") and the relatively simple nature of the medical procedure in question. But the language of the Kansas court was much more expansive in articulating the rule: "The sufficiency of a minor's consent depends upon his ability to understand and comprehend the nature of the surgical procedure, the risks involved and the probability of attaining the desired results in the light of the circumstances which attend."[49]

Although the latter criteria for determining the validity of a minor's consent to medical treatment parallel those usually invoked with respect to the doctrine of informed consent,[50] the court's focus on the individual minor's ability to understand the nature of the procedure goes further toward protecting the patient than does the model of informed consent customarily applied to adults.[51] This additional protection provides a safeguard against unwarranted or ill-advised availability of medical care for immature minors. It also centers courts' and physicians' attention on the individual minor and only allows a legally binding consent to be given by those minors who are able sufficiently to comprehend the proposed treatment.

The inaccessibility of a parent is not an absolute prerequisite to turning to a minor for a decision about his or her

---

[49]*Id.* at 300, 469 P.2d at 337.

[50]*See* Canterbury v. Spence, 464 F.2d 772 (D.C. Cir. 1972).

[51]*See generally* Capron, *Informed Consent in Catastrophic Disease Research and Treatment*, 123 U. PA. L. REV. 340 (1974).

own medical care. In *In re Green*[52] the seventeen-year-old patient suffered from severe curvature of the spine which resulted in an inability to stand or walk. The child's doctors recommended corrective surgery, which was approved by his mother. Because of her religious beliefs, however, she would not consent to the required blood transfusions. The doctors instituted a legal action to have the child declared "neglected" so the court could order the necessary procedures. The requested order was refused and the case was remanded to the trial court to determine the minor patient's feelings toward the proposed operation. The court reasoned that "it would be most anomalous to ignore Ricky [the patient] in this situation when we consider the preference of an intelligent child of sufficient maturity in determining custody."[53]

The *Green* case also suggests that judges are willing to extend the mature-minor rule to more complex medical interventions. Similarly, in *Lacey v. Laird*,[54] a 1956 decision, the Ohio Supreme Court acknowledged the Michigan court's decision in *Bakker* but felt constrained by Ohio's formal requirement of parental consent and awarded nominal damages. It did, however, refuse to ignore the eighteen-year-old plaintiff's "knowing and understanding" consent to cosmetic sur-

---

[52]220 Pa. Super. 191, 286 A.2d 681 (1971), rev'd and remanded 448 Pa. 338, 292 A.2d 387 (1972), dismissal on remand aff'd, 452 Pa. 373, 307 A.2d 279 (1973). A physician petitioned to be appointed guardian of Ricky Ricardo Green, then sixteen years old, in order to approve of the corrective operation and, if needed, blood transfusions. This petition was originally denied by Judge Hazel H. Brown of the Family Division (Juvenile Branch) of the Court of Common Pleas of Philadelphia County (No. 174612, December Term, 1970). The Superior Court of Pennsylvania reversed, but was itself subsequently reversed by the Supreme Court of Pennsylvania which remanded the case to the Court of Common Pleas, with instructions to conduct an evidentiary hearing on the wishes of the child. Ricky, by then seventeen years old, expressed clear opposition to the proposed operation. The lower court dismissed the petition, a decision then affirmed by the Supreme Court, which had retained jurisdiction.

[53]*Id.* at 349, 292 A.2d at 392.

[54]106 Ohio 12, 139 N.E.2d 25 (1956).

gery and hence did not allow more substantial damages.[55] Although plastic surgery on a nose might be found by a jury a relatively "simple operation,"[56] it is still much more than routine. Thus the emphasis is on whether the patient can sufficiently understand the procedure and compare its risks and benefits, not on a rigid rule about the types of procedures or the age of the patients.

Because of the considerable body of precedent that has developed around the physician's obligation to secure parental consent before treating a minor, it has been necessary to draw support for the mature-minor exception from many diverse areas of the law in addition to arguing that the old requirement has become outdated in modern society. For example, the court's opinion in *Lacey* criticized the general rule for being based on the rights of the parents and the accompanying financial responsibility while ignoring the capacity of the minor to consent. The general rule allows all the rights of a minor to be obscured in the discussion of parental prerogatives. Judge Kingsley Taft, joined by two other judges, wrote a concurring opinion in *Lacey* that points to a series of anomalies: a minor could give an effective consent for the purpose of deciding whether there was an assumption of risk in a tort action[57] or whether a forcible rape had occurred[58] and could also be found to have criminal capacity,[59] but could not give an effective consent to secure medical care. His conclusion was that performance of a surgical operation on a mature girl with her "consent" would ordinarily not amount

[55]The court allowed only nominal damages, characterized them as usually amounting to no more than one or two dollars, and said "[a] verdict for $100 or $200 or more does not come within the definition of nominal damages." *Id.* at 19, 139 N.E.2d at 31.

[56]*Id.* at 16, 139 N.E.2d at 28.

[57]Porter v. Toledo Terminal Co., 152 Ohio St. 403, 466, 90 N.E.2d 142, 143 (1950) (Jury should have been charged with respect to thirteen-year-old plaintiff's possible assumption of risk.); Centrello v. Basky, 164 Ohio St. 41, 128 N.E.2d 80 (1922) (ten-year-old plaintiff).

[58]*See, e.g.,* Smith v. State, 12 Ohio 466 (1861).

[59]*See* text accompanying notes 100–103 *infra*.

to an assault and battery even if parental consent had not been secured.

Several states have recognized the advantages of a mature-minor rule and have enacted statutes based on the common law. The codifications of the rule represent a marked improvement over the emancipation statutes discussed above. Many of the events that establish grounds for emancipation are poor indicators of the level of understanding needed to render a knowing and intelligent consent to the provision of health care.

The degree of specificity with which mature-minor statutes speak varies greatly from state to state. Mississippi's statute allows a minor "of sufficient intelligence to understand and appreciate the consequences of the proposed surgical or medical treatment or procedures" to give a valid consent.[60] This provision does little more than codify the common law and does not give the treating professional any useful guidelines to determine exactly what level of understanding the patient must demonstrate. It goes further than the common law, however, since possible treatments are not limited to simple procedures nor is its application dependent on the impracticality of parental consent. Idaho has a somewhat more comprehensive statute and provides that consent is valid when given by a minor who is of ordinary intelligence and awareness, sufficient to comprehend the need for, the nature of, and the significant risks ordinarily inherent in the proposed treatment.[61] Thus the law seems to require a determination that the minor patient is able to give a valid informed consent. But some commentators have suggested that this type of language is too ambiguous because it does not exactly define what terms the patient must understand, that is, standard laymen's terms, calculated to be understood by a reasonable person under similar circumstances,[62] or terms

[60]Miss. CODE ANN. §41-41-3(h) (1972).

[61]IDAHO CODE §39-4302 (1976).

[62]See, e.g., Wilkens, Children's Rights: Removing the Parental Consent Barrier to Medical Treatment of Minors, 31 ARIZ. ST. L. J. 31 (1975).

understood by the particular patient being treated. If, however, the courts were to follow a formula such as the one set forth in *Lacey*, attention would be given to the last of these alternatives whenever a minor was the subject of the litigation.[63] It has also been argued that these statutes give the physician too much opportunity to overreach the legislature's intended bounds and administer treatment to all minors who present themselves.[64] It seems likely that reference to the existing body of precedent surrounding the doctrine of informed consent, careful scrutiny of the specific patient in question, and the specter of potential liability would alleviate any problems of this nature.

The mature-minor exception plainly has significant impact not only on the content of the "rule" that all minors are incompetent but also on the logical starting point of that rule, which presumes that all persons under the age of eighteen lack the capacity to make decisions for themselves concerning medical matters. Moreover, this impact is much more direct than that of the "emancipation exception," since the latter grew out of situations in which the law was responding to the cessation of parental rights and obligations rather than to evidence of a child's maturity. As formulated by the more liberal judicial opinions and statutes, the mature-minor rule alters existing law to such an extent that the "rule" on minors' decision-making authority might be stated thus: a child who is capable of understanding the nature and consequences of a particular medical intervention, and of its primary alternatives including nonintervention, may give consent, and one

---

[63]This formula is legislatively recognized in the Idaho Code which, in addition to providing a comprehensive definition of who may consent, attempts to alleviate any confusion with respect to the terms required to be understood by providing that the health care may only be provided "if the *consenting person* appears to the physician or dentist securing the consent to possess such requisite intelligence and awareness at the time of giving it." IDAHO CODE §39-4302 (1976) (emphasis added).

[64]Wadlington, *Minors and Health Care: The Age of Consent*, 11 OSGOODE HALL L. J. 115, 125 (1973).

who is not may not. Although the courts have for the most part hedged in the exception more than this reformulation would acknowledge, the strains in maintaining the present view of the incompetence of minors are unmistakable. And they are being increased by other legal developments, especially those involving such highly charged areas as the medical treatment of reproductive and drug problems in minors.

Specialized Consent Statutes

Although only five states have enacted "mature-minor" statutes, every state has empowered minors with the right to obtain medical treatment for specific diseases or conditions on their own authority. The conditions and diseases that are most often provided for are of a sensitive nature or of grave public concern. The statutes appear to have been enacted because minors would be hesitant to seek treatment for the disease if prior parental consent were required. Consequently, little can be concluded from these statutes about society's view of the extent and limits of minors' competence. Instead, the statutes are probably better viewed as a legislative response to the public outcry over the social consequences of the particular conditions, principally venereal disease and drug abuse. Other diseases and conditions that have been statutorily recognized include alcohol abuse, pregnancy, mental disorders, and communicable diseases. Many states also allow minors to receive birth control counseling and devices without parental consent.

Although they were enacted for public health reasons and probably do nothing more than explicitly recognize the applicability of the "emergency nonexception" to a particular group of diseases (i.e., under the case law a physician would probably be successful in defending an action for failure to obtain parental consent for treatment for venereal disease in a minor who declined treatment if his or her parents would have to be informed), the specialized consent statutes by the fact of their existence give further impetus to a reformulation of the traditional view of minors' incompetence.

If a minor is competent to give a valid consent to procedures associated with a condition as complex as pregnancy, it follows that she should also be able to understand and consent to matters of less importance, such as physical examinations or common illnesses. If judges and legislators were to focus their attention on the logical inconsistency in the present "rule" and "special consent exceptions" they might decide that the guidepost should be the ability of each minor to effect a valid "informed consent" thereby removing the need for specialized consent statutes.

Of course, the desire to assure the availability of health care to minors is likely to be tempered with the paternalistic concern for the wisdom of minors in availing themselves of such care. The latter concern is manifested in the specialized statutes of some states, which impose minimum age requirements on the minor's ability to consent. These age requirements are designed to prevent children who the legislators feel are totally incapable of understanding the nature of their problem from securing medical care without the knowledge and consent of their parents.

Constitutional Considerations

Although society's attitude toward the legal competence of minors emerges primarily in the common law of torts and contract, recent Supreme Court decisions have begun to create constitutional law touching on this issue. The holdings of these cases tend to favor an expanded view of children's decision-making abilities. Perhaps more important, the language in which the issue has been discussed seems likely to contribute to changing the vantage point from which the law approaches minor's decision-making authority. Thus these decisions (which—like the specialized medical treatment statutes—formally address only a limited question) fall like a stone into the waters of the law, creating ever-broadening ripples that may lap against unexpected shores.

In constitutional litigation the issue of interest here is typically framed as a dispute about the extent of state authority to control the lives of children in ways to which their parents object. Yet, as Justice Douglas in partial dissent pointed out in the Amish school case in 1972,[65] the right of the children to decide was the underlying issue.

> The Court's analysis assumes that the only interests at stake in the case are those of the Amish parents on the one hand, and those of the State on the other. The difficulty with this approach is that, despite the Court's claim, the parents are seeking to vindicate not only their own free exercise claims, but also those of their high-school-age children.
>
> . . . Although the lower courts and a majority of this Court assume an identity of interest between parent and child, it is clear that they have treated the religious interest of the child as a factor in the analysis.
>
> . . . If the parents in this case are allowed a religious exemption, the inevitable effect is to impose the parents' notion of religious duty upon their children. Where the child is mature enough to express potentially conflicting desires, it would be an invasion of the child's rights to permit such an imposition without canvassing his views.[66]

Likewise, when the issue is framed in terms of the state power to compel children's behavior at their parents' behest, as in *Kremens v. Bartley*,[67] the explicit issue of allocating decision-making authority must rest on implicit or explicit resolution of the boundaries of minors' competence.

Although the Supreme Court's decisions have already begun affecting the resolution of the issue of minors' competence, the many questions of minors' constitutional rights are not ones that the Court has eagerly essayed to resolve, as Justice Marshall, joined by Justice Brennan, observed in

[65]Wisconsin v. Yoder, 406 U.S. 205 (1972).

[66]*Id.* at 241-2 (Douglas, J., dissenting in part).

[67]402 F. Supp. 1039 (E. D. Pa. 1975), *remanded*, 431 U.S. 119 (1977), *reconsidered sub. nom.* Institutionalized Juveniles v. Secretary of Public Welfare, 459 F. Supp. 30 (E. D. Pa. *rev'd*, 442 U.S. 640 (1979) (States revised statute and regulations for civil commitment of children for mental health treatment at parents' request satisfy due process standards).

dissenting from the denial of certiorari in a recent case raising one such issue.[68] Nevertheless, the recognition that decisions about medical care are matters of fundamental importance protected from state intervention by the constitutional umbrella of "privacy" has made it inevitable that the Court would be petitioned to dispose of cases about children's role in decision making.

The notion that matters involving health and family are constitutionally regarded as "private" was first raised in *Griswold v. Connecticut*[69] in 1965 and then expounded more fully in the 1973 abortion decisions.[70] The Court in other contexts had held that children as well as adults are protected by the Bill of Rights,[71] while acknowledging a broader scope for permissible state regulation.[72] Thus a question arose about children's rights concerning decisions about their own medical care, and in 1976 the justices were squarely presented with a dispute turning on the extent of minors' decision-making authority.

In *Planned Parenthood of Missouri v. Danforth*[73] the Court reviewed a state statute that sought to give the parents of *unmarried* women under eighteen years of age a controlling power over the abortion decision that the state could not, after *Roe v. Wade*, exercise directly. It had been argued in support of the statute that it was a permissible means of supporting parental authority and the family unit. Justice Blackmun, writing for the majority, found such reasoning unpersuasive; family structure is likely to have "already [been] fractured" when the pregnancy has led to a fundamental conflict between a woman and her parents. Furthermore, the court held that "any independent interest the parent may have in the termination of the minor daughter's

[68]Bykofsky v. Borough of Middletown, *cert. denied,* 429 U.S. 964 (1977).
[69]381 U.S. 479 (1943).
[70]Roe v. Wade, 410 U.S. 113 (1973); Doe v. Bolton 410 U.S. 179 (1973).
[71]*In re* Gault, 387 U.S. 1 (1967).
[72]McKeiver v. Pennsylvania, 403 U.S. 528 (1971).
[73]428 U.S. 52 (1976).

pregnancy is no more weighty than the right of privacy of the competent minor mature enough to have become pregnant."[74]

As this quotation displays, the majority opinion treats the central issue—whether the state may deprive a minor of decision-making power about a "private" medical matter in order to protect the minor from her own folly—only obliquely and unclearly. The Court might be read as saying that a girl's reproductive maturity renders her a competent decision maker about medical care related to reproduction. But the companion case, *Bellotti v. Baird*,[75] eliminates that possibility; the Court remanded *Bellotti* to the Supreme Judicial Court of Massachusetts for clarification of a statute that made a court order an alternative to parental consent for unmarried women under eighteen seeking abortions. No construction that could have been made by the Massachusetts court would have rendered the statute constitutional if *Danforth* required a pregnant girl to be regarded as legally competent *because* she was capable of becoming pregnant. Alternatively, Justice Blackmun's reference to "the right of privacy of the competent minor" might be read as simply adopting the definition of competence used by the common law. But such a reading would beg the entire issue, since the age of competence is set at eighteen years and the statute *only applied* to unmarried persons under the age of eighteen years.

In his dissenting opinion in *Danforth*, Justice White protests that the majority has expressed "absolutely no reason" why a state may not utilize the "traditional way" of "requiring parental consultations and consent"[76] to protect minors from making a decision not in their own best interest. In answering White, the majority seems to accept as a part of *constitutional* jurisprudence the change in vantage point toward minors'

[74]*Id.* at 95.
[75]428 U.S. 132 (1976).
[76]Danforth v. Planned Parenthood Assoc. of Mo., 428 U.S. 52, 95 (1976) (White, J., dissenting).

competence described in this chapter. For the fault of the
Missouri statute in the Court's view is that it imposes a "blan-
ket provision" of parental consent for unmarried minors.
Once it is established that the right of privacy protects pregnant females from any state interference in their decision to
abort during the first twelve weeks of pregnancy, the removal
of this protection from any group (e.g., unmarried women
under 18) is unacceptable "without a sufficient justification."[77] And it is thus apparent that Justice Blackmun and his
colleagues take it for granted that society does *not* automatically regard all seventeen-year-olds—nor even *all* ten- or
eleven-year-olds—as incapable of making important medical
decisions. A state thus seems to be required to overcome a
presumption (of constitutional as well as common law dimensions) of patient autonomy by showing that a particular
patient is *not* "capable of giving informed consent."[78]

REEVALUATING THE VANTAGE POINT

The picture of the decision-making authority of children
regarding medical research and treatment that emerges from
this survey of rules and exceptions is one clouded by conflicting aims. Although there has been no abandonment of

---

[77]*Id.* at 75.

[78]Bellotti v. Baird, 428 U.S. 132, 139 (1976). The interests inherent in the
parent–child relationship (*e.g.*, family integrity, protecting adolescents, etc.)
continue, however, to be given weight as a basis for treating pregnant
minors differently from women over 21 years old. In *H.L. v. Matheson*, U.S.
67 L.Ed.2d 388, 101 S.Ct. 1164 (1981), the Supreme Court court upheld a
Utah statute requiring a physician to "notify, if possible" the parents of a
minor upon whom an abortion is performed. As applied to unemancipated
minors, living with and dependent upon their parents and making no claim
of maturity, the Utah statute was found not to restrict unconstitutionally
minors' right of privacy (to obtain an abortion) or right to enter a physician–patient relationship. A minor's decisionmaking authority, as recognized in *Bellotti* and *Danforth*, was held not to be defeated by the mere
requirement of notifying parents when possible.

the intention to protect children's well-being, a second aim—preservation of parental control over the person and property of children—which often mingled with the protective one and lent it controlling force in the shaping of the rules, seems now to be given less deference. The social context in which the parental-control rule developed and the economic reality on which it was founded (all members of the family working, in shop or field, as a united productive entity) are largely historical relics. Moreover, the potential for parental exploitation—occasionally manifested dramatically—seems to have made the parental-control rationale less attractive.[79] The framers of rules have therefore been left to balance the objective of individual autonomy against solely the objective of protection. This fact may explain why recent statutes and judicial decisions have given greater weight to minors' own wishes, even though to do so increases the risk of improvident decisions. This trend is likely to increase as the constitutional protection of "privacy" is applied to medical and other significant personal decisions besides the choice to bear or not to bear children.[80]

As the *exceptions*—the "mature-minor rule" and the constitutionally protected authority to obtain medical care for "private" (i.e., significant) matters without parental veto—come to be more important in shaping the *rule*, it becomes necessary to return to the beginning and reexamine the law's basic vantage point: that children, unlike adults, are

[79]One example of this exploitation was the alleged misuse of money earned by child actors by those children's parents and guardians. Such a case involving child actor Jackie Coogan was widely publicized in the press in the 1930s. Shortly thereafter, the California legislature enacted legislation permitting judges who had been called on to review contracts involving minor actors and actresses to require the minor's parent or guardian to set up a trust fund or savings plan, thereby conserving as much as half of the minor's earnings. Cal. Civ. Code §36.1 (West 1939). *See generally* Kingsley, *The Work of the 1939 California Legislature: Personal and Domestic Relations*, 13 S. CAL. L. REV. 37, 44 (1939).

[80]*See The Minor's Right to Consent to Medical Treatment: A Corollary of the Constitutional Right of Privacy*, 48 SO. CAL. L. REV. 1417 (1975).

to be presumed incompetent. Such a reexamination reveals that the American law has been far from consistent in employing this vantage point, and that foreign jurisdictions, particularly Commonwealth countries, have explicitly approached the matter of minors' decision-making authority from a contrary point of view. Thus a more individually based rule—starting with presumptive competence for at least some groups of minors and removing decision-making authority only as required by particular immaturity or incapacity—is workable although perhaps more difficult to administer.

Commonwealth Jurisprudence

Although American courts have established a presumption that a child is incompetent to give a valid consent for the provision of medical care, Commonwealth courts seem to have approached the issue from a different perspective. In 1969 the United Kingdom enacted a statute allowing minors sixteen and over to consent to medical care,[81] and the same age has also been advanced on the basis of analogy to statutes governing sexual offenses.[82] Yet there is no direct common law basis for choosing sixteen as the age at which minors have power to consent to treatment. The increasingly widely held opinion is that in the Commonwealth, "[t]he common law does not fix any age, below which minors are automatically incapable of consenting to medical procedures. It all depends on whether the minor can understand what is involved in the procedure in question."[83]

---

[81]Family Law Reform Act, 1969, c. 46, §8(1). Quebec, moreover, has enacted legislation that allows even younger minors (those over fourteen) to consent to medical care. Pub. Health Protection Act, Que. Stat. Ch. 42, §36 (1972).

[82]Skegg, *Consenting to Medical Procedures on Minors,* 36 MOD. L. REV. 370, 372-373 (1973).

[83]*Id.* at 373; *See also* Goose, *Consent to Medical Treatment: A Minor Digression,* 9 U.B.C. L. REV. 56 (1974).

This view, which is still not universally taken,[84] finds some support in Commonwealth cases. In 1910 the Ontario Court of King's Bench ruled that a teen-age boy could give a valid consent to a throat operation.[85] The court refused to hold the hospital or physician liable for damages for failing to obtain the consent of the boy's parents, since the boy himself had consented, even though he was a minor and subject to epileptic seizures. In finding that consent valid, the court said, "He is not of the highest intelligence, but it appears that he was nineteen years of age and capable of taking care of himself."[86]

Two cases involving tattooing are further examples of judicial inquiry into capacity. In the first case[87] the court found that a thirteen-year-old boy gave a valid consent to being tattooed. It should be noted that the tattoo complained of was the boy's twenty-third, and the principal objection was that it depicted a musclewoman. The judge noted that the boy had sought out the artist, commissioned the work, and accepted it at the time. The consent of two boys, ages twelve and thirteen, to tattooing was held invalid in a case two years later because of the minors' incapacity. "If a child of the age of understanding was unable to appreciate the nature of the act, apparent consent to it was no consent at all."[88]

The best judicial statement of the view that a minor's capacity to understand a medical procedure should determine the legal sufficiency of that individual's consent is found in the Ontario High Court decision in *Johnston v. Wellesley Hospital*.[89] A twenty-year-old patient sued the treating physician

---

[84]*See, e.g.*, O'Bryan, *The Consent of the Patient to Surgical and Medical Procedures*, 8 Proc. Med-Leg. Soc. Vict. 138 (1961).

[85]Booth v. Toronto Gen. Hosp., 17 O.W.R. 118 (Ont. K.B. 1910).

[86]*Id.* at 144.

[87]R. v. Dilks, 4 Med. Sci. L. 209 (1964).

[88]Burrel v. Hammer, 116 New L. J. 1658 (Q.B. 1966) (decision not reported officially).

[89]17 D.L.R.3d 139 (1970).

for failing to obtain parental consent after a novel dermatologic treatment, to which he had consented, left him badly scarred. Writing for the court, Judge Addly stated that he could "find nothing in any of the old reported cases, except where infants of tender age or young children were involved, where the Courts have found that a person under 21 years of age was legally incapable of consenting to medical treatment."[90] He noted that in the analogous area of consent to sexual intercourse, minors under the age of fourteen had been found to give valid consent. Judge Addly approved of the view of the law, as expressed by Lord Nathan,

> that the most satisfactory solution of the problem is to rule that an infant who is capable of appreciating fully the nature and consequences of a particular operation or of particular treatment can give an effective consent thereto, and in such cases the consent of the guardian is unnecessary; but that where the infant is without that capacity, any apparent consent by him or her will be a nullity, the sole right to consent being vested in the guardian.[91]

Lord Nathan's bold view carried the court in part because it was so forcefully expressed, but also because the "general rule" from which he proposed to offer relief (that "the consent of the infant's guardian must be obtained before the infant is subjected to medical treatment")[92] found so little support either in the law of decided cases or in sound reasoning as applied across the board to "infants" of all ages.

One commentator has described *Johnston* as merely a Canadian statement of the mature-minor rule,[93] but that is not wholly accurate. First, reliance on the rule articulated in *Johnston* is not limited to simple procedures or to occasions in which parental consent is not easily obtainable. Second, the court indicated the test is always the ability of the child

[90]*Id.* at 144.

[91]H. L. NATHAN, MEDICAL NEGLIGENCE 176 (1957).

[92]*Id.* at 177.

[93]Wadlington, *Minors and Health Care: The Age of Consent*, 11 OSGOODE HALL L. J. 115 (1973).

to understand the procedure, that is, there is no lower age limit for application of the rule. Thus the commentators who claim that *Johnston* is merely a restatement of the common law are plainly reading it too narrowly or are overstating the common law. It would be better to say that the Ontario court, in accepting Lord Nathan's view, was adopting a vantage point neither clearly supported nor refuted by prior cases. As a rule of law it is a practical solution that supplants only unsupported assumptions about incompetence, not good law.

Custody Proceedings

Examples can also be found in branches of American jurisprudence in which the "competence" rather than the "incompetence" vantage point is employed. In legal proceedings to determine the custody of children, for instance, the law has taken a stance flexible enough to give consideration to wishes of the children involved. If a child is below the so-called "age of discretion" at which he has the legal capacity to make a binding choice between competing potential custodians, then the child's feelings will be entitled to the "most serious consideration."[94] The expressed wishes of these children are not considered to be controlling, however.[95] There is no fixed age that clearly establishes the "age of discretion," which is said to be dependent on the individual child's mental development.[96]

Thus in this field the law has abandoned administrative convenience in favor of a subjective determination of the propriety of an individual minor's participation in an important

[94]Snellrose v. Harris, 432 Pa. 158, 247 A.2d 596, 600 (1968); Rosenberger v. Rosenberger, 21 Ill. App.3d 550, 316 N.E.2d 1 (1974).
[95]Commonwealth *ex rel* Goldbaum v. Goldbaum, 161 Pa. Super. 131, 53 A.2d 796 (1947).
[96]State v. Kinne, 8 Wash.2d 1, 111 P.2d 222 (1941). Some state courts, however, have established a specific "age of discretion," from which judges depart on a case-by-case basis.

decision. Of course, a smaller issue is at stake than in the determination of competence to make health care decisions, for in custody cases the issue is only a child's participation in a judicial proceeding not his or her authority to make possibly momentous choices as freely as an adult could.

Evidence

The law of evidence provides a further instance. The competence of a minor to give testimony is determined subjectively, based on an examination of the individual by the court.[97] The Supreme Court examined this issue in a nineteenth-century case, *Wheeler v. United States*,[98] and established the criteria for determining competence to testify that remain controlling today.[99] In *Wheeler*, the Court upheld a murder conviction based in part on the testimony of a five-and-a-half-year-old boy who had witnessed the crime a few weeks before his fifth birthday. The Court found that age is never an absolute bar to competence to give testimony: "While no one would think of calling as a witness an infant only two or three years old, there is no precise age which determines the question of competency."[100] Instead, the Court said, competence "depends on the capacity and intelligence of the child, his appreciation of the difference between truth and falsehood, as well as of his duty to tell the former."[101]

This test is really a two-part one. First, does the child have the requisite cognitive ability to be a useful witness (that is, can he or she accurately observe, recollect, and communicate facts)? Second, does the child know the difference between truth and falsehood and understand the obligation to

[97]*See generally* McCORMICK, EVIDENCE §62 (2d ed. 1972).
[98]159 U.S. 523 (1895).
[99]United States v. Perez, 526 F.2d 859 (5th Cir. 1970); State v. Grossmick, 153 N.J. Super. 190, 379 A.2d 454 (1976).
[100]Wheeler v. United States, 159 U.S. 523, 524 (1895); *see also* Radiant Oil Co. v. Herring, 146 Fla. 154, 300 So. 376 (1941).
[101]Wheeler v. United States, 159 U.S. 523, 524 (1895).

tell the truth? If a court finds, on questioning the child, that the answer to both these questions is affirmative, the child will be permitted to testify.[102] Children as young as four have been found competent under this test.[103]

Some states have statutes concerning the competence of minors to give testimony, but they appear to be no more than enactments of the common law rule. For example, Washington's statute pronounces children under ten incompetent if they "appear incapable of receiving just impressions of the facts, respecting which they are examined, or of relating them truly."[104] There are at least two reasons why the law views this area from the vantage point of competence rather than incompetence. First, inquiring into the competence of a child to testify is not administratively difficult: children are rarely needed to testify and when they are needed, the judge conducting the trial can easily take a few minutes to make the inquiry. Second, a rule barring children from testifying would throw up too great an obstacle to the adjudication of cases, particularly in prosecution of crimes in which the children are themselves victims.

Criminal Law

Criminal law supplies another illustration from the American legal system of the more expansive view of children's competence. A person must be capable of entertaining criminal intent or must understand the nature or illegality of his acts before he may be considered legally responsible for a crime. The test of responsibility turns on the actor's discretion and ability to discriminate right from wrong and not merely on age.

[102]Wheeler v. United States, 159 U.S. 523 (1895); Pocatello v. United States, 394 F.2d 115 (9th Cir. 1968); State v. Segerberg, 131 Conn. 546, 41 A.2d 101 (1945).
[103]*In re* Lewis, 88 A.2d 582 (D.C. Mun. Appl. 1952); Jackson v. State 239 Ala. 38, 193 So. 417 (1940).
[104]Wash. Rev. Code Ann. Tit. 5.60.050 (1965).

For reasons of convenience and administrability the period of infancy, at common law, has been divided into three subperiods. If a child is below the age of seven he is conclusively presumed to be incapable of committing a crime.[105] From the ages of seven to fourteen years a prima facie presumption of incapacity replaces the conclusive presumption.[106] During this period, if an infant is of "sufficient intelligence and discernment to comprehend the nature and consequences of his evil acts"[107] or, as Blackstone explains, has a clear appreciation of the wrong done,[108] he may be convicted and punished. At the age of fourteen under the common law a person charged with a crime is presumed to possess criminal capacity. It is obvious from the law's attitude toward minors' "competence" as criminal defendants that a child's mental ability before the age of majority does not pose an insurmountable barrier to giving children the power to make fundamental decisions or expecting them to understand complicated situations.

Conclusion

Obviously, all three of these illustrations of "competence" vantage points differ in several important aspects from the situation usually pertaining in treatment of or experimentation with minors. All three involve courtroom settings in which someone trained in determining competence (and

---

[105]Commonwealth v. Green, 396 Pa. 137, A.2d 241 (1959); People v. Fields, 20 N.Y.S.2d 702, 174 Misc. 309 (1940). *See also* W. BLACKSTONE, COMMENTARIES *22–24.

[106]Some states have enacted statutes that have slightly modified the common law limits. *See, e.g.,* Tex. Penal Code Ann. §8.07 (Vernon West 1975) (presumption of competence does not attach until fifteen years of age); Cal. Penal Code §26 (West Supp. 1981) (if the minor is less than fourteen years of age there is a presumption of incompetence that can only be rebutted on proof that the minor knew the "wrongfulness" of the act).

[107]Hampton v. State, 1 Ala. App. 156, 55 So. 1018 (1911).

[108]W. BLACKSTONE, COMMENTARIES *24.

authorized, virtually without fear of liability,[109] to do so) is immediately available to lay any question to rest. Furthermore, the occasions when these questions arise are relatively infrequent when compared to medical decisions. Nevertheless these rules, like the approach of several Commonwealth courts faced with the issue, demonstrate that a stance different than that commonly employed is feasible and even appropriate.

The orthodox answer, then, to the question addressed by this chapter—when the authority to make medical decisions will be denied to children on grounds of "incompetence"—is "always" or "almost always." But a discernible trend has been set in motion by the ever-broadening case and statutory law "exceptions" to the rule of incompetence, pushed forward by constitutional law decisions that give greater scope to the "privacy" and self-determination of minor as well as adult patients, and given credibility by comparable rules in other areas of American law and the jurisprudence of other countries. Projecting its further development, an unorthodox but defensible answer to the question at issue would be: a child with the capacity to give informed consent has the legal authority (i.e., "competence") to do so.

Such a rule would make competence dependent on the individual child's capacity first to understand the procedure, second to reach an intelligent judgment about it in light of its risks, benefits, and alternatives, and third to possess sufficient independence to articulate and maintain any judgment voluntarily made, even when it differs from those taken by others, such as relatives and professionals. In many ways this standard is a difficult one to meet; it goes beyond that established in the law of informed consent regarding adult patients and subjects. The difference is justifiable, for there is no reason for society completely to dismiss a realistic concern to protect people who lack sufficient self-protective ability. But approaching the question from the vantage of competence

---

[109]*See, e.g.,* Stump v. Sparkman, 98 Sup. Ct. 1099 (1978).

rather than incompetence means that each child is assumed to be a possible self-decider (if he or she is capable of giving informed consent) rather than being presumed incapable and permitted to show otherwise in only certain limited circumstances.

Formulating the rule of medical decision making for minors in the newer way should not pose a heavy burden on physicians and biomedical scientists. In effect the task of the professional is comparable to that already existing under the law of informed consent. A professional would be reasonable in expecting to find few, if any, seven-, ten-, or even fourteen-year-olds with the requisite ability to give informed consent—but the law need not require the professional to insist on transferring authority to someone else in the case of a child who *does* possess such ability. Conversely, the professional may encourage even older minors to involve their parents (or other relevant adults) in the decision-making process; furthermore, in nonemergent situations, nothing prevents a physician or other professional from declining to go ahead on the sole authority of a minor who asserts, but does not convince the professional of, his or her adequacy as a self–decision maker. As elsewhere, this right of "conscience" can be preserved without jeopardizing the interest of all people in not being deprived of their autonomy by application of state power. Rules of thumb adopted by individuals although occasionally burdensome are seldom as oppressive as rules of law applied across the board. The vantage point discerned to be emerging in this chapter replaces the rule of law that viewed young people as inherently incapable of understanding and analyzing matters affecting their own welfare with one that begins with at least an open mind about each person's capabilities. Through such a change in official rules may come changes in personal attitudes and behavior, for the law not only symbolizes the present but molds the future.[110]

[110]Supported in part by GM 20140, National Institutes of Health. The research assistance of Richard D'Avino and Joseph Seiler, University of Pennsylvania Law School Class of 1980, is gratefully acknowledged.

Acknowledgments

The assistance of Richard D'Avino and Joseph Seiler, of the University of Pennsylvania Law School, Class of 1980, and of Jeffrey Stryker, of the University of Pennsylvania, Class of 1974, in the preparation of the Appendix is gratefully acknowledged.

APPENDIX

State Statutes on Minors' Competency to Consent

The text discusses generally the common law and statutes governing the ability of minors to consent to medical care. This Appendix consists of a detailed compilation (Table A–1) of the specific statutes that states have enacted to permit minors to give valid consent for such care beyond that permitted by the common law. Although we have attempted to make this Appendix as inclusive as possible, it is important, before relying on the information contained in it, to recognize its internal and external limitations.

First, the compilation contains only *statutory* provisions without attempting to identify the existence of common law rules or exceptions. For example, a physician in Ohio can raise a valid consent defense to a charge of technical battery on a married minor patient although that state does not have a statute empowering such minors to consent.

Second, we have included statutes that define the general age of majority. Persons who have reached their majority are presumed to be competent to consent to medical care until there is a showing of reasons to find them incompetent. We have not included statutes, found in several states, that specify only the age at which a person may consent to medical care, unless the medical age of majority is different from the general age of majority. (Also listed are medical age of majority statutes for Indiana, Missouri, and New York because, though these states have various statutes listing the age of majority for different, limited purposes, they have no general age of majority statutes.) Under the heading of "Emancipation," another type of general majority statute is listed—those giving minors who marry full rights of majority, including the right to consent to medical care. Statutes granting minors who marry the specific, but limited right to consenting to such care are also cited. These statutes reflect legislative determinations that married minors, either because of their presumed majority or because of practical necessity, should have such power.

Finally, certain statutory provisions are excluded despite their direct relevance to medical care. Most notable are the various legislative enactments that have followed the U. S. Supreme Court's several abortion opinions. Since the constitutional validity of many of these statutes, as well as those limiting the availability of family planning services, is in doubt, and since these statutes seem to be responding to a different set of concerns than those discussed in this chapter, we have not included them in this compilation.

As a final caveat to readers interested in knowing the current law in a state, we recommend consultation with the latest state statutory supplement and session laws, since statutes in this area have of late been frequently revised, and with the digests of judicial opinions, based on the overview of the common law rules provided in the text.

Key to Table A-1

I. Age

General—Age at which the rights of majority are granted for all purposes.

Medical—Age at which a minor can legally consent specifically for medical purposes. (Included when different from general age of majority.)

II. Emergency Rule—These provisions allow a physician to provide medical care to an otherwise incompetent minor in emergency situations.

General—Indicates an emergency provision which is not directed specifically at minors.

Minor—Indicates an emergency provision directed solely at minors.

Implied Consent or No Consent—Although the legislatures have employed two statutory formulas—"Implied consent," which presumes as a matter of law that consent would be given, and "No consent," which abolishes the consent requirements in emergent situations—the statutes are functionally equivalent.

Self-Consent—These provisions allow a minor to consent for himself in an emergent situation.

I.L.P. (In loco parentis)—These statutes allow any person standing in such a capacity to give consent before medical treatment may be given to minors.

III. Emancipation—These statutes extend the adult's capacity to consent to minors who possess specified characteristics.

   A. *Marriage*—Two types of statutes permit minors who are married to consent to medical care. Any other qualifications to this general rule are noted parenthetically.

   General—These statutes grant married minors all rights generally held by adults.

   Medical—These statutes only give married minors the power to consent to medical care. They effect none of the other disabilities of minority.

   B. *Other Bases*

   Common law—Minors emancipated by common law are given the statutory right to consent.

   High School Graduate—Minors who have received a high school diploma are given the legal capacity to consent.

   Military Service—Minors who have entered the armed forces are given the legal capacity to consent.

   Self-Management—Minors who are living away from their parents or guardian and manage their own income (regardless of source) are given the capacity to consent.

   Self-supporting—Minors who are living away from their parents or guardian and are not supported by their parents or guardian are given the capacity to consent.

   There are five situations in which a minor's biological or legal relationship to a child provides the basis for the minor's competency to consent for medical procedures for him or herself:

   Borne a Child—A minor woman who has given birth.

   Custodian—Person having legal custody of a child.

   Mother—Women who have children are given the legal capacity to consent.

   Parenthood—Minors who are the parents of children are given the legal capacity to consent.

Pregnancy—These provisions give pregnant (or once pregnant) minors the legal capacity to consent to all medical procedures unless specifically exempted; they may be contrasted with the "pregnancy statutes" (collected under V. Specialized Consent) which only give the minor the right to consent to medical treatment related to the pregnancy.

IV. Subjective Rules
Conditional Minor—A minor may consent if he will be in serious danger unless health care services are provided.
Mature Minor—A minor may give consent if he understands the nature and purposes of the proposed treatment.
Physician's Judgment—No consent is required if the risk of delay to life or health is of such a nature that treatment should be given immediately.

V. Specialized Consent—Minors are given the right to consent to specified medical treatment or to medical treatment related to the specified physical or mental conditions. These treatments and conditions are:
Alcoholism
Blood Donation—Statutes giving minors the ability to consent to the donation of blood do not all give the minor the power to consent to the sale of blood.
Drug Abuse
Emotional Disturbance
Mental Illness
Pregnancy
Rape Victim
Sexual Assault
Transplantation
VD—The specific venereal diseases are often defined by statute and may be collectively referred to as venereal, contagious or communicable diseases.

Table A-1

State	I. Age of majority	II. Emergency rule[a]	III. Emancipation		IV. Subjective rules	V. Specialized Consent
			A. Marriage	B. Other bases		
ALABAMA Ala. Code (1975 & Supp. 1981)	14 years Medical §22-8-4 19 years General §26-1-1		Medical §22-8-5	Borne a child §22-8-5 High school graduate §22-8-4 Pregnant §22-8-4	Physician's judgment §22-8-3	Pregnancy Drug abuse VD Alcoholism §22-8-6 Bone marrow transplantation (14 years, high school graduate, married, divorced or pregnant) §22-8-9
ALASKA Alaska Stat. (1977 & Supp. 1980)	18 years General §25.20.010	General No consent §09.65.090	General (16 years) §25.20.020	Self-management §09.65.100(1) Parenthood §09.65.100(3)	Conditional minor §09.65.100(2)	Pregnancy VD §09.65.100(4)

[a]Not included are good samaritan statutes that limit or preclude civil liability for "any acts or omissions in rendering emergency care" (*See, e.g.*, Calif. Bus. & Pro. Code §2144). Such statutes arguably remove the need for consent, but their aim is to encourage health professionals to render care in emergent situations where regular emergency care may not be available without fear of liability for negligence in rendering the care. Supporting this construction that the statutes are not directed to fear of liability for battery is language in some imposing liability for gross negligence and the absence of language concerning consent. Further, the statutes often have language making them specifically inapplicable to care rendered in hospitals or physician's offices where doctors and assistants are employed to give such care.

Continued

Table A–1 Cont.

State	I. Age of majority	II. Emergency rule	III. Emancipation A. Marriage	III. Emancipation B. Other bases	IV. Subjective rules	V. Specialized Consent
ARIZONA Ariz. Rev. Stat. Ann. (1967 & Supp. 1980)	18 years General §1-215(2)	Minor ILP §44-133[b] Minor No consent (Surgery) §36-2271(c)	Medical §44-132	Common law §44-132		Alcoholism §36-2024(A)VD §44-132.01 Drug abuse (12 years) §44-133.01 Rape victim (12 years) §13-1413
ARKANSAS Ark. Stat. Ann. (1971 & Supp. 1981)	18 years General §57-103	General Implied Consent §82-364	Medical §82-363(c)	Common law §82-363(f)	Mature minor §82-363(g)	Blood donation (17 years) §82-1606 Pregnancy §82-363(d) VD §82-629 §82-630
CALIFORNIA Cal. Civ. code (West 1954 & Supp. 1981)	18 years General §25.1	General[c] No consent Bus. & Prof. Code	Medical §25.6	Self-management (15 years) §34.6		Pregnancy §34.5 VD (12 years) §34.7

	§2144.3	Military service (Active duty) §25.7	Sexual assault §34.9 Rape victim §34.8 Drug abuse (12 years) Alcoholism (12 years) §34.10 Therapeutic Research (concurrent with parental consent for children over 7) Health & Safety Code §26668.4
COLORADO Colo. Rev. Stat (1973 & Supp. 1980)	21 years General §2-4-401 18 years Medical §13-22-101(d)	Medical §13-22-103	Self-manage- ment (15 years) §13-22-103	Alcoholism §25-1-308 Drug abuse §13-22-102 VD §25-4-402 Mental illness (15 years) §27-10-103

[b]In a nonemergency situation, failure to obtain consent for surgery is declared to be a misdemeanor for which the surgeon can be criminally prosecuted. ARIZ. REV. STAT. ANN. §36–2271 (Supp. 1978).
[c]This section of the California code dealing with the medical profession explicitly removes only the obligation to inform the patient, or person authorized to consent for one incapable of doing so, when an emergency arises in a physician's office or a hospital, but it seems to assume that in emergent circumstances consent is not needed.

Continued

Table A–1 Cont.

State	I. Age of majority	II. Emergency rule	III. Emancipation		IV. Subjective rules	V. Specialized Consent
			A. Marriage	B. Other bases		
						Transplantation §13-22-104
CONNECTICUT Conn. Gen. Stat. Ann. (West 1977 & Supp. 1980)	18 years General §1-1(d)					VD §19-89a Drug abuse §19-496c Alcoholism §17-155t
DELAWARE Del. Code Ann. (1974 & Supp. 1980)	18 years General tit. 1 §701	Minor Self-consent tit. 13 §707(a) (5)	Medical tit. 13 §707(a) (2)			Blood donation (17 years) tit. 13 §709 Pregnancy (12 years) VD (12 years) tit. 13 §708
DISTRICT OF COLUMBIA D.C. Code Ann. (1973) & Supp. 1978)	18 years General §21-104		General §21-104			VD §6-119j-1

	Age of majority	General	Minor	Medical	Specific conditions
FLORIDA Fla. Stat. Ann. (West 1973 & Supp. 1980)	18 years General §743.07	General §743.01	No consent §458.21		VD §384.016 Drug abuse §397.099 Blood donation (17 years) §743.06 Pregnancy §458.25 Alcoholism §396.082
GEORGIA Ga. Code Ann. (1979 & Supp. 1981)	18 years General §74-104	General Implied consent §88-2905		Medical §88-2904(c)	VD Drug Abuse §74-104.3 Alcoholism (14 years, limited to observation and diagnosis, excepting inpatient treatment) §88-403.1 Mental Illness (12 years, limited to observation and diagnosis) §88-503.1

Continued

Table A–1 Cont.

State	I. Age of majority	II. Emergency rule	III. Emancipation A. Marriage	III. Emancipation B. Other bases	IV. Subjective rules	V. Specialized Consent
HAWAII Haw. Rev. Stat. (1976 & Supp. 1980)	18 years General §577-1		General §577-25			Pregnancy (14 years) §577A-1 VD (14 years) §577A-2 Alcoholism Drug Abuse (diagnosis & counseling) §577-26
IDAHO Idaho Code (1976 & Supp. 1981)	18 years General §32-101(1)	General No consent §39-4303(c)	General[d] §32-101(3)		Mature minor §39-4302	Drug abuse §37-3102 VD (14 years) §39-3801 Alcoholism §39-307
ILLINOIS Ill. Rev. Stat. (1966 & Supp. 1980)	18 years General ch. 3 §11-1	Minor No consent ch. 111 §4503	Medical ch. 111 §4501	Pregnancy ch. 111 §4501		Blood donation (17 years) ch. 111 1/2 §600 VD (12 years) Drug abuse (12 years) Alcoholism (12 years) ch. 111 §4504

State / Citation					
INDIANA Ind. Code Ann. (Burns 1973 & Supp. 1980)	18 years Medical §16-8-3-1 18 years General (property) §32-1-2-2 (contract) §34-1-2-5.5 (rules of construction) §34-1-67-1	General No consent §16-8-3-2	Medical §16-8-4-1	Common law §16-8-4-1	Blood donation (17 years) §16-8-2-1 VD §16-8-5-1 Drug abuse Alcoholism §16-13-6.1-23
IOWA Iowa Code Ann. (West 1950 & Supp. 1980)	18 years General §599.1		General §599.1		VD §140.9 Alcoholism Drug abuse §125.33
KANSAS Kan. Stat. (1973 & Supp. 1980)	18 years General §38-101	Minor No consent §65-2891	General (16 years) §38-101	16 years or older if parent not "immediately available"	Pregnancy §38-123 Blood donation (17 years)

[d] Although described here as "General," this Idaho statute grants the married minor competence only to enter a contract. Most general marriage statutes explicitly grant to the married minor, sometimes with limitations as to age of the minor or his spouse, all rights generally held by adults, including the right to contract.

Continued

Table A–1 Cont.

State	I. Age of majority	II. Emergency rule	III. Emancipation		IV. Subjective rules	V. Specialized Consent
			A. Marriage	B. Other bases		
				§38-123(b)		§38-123(a) VD §65-2892 Alcoholism §65-4025 Drug abuse §65-2892a
KENTUCKY Ky. Rev. Stat. (1971 & Supp. 1978)	18 years General §2.015		Medical §214.185(2)	Common law §214.185(2) Borne a child §214.185(2)	Physician's judgment §214.185(3)	VD Pregnancy Alcoholism Drug abuse §214.185(1)
LOUISIANA La. Rev. Stat. Ann. (West 1972 & Supp. 1980)		General Implied consent §40:1299.54	Medical §40:1299.53(c)		Mature minor §40:1095	VD §40:1065.1 Drug abuse §40:1096 Pregnancy §40:1299.53(g) Blood donation (17 years) §40:1097
La. Civ. Code Ann. (West 1972 & Supp. 1980)	18 years General art. 37		General art. 379			

State / Statute	Age of majority	Minor	Medical	Parenthood / Self-management	Physician's judgment	Specific conditions
MAINE Me. Rev. Stat. (1965 & Supp. 1980)	18 years General tit. 1 §72					VD Drug abuse 　tit. 22 §1823 　tit. 32 §3292 　tit. 32 §2595 Alcoholism 　tit. 22 §1371
MARYLAND Md. Ann. Code (1976 & Supp. 1980)	18 years General art. 1 §24		Medical art. 43 §135(1)	Parenthood art. 43 §135(1)	Physician's judgment art. 43 §135(3)	VD Pregnancy 　art. 43 §135(2) Drug abuse 　art. 43 §135(4) Alcoholism 　art. 43 §135(5) Mental illness 　(16 years) 　art. 43 §135A Rape victim Sexual assault (need only be alleged) 　art. 43 §135B 　art. 43 §135(6)
MASSACHUSETTS Mass. Gen. Laws Ann. (West 1974 & Supp. 1980)	18 years General ch. 231 §85P	Minor No consent ch. 112 §12F	Medical ch. 112 §12F(i)	Self-management ch. 112 §12F(v) Parent		Drug abuse (12 years and two physicians must agree that minor is drug dependent)

Continued

Table A–1 *Cont.*

State	I. Age of majority	II. Emergency rule	III. Emancipation		IV. Subjective rules	V. Specialized Consent
			A. Marriage	B. Other bases		
				ch. 112 §12F(ii) Military service ch. 112 §12F(iii) Pregnancy ch. 112 §12F(iv)		ch. 112 §12E VD ch. 111 §117 ch. 112 §12F(vi)
MICHIGAN Mich. Comp. Laws Ann. (1974 & Supp. 1980)	18 years General §722.4(b) §722.52		General §722.4(a)	Military service §722.4(c)		VD §329.221 Drug abuse §335.231
MINNESOTA Minn. Stat. Ann. (West 1947 & Supp. 1980)	18 years General §645.451	Minor No consent §144.344	Medical §144.342	Self-management §144.341 Borne a child §144.342		Pregnancy VD Alcoholism Drug abuse §144.343 Blood donation (17 years) §145.41

	General	Medical	General	Medical	Common law	Mature minor	
MISSISSIPPI Miss. Code Ann. (1972 & Supp. 1980)	21 years General §1-3-27 §1-3-21		Implied consent §41-41-7	Medical §41-41-3(c)	Common law §41-41-3(g)	Mature minor §41-41-3(h)	VD §41-41-13 Pregnancy §41-41-3(i) Blood donation (17 years) §41-41-15 Alcoholism Drug Abuse (15 years, when resulting in mental or emotional problems) §41-41-14
MISSOURI Mo. Ann. Stat. (Vernon 1956 & Supp. 1980)	18 years General (Contract) §431.055 18 years Medical §431.061(1)(1)		Implied consent §431.063	Medical §431.061(1)(3) §431.065	Parenthood §431.061(1)(3) §431.065 Custodian §431.061(1)(3)		Pregnancy §431.061(1)(4)(a) VD §431.061(1)(4)(b) Drug abuse §431.061(1)(4)(c) Alcoholism (16 years) §431.061(1)(4)(c) Mental illness (16 years) Drug abuse (16 years) §202.115(1)(1)

Continued

Table A–1 Cont.

State	I. Age of majority	II. Emergency rule	III. Emancipation A. Marriage	III. Emancipation B. Other bases	IV. Subjective rules	V. Specialized Consent
MONTANA Mont. Rev. Codes. Ann. (1969 & Supp. 1977)	18 years General §64-101	Minor Self-consent §69-6101 (1)(d)	Medical §69-6101(1)(a)	Self-supporting §69-6101 (1)(b) Borne a child High school graduate Common law §69-6101(1)(a)	Physician's judgment §69-6104(2)	Pregnancy VD Drug abuse Alcoholism §69-6101(1)(c) Mental illness (psychiatric counseling) §69-6106
NEBRASKA Neb. Rev. Stat. (1976 & Supp. 1978)	19 years General §38-101	General No consent §71-5512	General §38-101			VD §71-1121 Blood donation (17 years) §71-4808
NEVADA Nev. Rev. Stat. (1979)	18 years General §129.010	Minor ILP §129.040	Medical §129.030(1)(b)	4 Months away from home §129.030(1)(a) Borne a child; mother §129.030(1)(c)	Conditional minor §129.030(1)(d) Mature minor §129.030(2)	Drug abuse §129.050 VD §129.060 §441.175

NEW HAMPSHIRE N.H. Rev. Stat. Ann. (1970 & Supp. 1979)	18 years General §21:44				Blood donation (17 years) §571-C:1 Drug abuse (12 years) §318-B:12-a VD (14 years) §141:11-a
NEW JERSEY N.J. Stat. Ann. (West 1976 & Supp. 1980)	18 years General §9:17B-1 §9:17B-3	Minor ILP §24-10-2	Medical §9:17A-1	Pregnancy §9:17A-1	Drug abuse VD §9:17A-4 Pregnancy §9:17A-1 Alcoholism §26:2B-15
NEW MEXICO N.M. Stat. Ann. (1978 & Supp. 1980)	18 years General §28-6-1	Minor ILP §24-10-2	Medical §24-10-1	Common law §24-10-1	VD §24-1-9 Drug abuse §26-2-14 Pregnancy §24-1-13
NEW YORK N.Y. [Pub. Health] Law (McKinney 1977 & Supp. 1980)	18 years Medical §2504(1) 18 years	General No consent §2504(3)	Medical §2504(1)	Parenthood §2504(1)	VD §2305 Blood donation (17 years) §3123

Continued

Table A–1 Cont.

State	I. Age of majority	II. Emergency rule	III. Emancipation		IV. Subjective rules	V. Specialized Consent
			A. Marriage	B. Other bases		
	General [Gen. Oblig.] §1-202 [Civ. Rights] §1-a [Dom. Rel.] §2					
NORTH CAROLINA N.C. Gen. Stat. (1975 & Supp. 1979)	18 years General §48A-2	Minor No consent (surgery re-quires a second opinion) §90-21.1 §90-21.3		Common law §90-21.5(b)		VD §90-21.5(a) (i) Pregnancy §90-21.5(a) (ii) Drug abuse Alcoholism §90-21.5(a) (iii) Emotional disturbance (excluding commit-ment) §90-21.5(a) (iv) Blood donation (17 years) §90-220.11

	Age	Self-consent	Medical	Self-support	Physician's judgement	Conditions
NORTH DAKOTA N.D. Cent. Code (1971 & Supp. 1977)	18 years General §14-10-01	Minor Self-consent §14-10-17.1				VD (14 years) Drug abuse (14 years) Alcoholism (14 years) §14-10-17
OHIO Ohio Rev. Code Ann. (Baldwin 1971 & Supp. 1980)	18 years General §3109.01					Sexual assault §2907.29 VD §3709.241 Drug abuse §3719.012
OKLAHOMA Okla. Stat. Ann. (West 1973 & Supp. 1978)	18 years General tit.15 §13	Minor Self-consent' tit.63 §2602(a) (7)	Medical tit.63 §2602(a) (1)	Self-support tit.63 §2602(a)(2) Common law tit.63 §2602(a) (1) Has a dependent child tit.63 §2602(a) (1) Military service tit.63 §2601(a)	Physician's judgement tit.63 §2602(a) (6)	VD Alcoholism Pregnancy Drug abuse tit.63 §2602(a) (3)

'This subsection, 63 OKLA. STAT. ANN. §2602(a)(6), provides that in an incompetent minor without known relatives or guardians may consent "to health services," if "two physicians agree" that such services are needed. The requirement for "concurrence from another physician" for "major surgery, general anesthesia, or a life-threatening procedure" does not apply in an emergency "in a community where no other surgeon can be contracted within a reasonable time" Tit. 63 §2604.

Continued

Table A-1 Cont.

State	I. Age of majority	II. Emergency rule	III. Emancipation A. Marriage	III. Emancipation B. Other bases	IV. Subjective rules	V. Specialized Consent
OREGON Or. Rev. Stat. (1977 & Supp.1979)	18 years General §109.510 15 years Medical §109.640 §109.660		General §109.520			Drug abuse Alcoholism §426.450 VD §109.610 Blood donation (16 years) §109.670
PENNSYLVANIA Pa. Stat. Ann. (Purdon 1977 & Supp. 1980)	21 years General Pa. Con. Stat. Ann. tit. 1 §1991 18 years Medical tit. 35 §10101		Medical tit. 35 §10101	High school graduate Been pregnant tit.35 §10101	Physician's judgment tit. 35 §10104	Pregnancy VD tit.35 §10103 Drug abuse tit. 71 §1690.112 Blood donation (18 years) tit. 35 §10001
RHODE ISLAND R.I. Gen. Laws (1976 & Supp.1980)	18 years General §15-12-1	Minor^f Self-consent (16 years or married) §23-51-1				Drug abuse §5-37-17 VD §23-11-11

	General	Medical	Self-support	Physician's judgment	Other
SOUTH CAROLINA S.C. Code (1976 & Supp.1980)	18 years General §15-1-320 16 years Medical (Not for operation unless essential and consulting physician, if available, agrees) §44-45-10	Medical §32-5-30		Physician's judgment §44-45-20	Blood donation (17 years) §44-43-20 Mental illness (16 years) §44-17-310
SOUTH DAKOTA S.D. Compiled Laws Ann. (1976 & Supp. 1980)	18 years General §26-1-1	General §25-5-17	Self-support §25-5-19 Common law §25-5-17		Blood donation (17 years, parental veto) §26-2-7 Alcoholism §34-20A-50 VD §34-23-16
TENNESSEE Tenn. Code Ann. (1979 & Supp. 1980)	18 years General §1-313				VD §53-1104 Alcoholism

[1]The Rhode island stature says that a minor who is at least 16 years of age or is married "may consent to routine emergency medical or surgical care." It is not clear what treatments fall into that category.

Continued

Table A–1 *Cont.*

State	I. Age of majority	II. Emergency rule	III. Emancipation — A. Marriage	III. Emancipation — B. Other bases	IV. Subjective rules	V. Specialized Consent
TEXAS Tex. Fam. Code Ann. (Vernon 1975 & Supp. 1980)	18 years General tit. 2 §11.01		General tit. 1 §4.03 tit. 2 §11.01	Self-management (16 years) tit. 2 §35.03(a)(2) Military service tit. 2 §35.03(a)(1)		Drug abuse[g] tit. 2 §35.03(a)(6) Pregnancy tit. 2 §35.03(a)(4) VD tit. 2 §35.03(a)(3) Withhold consent to examination for child abuse tit. 2 §35.04
UTAH Utah Code (1973 & Supp. 1979)	18 years General §15-2-1		General[h] §15-2-1			VD §26-6-39.1 Pregnancy §78-14-5(4)(f)
VERMONT Vt. Stat. Ann. (1972 & Supp. 1980)	18 years General tit 1 §173					Drug abuse (12 years) VD (12 years) Alcoholism (12 years) tit. 18 §4226

VIRGINIA Va. Code (1979 & Supp. 1981)	18 years General §1-13.42	Minor Self-consent (14 years) No consent (less than 14 years) §54-325.2(C)	Medical §32-137(9) (excepting surgical sterilization) §54-325.2(E)	Pregnancy §54-325.2(D)(2) Drug abuse Alcoholism §54-325.2(D)(3) Blood donation (17 years) §54-325.2(F) VD §54-325.2(D)(1)
WASHINGTON Wash. Rev. Code Ann. (1965 & Supp. 1980)	18 years General §26.28.010 §26.28.015	General No consent §18.71.220	General (if married to a person of full age) §26.28.020	VD (14 years) §70.24.110 Drug abuse (14 years) Alcoholism (14 years) (except becoming a treatment center resi- dent) §69.54.060

*An earlier Texas provision, §447i, which contains a minimum age of 13 years for consent to treatment of drug abuse, has not been repealed. The more recent statute, cited in the appendix, has no minimum age.

hUtah statute §15-2–1 provides that a person is an "adult" when he or she either reaches age 18 or marries. Under the common law, any adult who is not mentally or physically incompetent can consent to medical treatment. Utah has a statute which defines who can consent to treatment; it states that "[a]ny patient eighteen years of age or over" may consent. §78–14–5(4)(e). It does not say any *adult* may consent. The statute does provide, however, that "[a]ny married person" may consent for a spouse. Thus, strictly construing the statute, a married minor could consent for his spouse, but not for himself. In light of the common law and the general provision giving married minors the rights of adults, such a reading seems inappropriate, though it might be argued.

Continued

Table A–1 *Cont.*

| State | I. Age of majority | II. Emergency rule | III. Emancipation | | IV. Subjective rules | V. Specialized Consent |
			A. Marriage	B. Other bases		
WEST VIRGINIA W. Va. Code (1977 & Supp. 1981)	18 years General §2-2-10(aa)		General (16 years) §49-7-27			Alcoholism §60-6-23 Drug abuse §60A-5-504 VD §16-4-10
WISCONSIN Wis. Stat. Ann. (West 1974 & Supp. 1981)	18 years General §48.02					VD §143.07
WYOMING Wyo. Stat. (1977 & Supp. 1981)	19 years General §14-1-101(a)	Self-consent §14-1-101(b)(iii)	Medical §14-1-101(b)(i)	Military Service §14-1-101(b)(ii)	Self-manage- ment §14-1-101(b)(iv)	Transplantation (donate all or part of body) (18 years) §35-5-102 VD §35-4-131

The Authority of Others to Decide about Biomedical Interventions with Incompetents

ALEXANDER MORGAN CAPRON

In the preceding chapter the question, When is a person competent? was examined as it relates to decisions about medical therapy and experimentation with children. If a child is determined through the application of the legal rules analyzed there to be incompetent to decide for him or herself about a biomedical intervention, who possesses the authority to permit or refuse the proposed intervention? John Locke once wrote that, since children are "born to" but not "born in" the full state of equality that characterizes free men, "their parents

ALEXANDER MORGAN CAPRON ● University of Pennsylvania Law School, Philadelphia, Pennsylvania 19104.

have a sort of rule and jurisdiction over them when they come into the world, and for some time after, but it is but a temporary one."[1] This observation both captures the necessary ambiguity about the precise scope of parental authority[2]— which *is* a "sort of rule and jurisdiction" in making biomedical choices, as all others—and serves as a reminder of the transient nature of children's incapacity and of the parents' role in preparing them for the full authority of maturity. Thus the usual response to the question of authority, namely, that the child's parents may choose whether to permit or refuse a biomedical intervention, is a good starting point but nothing more. What, then, is the basis for the authority vested in parents?

PARENTS' VERSUS CHILDREN'S "RIGHTS"

The authority of parents might be grounded on an independent "right" they possess to make decisions about all dependent members of their family. Such a right would follow if the central interest were the welfare and well-being of the parents. They are clearly the best judges of what is good for themselves, so the law's underlying notion of self-determination would lead to the conclusion that parents are entitled to make medical decisions about their children to achieve the greatest "good" for themselves as they define it. Parental authority might also follow were the central interest taken to be the attempted maximization of the child's welfare and well-being. If it is admitted that there is no objectively verifiable measure of the "best outcome" for all children, and if it is further assumed that parents are the preferred estimators of what is best for each individual child, then a parental "right" to decide emerges.

[1]J. LOCKE, TWO TREATISES OF CIVIL GOVERNMENT, 322 (2d ed. 1697).
[2]The term "parental authority" is intended to encompass guardians or other persons who have legal custody and control of a child independently of any dispute over a biomedical intervention.

The starting point for the entire discussion, however, is that some people (e.g., most children) lack the capacity to decide about significant matters (e.g., medical interventions) for themselves. From this fact it might follow that there is no independent parental "right" to make biomedical decisions for children; instead, there is a "right" of the children to decide, which under the circumstances is delegated to the parents, to be exercised in a fashion as close as possible to the one the child would him or herself choose. Parents achieve their position as substitutes because they are likely best to know their child's *existing* views and the value preferences of the family unit, which typically play the leading role in molding the child's *future* views.

Unarticulated Contradictions

The fundamental difference between these two versions of the underlying goals and resulting rights of the participants in biomedical decision making often goes unrecognized or at least unarticulated. As with the competence issue, legal analysis here rests on the dual basis of constitutional law (primarily "privacy" and First Amendment religious liberty) and private law (primarily the tort law of "informed consent"). In both settings, the issue of authority is usually framed as parent versus state. As was previously discussed,[3] it is seldom that the conflict is seen as one between parent and child as it was by Justice Douglas in *Wisconsin v. Yoder*.[4] Although attention is usually drawn to instances of conflict, it is apparent that in many (perhaps most) situations the interests of parents and children are complementary or congruent. But in at least some cases—perhaps those involving the most difficult choices—the difference between the perspectives of "parents' right" and "child's right" will be determinative of

---

[3]*See* Ch. 3.
[4]Wisconsin v. Yoder, 406 U.S. 205, 242 (1972) (Douglas, J., dissenting).

the outcome. Hence it may be helpful to look to other areas of the law to see how similar questions have been resolved.

Differentiating Private and Public Law Roots

As has been previously suggested, the strands of tort and constitutional law are interwoven on the subject of medical decision making. Indeed, it is remarkable how similar statements of principle sound whether promulgated in private or public law contexts. In disposing of a damage action against a *surgeon*, Judge Benjamin Cardozo declared for the New York Court of Appeals in 1914 that "Every human being of adult years and sound mind has a right to determine what shall be done with his own body."[5] Nearly a half century later, a New York trial judge, in articulating the limits of the *state's* authority to insist on treatment, wrote that "it is the individual who is the subject of a medical decision who has the final say and . . . this must necessarily be so in a system of government which gives the greatest possible protection to the individual in the furtherance of his own desires."[6]

Despite the overlap of public and private law reasoning on the general issue of consent and on the more specific issue of one person giving permission for an intervention with another, it is possible to differentiate factually the types of cases that most directly implicate one strand or the other of the law. The most important point in determining the range of legal issues is whether the physician and parents agree about the course to be followed. When they do agree, the issue presented to the court is typically framed as whether the "consent" given by the parents is valid, that is, whether it will insulate the physician from liability should a suit for an unconsented medical intervention later be brought by or on behalf of the child.

[5]Schloendorff v. New York Hospital, 211 N.Y. 127, 129, 105 N.E. 92,93 (1914).
[6]Erickson v. Dilgard, 44 Misc. 2d 27, 28, 252 N.Y.S. 2d 705, 706 (Sup. Ct. 1962).

When the parents' view is not shared by the treating physician and for some reason the matter is not simply avoided by the parents transferring the child to the care of a physician with whom they do agree,[7] the issue for judicial resolution will probably be framed as whether the state has grounds for superseding parental control and custody of the child, at least temporarily. We turn first to see what light the law can shed on the question of what is rather inaptly termed "proxy consent"[8]; we shall then return to the question of state authority.

THE VALUE OF ANALOGIES

Several problems inhere in the manner in which the consent issue has arisen in the case law. First, the cases are unusual in that something about the medical procedure (e.g., that it involves research not aimed directly at benefiting the minor patient–subject) is seen as raising a question that would not be addressed were it assumed, as in a standard, "accepted" form of treatment, to be "for the benefit of" the minor. This result is understandable as a practical matter, since physicians and parents alike take the law clearly to have established parental authority on therapeutic interventions. Yet any analysis of parental permission must take some account of the noncases that are never brought because the *underlying rationale* should be the same in all contexts.

---

[7]There may be no such physician, or at least not readily accessible; or the child may already be deeply implicated in a course of treatment to which the parents do not otherwise object and which they indeed do not want interrupted; or, although the parents are able to discharge the physician with whom they disagree, officials from the welfare agency having responsibility for protecting "abused" or "neglected" children may already have entered the scene, and they are not subject to "dismissal" by parental choice.

[8]The term "third-party (or "parental") permission" would be more descriptive; "proxy" inaccurately suggests express agency or deputization, and "consent" connotes self-choice in medical matters.

Second, the cases that do arise seem to manifest physicians' desire to be protected from future liability (in a suit brought by the child after he or she reaches majority) by advanced judicial certification that the parental permission is legally valid "consent," binding the minor.[9] These suits are not brought because the physicians fear that the parental decisions have in fact exposed the child to an improper risk—on the contrary, the health professionals are typically poised to undertake the procedure as soon as their assurance of nonliability is in hand. Thus it would be surprising if such "sweetheart" lawsuits provided a great opportunity for probing deeply into the bases of parental capacity and authority to act in place of the "incompetent."

Nevertheless, analogous issues have arisen in other legal contexts in which they have been pursued with adversary vigor. An examination of the legal theories that have emerged from such settings provides a helpful supplement to the law of "proxy consent." That does not mean one will find any hard and fast legal rules that will determine how biomedical decisions should be made. Instead, by looking at other types of choices that one person is enabled by the law to make for another, contexts may appear in which the interests and relationships are analogous to the ones that concern us. Indeed, the purposes of rules on third-party permission in the biomedical context appear to be the same as those being served by the law in analogous areas—namely, to permit choices to be made while protecting incompetents from undue harm—although some differences in the purposes will need to be noted.

Among the legal analogies are examples of the three major explanations for allowing third-party permission: first, that the person giving permission is able to express the choices the incompetent would in fact have made because of indivi-

---

[9]*See, e.g.*, Hart v. Brown, 29 Conn. Supp. 368, 289 A.2d 386 (Super. Ct. 1972); W. Curran, *A Problem of Consent: Kidney Transplants in Minors*, 34 N.Y.U. L. REV. 891 (1959) (summarizing early Massachusetts cases).

dualized, subjective knowledge of the incompetent; second, that the person giving permission will make an objectively reasonable choice that comes close to being what the incompetent, as a reasonable person, would want or that will at the least serve the incompetent's interests; or third, that the interests of the third party and those of the incompetent are so close that in pursuing his or her own interests the third party will protect the interests of the incompetent. A fourth explanation for parental power over children—that the children are akin to the parents' other property—need not be discussed here, since it does not illustrate the phenomenon of A choosing for B. If B is regarded as property, one would not usually think of B as having independent interests that needed to be protected by self-choice or its equivalent.

SUBJECTIVE RULES

Parents are not expected to be mind readers in the sense of clairvoyants, but it is generally thought that they know their children well enough to discern what the latter would choose were they able to do so. Thus it is interesting to discover that examples of this situation are scanty in the law. And even these depend on prior actions of the incompetent, such as in the doctrine of substitute judgment from the law of trusts, or on express delegation, such as in the attorney–client relationship.

Substitute Judgment

Suppose a person with a substantial estate becomes incompetent to manage his or her own affairs, and that a trustee is appointed by a court to administer the property. It is obvious that the trustee is authorized to pay from the estate any amounts lawfully owed for the maintenance and care of the incompetent and any other people whom the incompetent is obliged to support. But what of a cousin, or a charity, to whom the incompetent had given money in the past, without legal necessity of doing so? May the trustee make *gifts* to such a person? What about a person of whom the incompetent has always been very fond but who only recently became needy, so that there is no pattern of past gifts from the incompetent? The answer given by the law to the question of whether such gifts are proper has been a guarded "yes." The trustee may petition the court of which the incompetent is a ward for permission to act as the incompetent would have were he or she capable of acting.[10] The request will be approved to the extent that it can be met out of excess income that will not be necessary now, or in the future, to meet the needs of the incompetent. The subjective nature of the doctrine is thus hemmed in by objective limitations. By imposing a standard of reasonable prudence on the actions the trustee is permitted to take in the incompetent's stead, the law assumes that no person would give away his property so as to endanger him or herself: a petition will be disapproved if it derogates from the fiduciary's primary duty, which is to preserve the incompetent's estate. Within those limits, the doctrine has been treated as "subjective" by the courts[11] because an attempt is made to act as the incompetent person would.

Thus, though initially attractive, the doctrine of substitute judgment is likely to be of only limited value in understanding the basis of third-party permission for biomedical interventions. First, in the hands of most courts the doctrine is taken to require some individualized evidence about what the incompetent would have done; in the case of a young child a judgment on this point would be speculative. Second, the doctrine is concerned with the donation of *property* to a *specific person;* by contrast, at least in the context of medical research, the patient–subject's *body* is placed at risk for *unspecified people*

---

[10]R. M. Engel, *Making Gifts from the Estate of an Incompetent: The Substitution of Judgment Doctrine,* 9 WAKE FOREST L. REV. 199 (1973).

[11]City Bank Farmers Trust Co. v. McGowan, 323 U.S. 594 (1945); *In re* Guardianship of Brice, 233 Iowa 183, 8 N.W.2d 576 (1943).

(the potential beneficiaries of the knowledge gained) or to "science," as an abstract entity. Third, the limitation that only the excess may be given may render the entire analogy inapposite since it is hard to know what the "excess" would be in a biomedical context, unless it means that only nonharmful interventions are permissible.

Attorney–Client Relationship

A second comparison—to the attorney–client relationship—provides some further insight, but is also not fully comparable. The prevailing view is that once a client has given an attorney directions about the goals to be sought and has agreed to the general manner of proceeding, the attorney possesses broad powers to make subsidiary choices on behalf of the client.[12] At the very least, since clients typically lack expertise in the law, the choice of which legal instruments will be used falls to the lawyer. But it is still necessary for the attorney, as a fiduciary, to disclose the options to the client and for the client to decide which among the various possibilities he desires. For reasons both of ethics and self-interest,[13] the lawyer should not attempt to make the basic substantive choices. The powers of the attorney, which can affect the client's person as well as his property, are closer to those of the "proxy" in biomedical intervention than those of most of the other analogies. Yet, although an attorney's power to speak for and bind his client[14] is premised on the attorney's thinking as his client actually would, the basis for the presumption is that the client has instructed his attorney, as he would any agent, how to carry out his affairs. Again, this factual premise of the analogy is absent in deciding about

[12]The prevailing view is summarized and criticized in M. Spiegel, *Lawyering and Client Decisionmaking: Informed Consent and the Legal Profession*, 128 U. PA. L. REV. 44 (1979).
[13]DOUGLAS E. ROSENTHAL, LAWYER AND CLIENT: WHO'S IN CHARGE? (1974).
[14]Link v. Wabash Railroad Co., 370 U.S. 626 (1962).

medical interventions with children too young to give competent directions or even indications of their value preferences. Nevertheless, the rules governing fiduciaries do provide one instructive point, the requirement that an attorney's own interests not be in conflict with those of the client.

OBJECTIVE RULES

If the hallmark of the subjective rules is that the decision-maker be personally familiar with the actual wishes and values of the incompetent person, one would expect in the case of objective rules to discover that anyone who behaves reasonably according to defined standards could be the decision-maker. This principle is well illustrated by the law concerning guardians *ad litem* (also called "next friends" in some cases) for infant parties to legal actions.

Guardian *Ad Litem*

Under the rules developed by the common law, any adult can act as a guardian, "regardless of his lack of kinship to the infant" in question.[15] Subject to the broad supervision of the court (of which the infant becomes a ward for purposes of the litigation), the guardian *ad litem* hires an attorney and makes decisions with the attorney just as a party would make for him or herself about the conduct of litigation. The guardian must "acquaint himself with all of the rights of the infant" whom he is supposed to be protecting and "not do any act which will prejudicially affect" those rights.[16] If the choices made by the guardian later prove detrimental to the infant, the latter is not bound by them (once he or she reaches maturity) unless they were approved as reasonable by the court.

[15]A. J. Kleinfeld, *The Balance of Power Among Infants, Their Parents and the State,* 4 FAMILY L. Q. 320 (1970).
[16]Lee v. Gucker, 186 N.Y.S.2d 245 (Ore. 1972).

This rule, which governs the interests that infants have in real estate, as beneficiaries under a will, and so on, comes particularly into play in determining whether decisions made about a lawsuit amount to binding waivers of the infants' rights. Thus the judgment rendered by the court in a case in which a child was represented by a guardian is as valid against the child as it would be if the child had been competent to represent him or herself, but a guardian's election of which remedy to pursue (a decision made without judicial supervision) will not bind the child.[17] The law opts for uncertainty—which is generally disfavored because of its disruptive effect on property and commercial transactions—in order to give maximum protection to the interests of those who cannot make decisions for themselves. A second safeguard is the requirement that the guardian be completely free of any conflicting entanglements that might make him adverse to the interests of the ward.

"Best-Interests" Doctrine

A second objective rule (although one with subjective undertones) is the rather vague and elastic doctrine of "best interests," which is invoked in two ways by courts in disputes concerning the care and custody of children. Its first use is in determining who should have decision-making authority for the children in question. Here "best interests" is arrayed against the competing and more traditional view that unless the natural parents are affirmatively shown to be unfit they are entitled to make all decisions about their children, as about any other item of property. A natural parent is, for example, typically permitted to withhold consent to a child's adoption by another adult even if there are good reasons to believe that the child would be better off with the adoptive parents; the parent's choice must actually be contrary to the child's inter-

---

[17]*See, e.g.,* Williams v. Briggs, 502 P.2d 245 (Ore. 1972).

ests before it will be overridden.[18] Such a presumption in favor of the natural parents has been upheld by the Supreme Court.[19]

The second use of the term "best interests" occurs when the natural parents, or others with a strong claim, dispute among themselves over the custody of a child and the judiciary must decide about the care and custody of children.[20] Although courts *may* take into account the wishes of mature children, they are left to their own discretion as to what disposition would best serve the child's welfare. Since there is no requirement that the decision reflect individualized knowledge about what is actually best suited for a particular child, the doctrine seems to rest on an "objective" standard of what a reasonable person would find appropriate for the ordinary child; in application, this standard may amount to a highly *subjective* decision, but subjective in the sense that it reflects the values and beliefs of the judiciary, not those of its individual wards. Moreover, by custom and by statute, the "best interests of the child" are taken to include the wishes of its parents and of children's-agency officials who are responsible for it, not just factors relating to the health and competence of its prospective custodians or the quality of the relationship it may already have developed with such custodians. "Many decisions are 'in-name-only' for the best interests of the specific child" and are fashioned instead "to meet the needs and wishes of competing adult claimants or to protect the general policies of a child care or other administrative agency."[21]

The safeguards built into "best-interests" judgments are surprisingly few, considering that the personal health and well-being of the incompetent, not merely his or her property,

---

[18]*Malpass v. Morgan: Determining When a Parent's Consent to an Adoption is Withheld Contrary to the Best Interests of the Child,* 60 VA. L. REV. 718 (1974).
[19]Armstrong v. Manzo, 380 U.S. 545 (1965).
[20]Note, *The Custody Question and Child Neglect Rehearings,* 35 U. CHI. L. REV. 478-492 (1968).
[21]J. GOLDSTEIN, A. FREUD, AND A. SOLNIT, BEYOND THE BEST INTERESTS OF THE CHILD, 54 (1973).

are at stake. What protection there is derives largely from the impartiality of the judiciary and from the full development of the relevant issues by counsel in the litigation, although the child is seldom represented separately.

IDENTITY OF INTERESTS

The final set of analogous legal rules to be canvassed are those that are premised on an identity of interest between the person who makes the decisions and the one who is affected by them. In most jurisdictions the premise that such an identity exists is taken to be a part of the rationale for leaving decisions about children to their parents. Of course, identity of interests does not tell the whole story, any more than the previous two rationales. But in common-sense terms parents *are* "in the same boat" with their children; risks that the latter experience will have direct and probably unavoidable effects—physical, psychological, and financial—on the former.Thus there may be something to be learned from such examples as the doctrine of virtual representation in the law of trusts, the rules governing class actions, and what is called "third-party consent" to searches and seizures by police officers. Since these doctrines relate to joint or similar interests in property, however, care must be taken in extrapolating them to biomedical interventions. As close as two individuals may be, it is hard to say that one has the same interest in the second's physical integrity as the latter has in his or her own; the parallel may be closer if the first person (who is giving the permission) is also willing to permit the procedure to be performed with his or her own body, but this situation would not often arise with medical treatment and research with children.

Virtual Representation

To be bound in a legal action, as some of the illustrations in previous sections may already have made apparent, a person has to take some part in that action either personally or through a representative. Usually, a representative must be appointed by the person (or by the court, as with a guardian *ad litem*) and be given the authority to act as the person's agent in the litigation. But in certain circumstances an incompetent person without an actual representative may nevertheless be bound by the outcome of the legal action if another party to the action stood in the same legal position vis-à-vis the questions at issue; this person is called the virtual representative of the incompetent. Typically, it will be the sibling of an unborn child who bore the same relationship to a testator or the granter of a trust; by pursuing his or her own selfish interests the virtual representative also promotes those of brothers and sisters yet unborn.

Beyond the threshold requirement of identity of interests, the law of virtual representation erects few protections. The sole basis for finding that a person's interests were not sufficiently represented is affirmative proof that the virtual representative acted in hostility to the absent beneficiary's interests. As the American Law Institute restated the accepted rule: "Evidence as to either the inactivity of the representative or the inadequacy of his conduct is material only as it conduces to establish the hostility of the conduct of the representative to the interest of the person represented."[22]

Class Actions

More rigorous requirements have been established for maintenance of class actions because of the profound effect the actions of the litigant can have on the rights and obligations of absent and otherwise unrelated persons. In class actions, the named party's decisions and the court's judgment are binding on all members of the class,[23] so that it is necessary

---

[22]RESTATEMENT, PROPERTY §185, at 747 (comment), American Law Institute Publishers, St. Paul, Minn. (1936).

[23]*See, e.g.*, Hansberry v. Lee, 311 U.S. 32 (1940).

that what the class representative has at stake is significant enough that he will pursue the case with the proper vigor and that he has the capability to undertake a massive and complicated lawsuit. Furthermore, his interests must be nearly identical with those of the whole class in order that the self-interested choices he makes as a litigant will truly represent the interests of the class. Although the notion of one party appearing in court on behalf of a larger group, in order to avoid repetitious litigation, is not a new one, it has recently taken on increased importance and it became the subject of a complex provision of the *Federal Rules of Civil Procedure*. Rule 23 provides that the named parties must "fairly and adequately represent the interests of the class." "Adequacy" means that they (and their attorneys) are qualified to conduct the litigation,[24] and "fairness" has been interpreted by the courts to require that they have the same interests,[25] or alternatively have no interests that are antagonistic to those of the class,[26] or both.[27] The second aspect of "fairness"—that the party has no conflict of interest with the class—is most often invoked when the party is also the attorney prosecuting the action; conflict obviously may arise between seeking the largest possible recovery for the class and bringing the litigation to a swift conclusion with a highly remunerative fee.[28] A similar problem arises when the person desiring to represent the class is involved in other, nonclass litigation with the opposing party.[29]

Note must also be taken of the law on "standing to sue." The rules on standing, by requiring a party to have a "concrete

---

[24]Comment, *The Importance of Being Adequate: Due Process Requirements in Class Actions under Federal Rule 23*, 123 U. Pa. L. Rev. 1217–1261 (1975).

[25]*See, e.g.,* Hettinger v. Glass Speciality Co., 59 F.R.D. 286 (N.D. Ill. 1973).

[26]*See, e.g.,* Williams v. Sheet Metal Workers, Local 19, 59 F.R.D. 49 (E.D. Pa. 1973).

[27]*See, e.g.,* Shulman v. Ritzenberg, 47 F.R.D. 202 (D.D.C. 1969).

[28]Graybeal v. American Savings & Loan Assoc., 59 F.R.D. 7 (D.D.C. 1973).

[29]duPont v. Wyly, 61 F.R.D. 615 (D. Del. 1973).

adverseness"[30] and precluding the assertion of a "generalized grievance"[31] shared by a large class of citizens, are closely related to those on class actions. Since the rights of others may be affected, the rules about standing not only look for a party who identifies with the legal questions at issue but who will also (or in consequence) be a vigorous advocate. This sort of question arose in the challenges to contraceptive and abortion statutes, in which physicians were sometimes found to lack, and sometimes found to have, the requisite standing to assert the interests of their patients. To have standing a person must allege such a personal stake in the outcome of a controversy with the defendant as to justify the exercise of the court's remedial powers on his or her behalf.[32] This requirement derives both from the limitation on federal courts' jurisdiction in Article III of the Constitution to adjudicating a "case or controversy," and from the judiciary's own "prudential limitations" on the exercise of its authority.[33] The issue of standing may arise in a class action suit, but standing itself is a more attenuated analogy here because, whatever effects the litigant's conduct of the suit may have on the interests of persons not party to the suit, nonparties are not legally bound unless the suit is a class action.

Although not strictly analogous to the making of decisions about biomedical procedures with minors, the rules on class actions serve to remind us of the importance the law attaches to having safeguards that will limit the harm one person can do to another, even when their legal positions seem coincident. In class actions only property is at stake, whereas in medical jurisprudence life and health may be endangered; thus greater care should be exercised in designating any representative. On the other hand, requirements of notice to members of the class, which are among the most difficult

---

[30]Flast v. Cohen, 392 U.S. 83, 99 (1963).
[31]Schlesinger v. Reservists Comm to Stop the War, 418 U.S. 208, 217 (1974).
[32]Baker v. Carr, 369 U.S. 186, 204 (1962).
[33]Warth v. Seldin, 43 U.S.L.W. 4906, 4908 (1975).

aspects of Rule 23, would be much simpler in the medical context; the persons for whom permission is to be given will usually be few in number and easily accessible—although, if they are incompetent, "notice" may be meaningless.

Search and Seizure

"Third-party consent" to search and seizure, the third example of rules grounded in an identity of interests, probably provides the least instructive analogy for several reasons. First, there is no unanimity among the courts on the basis for regarding a third party's consent to the search of the defendant's premises as a valid exception to the Fourth Amendment's requirement of a search warrant from a judicial officer. The Supreme Court initially suggested that the proper grounds for third-party permission would be express agency,[34] a view that has been explicitly followed by many courts and that has much to recommend it.[35] Since such agency is lacking in the medical setting with an incompetent (incompetence terminates an existing agency), the same problems are presented as were found, for example, in drawing a comparison to the attorney–client relationship. Subsequent opinions of the Court, however, have approved third-party consent for searches based on the mutual relationship between the parties and the premises: if the user of a duffel bag[36] or the occupant of a building[37] gives permission for a search, the items seized are admissible against joint users or occupants. Since the evidence can be used against all those with joint authority, there is an identity of interest to validate the nondefendant–third party's consent.

Even if the latter view is taken, however, more basic problems remain with this analogy. On the one hand, the

[34]Stoner v. California, 376 U.S. 483 (1964).
[35]*Recent cases*, 79 HARV. L. REV. 1513 (1966).
[36]Frazier v. Cupp, 394 U.S. 731 (1969).
[37]United States v. Matlock, 415 U.S. 164 (1974); United States v. Stone, 471 F.2d 170 (7th Cir. 1972).

search-and-seizure cases may set rules that are too high since the interests involved enjoy constitutional protection. The courts and commentators who object to the joint-control theory do so, at least in part, because the defendant's Fourth Amendment rights are private[38] and can only be waived "knowingly."[39] Although an express authorization to an agent to permit officials of the state to inspect one's premises might meet this standard, merely sharing control over those premises with someone else does not amount to a waiver of the right to refuse a warrantless search. Although one's interest in being protected against unauthorized bodily invasions—for example, a "search and seizure" of fluid on which to conduct genetic studies[40]—is undeniably greater than the interest in privacy of property, the consequently greater limitations on intervention would not be relevant were the party conducting the interventions not an agent of the government.

The third and final objection, which cuts the other way, is that the purposes to be served by rules in the medical and search areas are so divergent that the rules developed for the latter would not adequately protect an incompetent party being subjected to a medical procedure. The question before the court in search and seizure cases is whether, in order to deter unconstitutional police conduct, evidence that would otherwise be admissible against the defendant should be "suppressed" because it was improperly obtained. As a matter of the administration of justice, such evidence might be allowed, even when the person giving permission for the search was not authorized to do so, if it were reasonable for the police who seized the items to have believed that the person giving permission was a proper person to do so. All of search-and-seizure law, but particularly the joint-control (i.e., identity of interests) theory, is therefore of doubtful help

[38]Boyd v. United States, 116 U.S. 616 (1886).
[39]*See, e.g.,* People v. Flowers, 23 Mich. App. 523, 179 N.W.2d 56 (1970).
[40]*See* J. M. Friedman, *Legal Implications of Amniocentesis,* 123 U. Pa. L. Rev. 92 (1974).

in the biomedical context, where the question is not the reasonableness of official conduct but the designation of a proper party to give permission for intervention with an incompetent.

BORROWED LESSONS

The differing purposes and origins of the law in the various areas surveyed here make it difficult or perhaps impossible to construct a unified theory of third-party permission. Nevertheless, this survey serves as a reminder that rules developed outside medical jurisprudence may prove useful in attempting to arrive at an understanding of the appropriate scope and limits of "proxy consent." The analogies suggest a number of procedural and substantive safeguards that might reasonably be taken as requirements for third-party permission to biomedical intervention with incompetent patients.

First and foremost, there should be no conflict of interest between the decision-maker and the incompetent person. It is just this perception of conflict that has led to prior judicial review in the various twin and sibling transplant cases.[41] The physicians and hospitals were concerned that they ought not to be relying on parental permission for a treatment intended to benefit one of the parents' offspring at the expense of another.

A second lesson about the characteristics of the decision maker can be derived from the law that is based on identity of interests, as well as some of the substitute-judgment examples such as guardians *ad litem*. They teach the importance of a capable and vigorous advocate of the incompetent's interests who maintains control of decision making throughout the intervention. The lowest formal requirements, which occur in the case of virtual representation, can only be justified by the complete identity of interests and the close familial

---

[41]*See* A. M. Capron, *Informed Consent in Catastrophic Disease Research and Treatment*, 123 U. PA. L. REV. 340, 423–429 (1974).

relationship between the representative and represented. The right to withdraw at any time is an important aspect of informed consent law for competent parties; similarly, a third party who has given permission on an incompetent's behalf should retain the right to withdraw it and the duty to remain vigilant in supervising the intervention and protecting the incompetent's interests.

The preceding "lessons" speak to the nature of the "proxy" who should be permitted to decide for a child or other incompetent. The analogies also suggest ways in which a decision can be reached and the outer limits of a decision, whoever is making it. The first of these emerges from the law on guardians *ad litem*. A guardian cannot waive any interest or right of the ward to the latter's detriment. One way to surmount the barrier to action that this rule could create is to seek judicial approval of the guardian's decision, which thereby becomes binding on the ward. But if the interests (such as protecting one's body from harmful invasions) are viewed as sufficiently important and if it is recognized that many of the points at which choices are made prior to the final decision will, in fact, never get *real* judicial scrutiny, greater protection could be assured if the guardian's permission did *not* bind the ward. Clearly, that would purchase greater protection for the incompetent at a high price of uncertainty for the guardian and the biomedical personnel conducting the procedure. To make it reasonable, it would clearly have to be limited in some measure. For example, recovery could be allowed for nonnegligent injuries (negligent injuries already being recoverable, even with valid permission) but not for the harm of an "unconsented touching" itself (i.e., assault and battery). It would also seem advisable to limit the application of the practice to nonbeneficial interventions, such as research, and perhaps especially to cases of sibling transplants. The question for the persons deciding to go ahead in such cases would then be: Are we sure enough of the probable outcome (no real harm to the incompetent but great benefit to someone else or to science) that it is highly unlikely that the incompetent party will, on achieving majority, have any reason to want to sue us? (In other words, is it likely that he or she will feel grateful not to have been prevented from helping someone else just because of being too young to give consent personally?) The probability of suit would further be diminished if the incompetent party were assured (through an insurance mechanism) of full, immediate medical and rehabilitative care for any untoward results of the intervention, without necessity of waiting until he or she comes of age to sue, although suit at that time (to collect for any additional expenses and for the pain and suffering associated with the injury) would not be precluded.

Second, in borrowing from the various areas of the law, one may wish to incorporate *both* the "subjectivity" about what a particular person would want to do (as in the "substitute-judgment" doctrine) and the "objectivity" derivable from a neutral party's judgment about what is reasonable under the circumstances. These twin objectives would be achieved through a two-stage procedure in which initial screening occurs when professionals (typically physicians) determine the objective outer limits (i.e., what procedures can reasonably be performed on *any* children), and then selection of individuals is made by parents, who are not likely to be neutral but who should be well informed about their children's idiosyncrasies as well as their family's ability to deal with any adverse consequences to the child from the choice made.

To increase appropriate "subjectivity," a final "lesson" would place greater emphasis on determining the wishes of the incompetent. If the procedures for determining competence (as discussed in the preceding chapter) lead to differentiation among classes of those found to be incapable of consenting for themselves, then there can also be variations in the rules about third-party permission. For example, third parties might be recognized as having authority to decide for or against participation in experimental procedures of children up to the age of eight to ten, at which point the latter could be found to be "mature enough"[42] to agree or decline to participate, although third-party permission would *also* still be required until the age of consent (which is now eighteen in a majority of American jurisdictions). In the *Seiferth* case, for example, the trial judge indicated that he would have been willing to order the operation on the cleft palate if the question had arisen before the fourteen-year-old patient, who was opposed to the surgery, had acquired convictions of his own.[43] A lesser role for children would be appropriate in nonexperimental care.

By analogy to the doctrine of substitute judgment, under which all gifts from the estate of an incompetent must be made from any surplus not needed for support and may not endanger the corpus, a biomedical intervention ought not to be permitted if it increases in anything more than the most minimal fashion the ratio of risks to benefits. Only the doctrine of substitute judgment encompasses the notion that steps may be authorized that are not intended to benefit the incompetent person. All the other legal rules surveyed assume that the person giving permission will act so as to benefit the incompetent; the legal rules then establish safeguards (of varying rigor) to reduce the probability that this assumption will prove erroneous. Thus, in the case of nonbeneficial (e.g., pure research) interventions, the severe limitation on risks seems appropriate. The assumption of an intent to benefit the child that would accompany therapy, even if unusual or risky, would probably remove it from the severe limits of "substitute judgment." Furthermore, the general approach would be enormously complex, not the least because the evaluation of risks and benefits is itself a highly subjective undertaking.

It is unlikely that the legal analogies can be expected to yield additional useful substantive guidelines for judging

---

[42]*See Developments—The Constitution and the Family,* 93 HARV. L. REV. 1156, 1380 (1980).

[43]*In re* Seiferth, 309 N.Y.80, 127 N.E.2d 820 (1955).

third-party permission in the biomedical context because the subject matters of the various areas differ in many ways from the concerns about bodily integrity and physical and mental well-being that are central to biomedical interventions.

STATE AUTHORITY TO SUPERSEDE PARENTS

If the analogies help to flesh out the contours of "proxy consent" that should be legally acceptable, the second branch of our initial inquiry remains: When, why, and how does the state have the authority to supersede the control exercised by the "proxy"? This problem is often analyzed in terms of the "competing interests" of the child, parent, and state.[44] Such an approach can be helpful,[45] but is also diverting from the main point. It seems particularly artificial to identify separate state interests; in these circumstances, the state is merely a means by which to protect the welfare of parties unable to act for themselves.[46] The presumption the law employs in favor of parental decision making for children does not establish a separate "privacy interest" of the parents to be protected for its own sake but only because, in line with the initial premise, respecting parents' choices serves the child's

[44]Custody of a minor, 1978 Mass. Adv. Sh. 2002, 379 N.E.2d 1053 (1978), *reviewed and aff'd,* 1979 Mass. Adv. Sh. 2124, 393 N.E.2d 836 (1979); *In re* Hofbauer, 65 A.D.2d 108, 411 N.Y.S.2d 416 (1978), *aff'd,* 47 N.Y.2d 1009, 419 N.Y.S.2d 936 (1979).

[45]Bennett, *Allocation of child medical care decisionmaking authority: A suggested interest analysis,* 62 U. VA. L. REV. 285 (1976); Note, *State Intrusion into Family Affairs: Justifications and Limitations,* 26 STAN. L. REV. 1383 (1974).

[46]Although most of the state's interests are derivative, that is, they consist in promoting the interests of members of society whose well-being conduces to the benefit and successful functioning of the state, *see Developments—The Constitution and the Family,* 93 HARV. L. REV. 1156, 1198–1248 (1980), the state has an independent interest in the wise use of collective resources, whether in the adjudicatory process or in the provision of services to citizens, *see* Parham v. J. R., 442 U.S. 584, 604–605 (1979).

interests.[47] It is this interest that the law seeks to protect until such time as the child is deemed capable of exercising it for him or herself. Beginning, then, with the assumption that the law follows nature and custom and assigns decision-making power over children to parents, the issue of state authority to supersede divides into three subsidiary questions: (a) In what circumstances should state intervention be initiated? (b) When is it appropriate to supplant the parents? and (c) How ought the decision to supersede be arrived at?

Basis for Initiation

Judicial intervention in any situation is costly, not only in expending professional resources (those of the state, in operating the courts and those of the parties, in retaining counsel) but also in requiring personal expenditure of time and emotional energy and in placing burdens on people and groups, such as families, whose normal, informal functioning is likely to be seriously disrupted by the glare of the adversary process.[48] Consequently, court scrutiny ought not be too readily invoked. On the other hand, substantial interests of in-

---

[47]The cases usually cited in support of "parental autonomy," e.g., Wisconsin v. Yoder, 406 U.S. 205 (1972) (parental right to determine child's religious upbringing), Pierce v. Society of Sisters, 268 U.S. 510 (1925) (parents' right to direct education of their children), Meyer v. Nebraska, 262 U.S. 390 (1923) (liberty of parents to raise child according to own beliefs), actually involve judicial protection of family integrity in which it is *assumed* that parents are the proper locus for decision making within the family. See Tribe, L., *The Supreme Court, 1972 term—Foreword: Toward a model of roles in the due process of life and law*, 87 HARV. L. REV.: 1, 33–41 (1973), which distinguishes the allocation of abortion decisions to family rather than state from the choice of the mother as the right decision maker within the family.

[48]The informality that reformers early in this century made a hallmark of juvenile proceedings, to protect young people in trouble from the rigors of normal court procedures, was found in time to have its own costs. *See In re* Gault, 387 U.S. 1 (1967).

competents, when health or even life may be at stake, would be jeopardized if judicial oversight were unavailable.

Disregarding for the moment situations in which parents and the biomedical personnel agree on treatment and any action is for a declaration of rights to forestall future liability and not to settle an actual disagreement,[49] the typical basis for initiating a proceeding "against" the parents is through a petition brought by a physician, hospital, or other person such as a representative of a state agency concerned with children's welfare in a court having special jurisdiction over juveniles or family matters. Such a petition contends that the state should assume custody of the child (or limited custody, for the purpose of providing medical care) and authorize someone other than the parents to consent to necessary medical care because the parents, by insisting on a course of action that the petitioners find improper, have "neglected" the child.[50]

The vague nature of the standards opens them to abuse,[51] but it is plainly very hard to adopt narrower ones that will encompass only appropriate cases. At least so far as the biomedical questions of interest here are concerned, a standard more likely to give proper protection would be to limit judicial scrutiny to allegations of irreversible harm of a substantial nature that cast doubt on the presumption that the third party (namely the parents) authorized to decide is actually competent to do so.

---

[49]*See, e.g.,* Madsen v. Harrison, Eq.No. 68651 (Mass., June 12, 1951), and cases cited in Baron, C. H., Botsford, M. and Cole, G. F., *Live organ and tissue transplants for minor donors in Massachusetts,* 55 B.U. L. REV. 159, 161 n. 15 (1975).

[50]*See, e.g.,* Cal. Welfare & Inst. Code §300(b) (West 1978); Mass. G.L. c. 119, §24 (1978); N.Y. Family Court Act §1012, 29A Judiciary Act, pt. 1 (McKinney 1975).

[51]J. GOLDSTEIN, A. FREUD, and A. SOLNIT, BEYOND THE BEST INTERESTS OF THE CHILD (1973); Day, *Termination of Parental Rights Statutes and the Void for Vagueness Doctrine: A Successful Attack on the Parens Patriae Rationale,* 16 J. FAM. L. 213 (1977).

The real protection of all interests involved depends not on the standard for triggering review but on the underlying standard that will be applied by the court in deciding whether to supersede the "proxy's" authority. The triggering standard must permit some cases to be brought before the court that are not, in fact, appropriate candidates for state supervention. Problems arise, however, when review is too easily triggered, since that disrupts private relations unnecessarily and, even worse, is likely to bring about a lowering in the standard for intervention. Like the trigger, the underlying standard is not capable of articulation with mathematical precision. As a larger number of cases are brought before the courts, the judges—operating on the understandable instinct that intervention is appropriate in a certain proportion—will probably intervene in a larger number. From the reasoning given in such cases of intervention (and *some* reason can be found in most cases), the standard for review would gradually broaden.

The mere petition by a relative for appointment as a guardian should not ordinarily occasion review of the propriety of state supervention. The law's requirement that *someone* be authorized to make decisions about matters such as medical care is the basis on which parents, for example, would seek to be appointed guardians of their child, once he or she had reached the age of majority, if the child were unconscious or otherwise unable to decide for him or herself. Considerable confusion on this point has been generated by the *Quinlan* case. Had Joseph Quinlan, the father of Karen Ann, who was twenty-one at the time she became comatose, simply sought to be appointed her guardian, many of the difficulties raised by the case would have been avoided—or at the very least, postponed until he and the physicians he chose to treat Karen disagreed and the latter declined to follow his instructions because they believed that such instructions would place Karen at an unacceptable risk of severe, irreversible injury or death.

Basis for Superseding the Third Party

From the case law one can see several possible views of the substantive rule on state authority to supersede parents. There is a substantial body of constitutional law establishing the notion of familial privacy and recognizing the need to treat with great deference the exercise of parental prerogatives to make decisions about family matters.[52] Yet this right is plainly a limited one. If it is seen as the counterweight to the state's interest in protecting helpless beings, then the scope for parental decision making will in all probability be regarded as narrow: parental conduct that "threatens a child's well-being" will be overturned. This approach was taken by the Supreme Judicial Court of Massachusetts in the Chad Green case in which the justices unanimously affirmed a superior-court judgment giving custody and control of a two-year-old child to the Department of Public Welfare in order to permit chemotherapy to be commenced for his leukemia.[53]

On the other hand, if the interest at stake is the incompetent patient's right to control his or her own treatment, a right that would be extinguished by his or her incompetence if the "proxy" is not permitted to exercise it,[54] the state should be put to a much greater showing in order to intervene. The "lessons" derived from the analogous legal rules suggest that the state should supersede only when the parent (or other guardian) is incompetent as a representative or is manifestly at odds with the interests of the child.

[52]See generally, Developments—The constitution and the family, 93 HARV. L. REV. 1156, 1161–1197 (1980), and note 47 supra.

[53]Custody of a Minor, 1978 Mass. Adv. Sh. 2020, 379 N.E.2d 1053 (1978), reviewed and aff'd, 1979 Mass. Adv. Sh. 2124, 393 N.E.2d 836 (1979).

[54]See In re Quinlan, 70 N.J. 10, 355 A.2d 647, cert. denied, 429 U.S. 922 (1976); Superintendent of Belchertown State School v. Saikewicz, 1977 Mass. Adv. Sh. 2461, 2482–2483, 370 N.E.2d 417, 427 (1977). Strictly speaking, if the "right to control treatment" is personal to the patient, it is destroyed by the fact of incapacity to choose and cannot be regenerated by the courts' allowing someone else to make the decision instead.

These two qualities are reflective of the review of the analogies regarding the characteristics of the decision makers in the preceding section: the need for a capable advocate and the prohibition on conflicting interests. The notion of "competence" of the parent ought to go beyond vigor of advocacy and manifest a comprehension of the reasons for, and consequences of, the alternatives available. More difficult is the question whether the standard *for superseding* should incorporate as a part of "competence" the lessons from the analogies about the nature of the choice that should be made. These lessons are clearly helpful in guiding the judge or other state official in making choices for the child once the decision to supersede the parents' authority has been made, but employing them to decide whether the parents are to be overridden introduces serious problems.

Certain of the desired limitations are likely to be inherent in biomedical decision making. The need for the cooperation of professionals places *objective* outer limits on choice. Moreover, parental choice can also be made "subjective" by providing for concurrent decision making by children who (because of their age) are marginally competent[55] and by not giving binding effect to the parents' "consent" on the child's behalf, which should have the effect of increasing the sensitivity of parents and professionals to arrive at decisions that are likely to be endorsed by the child when he or she comes of age.

Difficulties arise if one takes the next step and permits a decision to supersede to be based on the conclusion that a parental choice is not *subjectively* what the child would have chosen. In many cases, especially for very young children, judicial conclusions on this point would be mere speculation. Of course, judicial insistence on an *objective* standard can oust parental decision making as completely as a subjective judgment by the courts. (In the *Storar* case, for example, the New York Court of Appeals refused to allow speculation on the

[55]*See* Chapter 3 for further elaboration of the issue of competence.

wishes of a profoundly retarded fifty-two-year-old man with a mental age of about eighteen months whose mother was, obviously, unable to provide any statement of the patient's own views.[56]) Nonetheless, when one sees the results of subjective reasoning in the making of decisions for an incompetent, as for example by the Massachusetts Supreme Judicial Court in the *Saikewicz* case,[57] one is not left with great confidence in the advisability of applying subjective reasoning to the decision whether to supersede parental choice, as illustrated by the same court's decision in Chad Green's case.[58] Any borrowing from the analogy of the doctrine of substitute judgment ought, therefore, probably be limited to the subjectivity that parents may be assumed to bring the choices they make on their child's behalf. If their role is to be taken over by the state it ought to be on firmer ground than judicial speculation about what the child would want.

Method for Superseding

The steps that should be followed to arrive at the decision that the state should supersede parental authority ought to

[56]Mrs. Storar's petition for an order prohibiting further blood transfusions (needed by her son because he was bleeding from a terminal cancer) was refused on the grounds that under New York law parents may never deprive a child of life-sustaining treatment. 438 N.Y.S.2d 266 (Ct.App. 1981). By way of contrast, in the *Quinlan* case the New Jersey Supreme Court also declined to accept anecdotal evidence of Karen Quinlan's attitude toward "extraordinary treatment"; relying instead on the standard of the average, reasonable person in similar circumstances, the court found it acceptable for Karen's father to order the discontinuation of life-sustaining treatment. *In re* Quinlan, 70 N.J. 10, 42, 355 A.2d 647, 644 (1976).

[57]Belchertown State School v. Saikewicz, 1977 Mass. Adv. Sh. 2461, 370 N.E.2d (1977). The court concluded that although most people in Mr. Saikewicz's condition *would* consent to treatment of leukemia, he would not because his low intelligence kept him from understanding what was being done and the reasons for his pain; the court hypothesized that Mr. Saikewicz might have to be restrained for treatment and so on, but made no move to *begin* treatment in order to test its suppositions.

[58]Custody of a Minor, 1978 Mass. Adv. Sh. 2002, 379 N.E.2d 1053 (1978).

reflect the standard being applied. The benchmark suggested in the preceding pages is a decision made by capable, non-adversary parents, which also comports with professional standards and, perhaps, with the actual wishes of children who are nearly mature.

Thus the court should primarily address its attention to the parents' process in reaching their decision. The greater the risk of a procedure, the higher the requirements of the care and completeness that may be applied. For a minor medical intervention, one would not be surprised if parents were content with a basic explanation from a single physician; before they took a very serious step, such as the withdrawal of lifesaving treatment, however, one would expect parents to have consulted a variety of sources, medical and nonmedical (such as other family members, the clergy, lawyers, social workers, and so on), and to indicate in their statements (however simply or elegantly articulated) an awareness of the options and the reasons for choosing among them.

Furthermore, inquiry should be made about any factors, in the relationship between parents and child or in the nature of the medical choice to be made, that demonstrate a conflict between the interests or wishes of the parents and child. Although parents "may at times be acting against the interests of their children,"[59] the presumption is that they "generally do act in [their] best interests."[60] Therefore, parental authority should be superseded only if the judge has been convinced by clear and convincing proof[61] that the parents, through lack of attention, incapacity, or adverse interest, are unable to represent their child's interests.

---

[59]Bartley v. Kremens, 402 F. Supp. 1039, 1047–1048 (E.D. Pa. 1975), *vacated and remanded*, 431 U.S. 119 (1977).

[60]Parham v. J.R., 442 U.S. 584, 602–603 (1979).

[61]*In re* Phillip B., 156 Cal. Rptr. 48, 52 (Ct. App. 1979); E. T. Horwitz, *Of Love and Laetrile: Medical Decision Making in a Child's Best Interests*, 5 AM. J. L. & MED. 271, 284–286 (1979). *Cf.* Eichner v. Dillon, 438 N.Y.S.2d 266 (Ct. App. 1981) (clear and convincing proof required when it is claimed that a person who has become incompetent had left instructions to terminate life sustaining procedures under certain circumstances).

This requirement may suggest an elaborate process and a serious intrusion into a private sphere. It is not meant to. Certainly, the judicial proceeding itself should not be unduly protracted or formalized. Counsel should, of course, have an opportunity to examine the parents and other witnesses, especially if a conflict of interest is the basis for urging the state to supersede parental authority. But the court may also wish to play an active role in questioning the parents, less to "cross-examine" them than to understand the motivation and thought processes that led to their choice. Properly handled, the process of articulation in the courtroom may be a helpful (if perhaps also painful) part of the actual decision-making for the parents and their medical advisers. The open and structured nature of the process also underlines for everyone the gravity of the matters at stake, and may thereby further protect the child's interest in fair and conscientious choices being made about his or her care.[62]

---

[62]A parent following his or her own *conscience* is not the same as *conscientious* weighing of the available options to select the one that is best for the child. The proper role for conscience is especially difficult because of the deference accorded by the Constitution to religious beliefs, which may be a large or perhaps dominant element in personal conscience. Courts have, nevertheless, been willing to override parental decisions that are based on the parents' religious objections to treatment of proved efficacy and favorable benefit–risk ratio, as for example lifesaving blood transfusions. *In re* Pogue, No. M-18-74 (D.C. Super. Ct., Nov. 11, 1974); *In re* Ivey, 319 So.2d 53 (Fla. D.Ct. App. 1976); John F. Kennedy Memorial Hosp. v. Heston, 58 N.J. 576, 279 A.2d 670 (1970). In some ways the usual protection of religious belief is stood on its head in these cases; religiously motivated choices seem actually to be disfavored. Of the two most likely explanations for this judicial attitude, one seems clearly improper. The religious beliefs in question are typically those of small sects, outside the mainstream of American religion; for a state official to disapprove on these grounds amounts to exactly the sort of state establishment of orthodoxy, and prevention of minority exercise of "deviant" religions, that the First Amendment forbids. On the other hand, it is neither a matter of religious persecution nor a violation of the general standard of judicial review of substitute decision makers described in this chapter for a court to disapprove of a choice determined by the parents' religion on the same basis that would disqualify a choice commanded by *any* principle that operated independently of the needs and

Although the inquiry should be a probing one, it invades parental authority and familial privacy much less than the process followed in the *Quinlan* or *Saikewicz* cases. In the former, the New Jersey Supreme Court went beyond examining the fitness of Joseph Quinlan to be his daughter's guardian, as evidenced by his carefully articulated reasoning, arrived at after conscientious consultation and personal ethical agonizing. Instead, it speculated about the choice Karen Ann would make if her ability to express herself were momentarily restored, and it further theorized about the choice "the overwhelming majority of [society's] members" would make.[63] The court thus assumed in turn the roles of Karen's own father and the father of the hypothetical average, irreversibly comatose patient. In either guise, the New Jersey court took the issue on which the judiciary should pass to be the appropriateness of the choice not of the chooser.

The setting of the Massachusetts case was significantly different, since the state had an unavoidable role in any decisions about the treatment of Joseph Saikewicz, a longtime resident of a state institution without any close relatives willing to make the decisions. But in approving a procedure of judicially promulgated substituted judgments for incompetent patients in need of medical care,[64] the Supreme Judicial

---

risks for a child in a particular case. A parental refusal to permit life-preserving treatment, for example, of any child born on a Wednesday, or any female, or any child intellectually incapable of enrolling at Harvard University, indicates that the parents are deciding solely *about* the child and not also *for* and *on behalf of* the child. Since there is no assurance that such highly unusual beliefs, religious or otherwise, would be shared by children and applied by them in such a fashion, it is wrong, in the Supreme Court's words, to allow the parents to "make martyrs" of the children before they are mature enough to "make that choice for themselves," although the parents are free to become martyrs for their own principles. Prince v. Massachusetts, 321 U.S. 158, 170 (1944).

[63]*In re* Quinlan, 70 N.J. 10, 41–42, 355 A.2d 647, 664 (1976).

[64]Superintendent of Belchertown State School v. Saikewicz, 1977 Mass. Adv. Sh. 2461, 370 N.E.2d 417 (1977).

Court did not confine its decision to people like Mr. Saikewicz.[65] If parental authority has been superseded, it would be appropriate for a court to apply the "best-interests" test in approving medical decisions for the incompetent patient, but employing the test as a means of second-guessing parental choices is inappropriate unless the parents have been disqualified as decision makers.

In addition to the issues before the court and the burden of proof, deciding what parties will appear is an important aspect of the procedure in these cases. A guardian *ad litem* should be appointed to represent the child only if this person (or the attorney he or she retains) is to be an active and independent participant in the litigation. A guardian *ad litem* would not appear to be necessary in all cases but *is* a necessity if the appearance of adversariness between the parents and the party objecting to their role as the child's representative (e.g., the treating physicians or hospital administrator) is merely an appearance.[66] The occurrence of such "sweetheart" lawsuits is likely to be diminished if no decision by the court makes the consent of the parent (or other guardian) binding on the child should the latter later disapprove and wish to sue (as was previously discussed). If courts were to confine themselves to the parents' role as decision makers, no explicit judicially created immunity would arise for the consequences of any particular decision. (To the extent that such immunity

---

[65]*But see In re* Dinnerstein, 1978 Mass. App. Ct. Adv. Sh. 736, 380 N.E.2d 134 (1978).

[66]Baron, C. H., Botsford, M. & Cole, G. F., *supra* note 49, at 186:

> Courts should be required to appoint guardians ad litem to represent prospective minor donors in all transplant proceedings. The guardian's role should be defined as that of an advocate of the child's interest in not acting as a donor; the guardian should be instructed to present all the evidence and arguments against his ward's donation and to oppose the positions taken by the hospital and family, regardless of the guardian's personal perception of the child's actual interests.

See also C. H. Baron, *Assuring Detached but Passionate Investigation and Decision: The Role of Guardians ad litem in Saikewicz-Type Cases*, 4 AM. J. L. & MED. 111 (1978).

is thought to exist under the present law of agency, modification in the rules for these circumstances would be needed.)

In its recent decision, *Parham v. J. R.*,[67] the Supreme Court of the United States set forth the role, mandated by due process, for another figure—a "neutral factfinder"—who might also have a place in making choices about children's medical care. In *Parham*, the issue was the review that was necessary before parents could have their children institutionalized for mental health care. *Parham* holds that a judicial hearing is not required for commitment of a juvenile but that "some kind of inquiry should be made by a 'neutral factfinder' to determine whether the statutory requirements for admission are satisfied."[68]

The function of psychiatrists (or other physicians) in this role seems even more dubious in the present context than in that established in *Parham*. Although denominated a "factfinder," the person actually has the power to approve or refuse admission, based on a judgment whether "the parents' decision . . . is proper from a medical standpoint."[69] It would hardly seem to require a high-court decision, much less the interpolation of this new "neutral factfinder," to establish that the staff of mental hospitals may limit their admissions to people who evidence mental illness suitable for treatment (to paraphrase the Georgia statute that was under scrutiny in *Parham*). Thus one would suppose that the probing for medical propriety, on which the factfinder is to base his judgment, invites him to inquire more extensively into the basis of the parental decision and the true interests of the child. Since the scope of the issues in general biomedical decision making involving children (and other incompetents) is broader than the single, statutorily established issue in hospitalization for mental health care, there would be grave danger of overreaching by a medical "neutral factfinder."

[67]442 U.S. 584 (1979).
[68]*Id.* at 606.
[69]*Id.* at 610.

Medical norms do have a legitimate place in protecting minor patients through the establishment of outer boundaries of "reasonableness" on parental choices of treatment options. The physicians caring for a child thus serve this "gatekeeping" function,[70] without need for each "case" to move from the medical to the legal arena for actual adjudication. Even when the physicians do not prefer the option chosen by the parents, they implicitly assure that it is within the range of acceptability by complying with the parental choice rather than challenging the parents' authority.[71]

If a challenge is brought to parental authority by physicians or (in the face of physician approval or acquiescence) by a public official (state prosecutor, representative of a child welfare agency, or the like), courts may wish, in unusual cases, to appoint a physician to act truly as a neutral factfinder, with the task of reporting to the court the medical norms that

---

[70]*See* R. C. Fox, and J. P. Swazey, The Courage to Fail, 5–39 (1974). Because health professionals place a very high value on the preservation of life, *see, e.g.,* John F. Kennedy Memorial Hosp. v. Heston, 58 N.J. 576, 582, 279 A.2d 670, 673 (1970), their role in the process set forth here protects children and other incompetents by bringing about judicial scrutiny of, and setting outer boundaries for, parental decisions for or against medical procedures that thereby place life at risk. Since health professionals may not balance the value of biological life against competing considerations in the same fashion as the general community, D. Crane, The Sanctity of Social Life: Physicians' Treatment of Critically Ill Patients (1975), the medical viewpoint is an appropriate trigger for review but not the final measure of the appropriateness of the parents remaining in control of the decisions. Courts will be likely to give great weight to the professionals' preferences when it is predictable that treatment will return the patient "to a normal, integrated, functioning, cognitive existence." *In re* Dinnerstein, 1978 Mass. App. Ct. Adv. Sh. 736, 746, 380 N.E.2d 134, 138 (1978).

[71]Physicians, nurses, and other health personnel providing care for a child have a legal duty to provide adequate care. Professor Robertson argues that they must continue care, for acquiescing in a parental decision to terminate care exposes them to prosecution for homicide by omission or for failure to report the parental "neglect" to child welfare authorities. J. Robertson, *Involuntary Euthanasia of Defective Newborns: A Legal Analysis,* 27 Stanford L. Rev. 213 (1975).

are relevant to the case. It would then be open to the court to supersede parental decision-making that was based on such a highly deviant medical subgroup or on such peculiar professional norms as not to be acceptable to the general community. As there are other means to render either of these situations unlikely,[72] a judgment of this type ought rarely to be rendered. Typically, the cooperation of the medical profession provides an adequate screen of parental choices for their conformity with objective standards.[73]

CONCLUSION

When a person is legally incompetent to decide about his or her own medical care, the authority to make the necessary choices must be vested in someone else. In the case of minors living with one or both parents (or other guardians), the person already charged with the child's care and welfare is the appropriate decision maker.[74]

Looking to areas of the law other than the rules on biomedical treatment and research, one finds several examples of third-party substitutes making decisions that affect an absent or incompetent person. The most commom elements in these disparate rules is that the substitute decision-maker should have no conflict of interest with the incompetent and should manifest the ability to participate in the decision in a vigorous, informed, and conscientious manner. The value of subjectivity in choice should be partially achieved by reliance on parents as decision-makers, since the common nature of

[72]"If the physician's clinical judgment is not acceptable, the appropriate state authority should prosecute not the parents for their reliance on it, but the physician." Horwitz, supra note 61, at 274, n. 13.

[73]Doe v. Bolton, 410 U.S. 179, 199 (1973); In re Hofbauer, 47 N.Y.2d 648, 655, 393 N.E.2d 1009, 1014, 419 N.Y.S.2d 936, 940 (1979).

[74]Rishworth v. Moss, 222 S.W. 225 (Tex. Comm. App. 1920); In re Roll, 117 N.J. Super. 122, 283 A.2d 764 (1971) (interpreting statute requiring appointment of next of kin as guardian absent demonstration that to do so would be "affirmatively contrary to best interests of incompetent").

their interests makes it probable they will reflect the views and values of their children. And the participation of physicians and other health professionals in any decisions about research and treatment help to assure that parental choice will be confined within the bounds of objective reasonableness, a further factor that emerges from some of the rules.

Although this formulation provides some scope for subjectivity (which could be increased by holding that parental permission does not preclude later action by the child and by according older children an increasing role in making medical choices short of full independence), it does not seem wise to adopt the practice established by the doctrine of substitute judgment in the law of trusts under which the court makes the truly subjective determination that the parents' choice is the same as the one the child would have made. Experience with cases in which the courts have undertaken this task confirm the fear that it is too time-consuming and difficult to be done well; furthermore, it is inherently at odds with the safeguards for a proper decision derived from all the other legal analogies, because in pronouncing the acceptability *vel non* of the parental decision the court is implicitly replacing the parents. Only if parents are unable to agree on what is right for their child or if no suitable decision-maker exists would a court have to arrive at its own conclusions about the child's "best interests." Restricting judicial oversight to whether parents are "fully informed 'and acting in good faith' "[75] for a particular child[76] rather than to the acceptability of the decision

---

[75]Ruby v. Massey, 452 F. Supp. 361, 371 (D. Conn. 1978) citing Hart v. Brown 29 Conn. Supp. 368, 371, 289 A.2d 386, 388 (1972). In *Ruby,* Judge Blumenfeld extended the statutory procedures for sterilization of the institutionally retarded (who may be sterilized by decision of the institution's director, subject to review by three physicians and approval of the probate court) to noninstitutionalized retarded children. Looking to *Hart,* the kidney transplant case involving seven-year-old twins, he suggested in *dictum* an appropriate standard for reviewing a parental judgment to sterilize. *See also In re* Grady, 170 N.J. Super 98, 405 A.2d 851 (1979) (recognizes authority of courts to approve parental decision to sterilize, to prevent child's permanent incompetence from extinguishing his or her right). In reviewing parents' decision, courts must consider the good faith of the applicants,

is also less intrusive on the interests in familial privacy and continuity of care that are important parts of our jurisprudence,[77] as portrayed by Joseph Goldstein in the next chapter.

The conclusions reached here will not, of course, remove the private agony and public concern that accompany those cases—few in number but dramatic in impact—in which a child's desperate straits or a parent's unusual views test the limits of judicial forbearance. When life-threatening or other serious, irreversible steps are involved, prospective review is particularly appropriate to afford the child adequate protection. But medical or judicial disagreement with the choice made by parents should not be equated with parental unsuitability as decision makers. The risk for children thus accepted is irreducible, in biomedical decision making as in all of life; attempts to reduce it further risk for us all the deadening encroachment of the beneficent tyranny that Justice Brandeis so eloquently decried.[78]

---

their interests, their motives, and the weight to be given their judgment. "Since there can be no objectively right or wrong answer, the burden should not be on the parents to establish that what is right for them is necessarily right for others." 405 A.2d at 865.

Because children as well as adults possess the right to decide whether to bear children, Carey v. Population Services International, 431 U.S. 678 (1977); Planned Parenthood of Central Missouri v. Danforth, 428 U.S. 52 (1976), a parental choice to have a child sterilized is as significant in legal terms as any, save perhaps one risking life. Several courts have held that courts do not have jurisdiction to approve decisions to sterilize, absent legislation. *See, e.g., In re* Tulley, 83 Cal. App. 698, 146 Cal. Rptr. 266 (1978), *cert. denied,* 440 U.S. 967 (1979); A. L. v. G. R. H., 325 N.E.2d 501 (Ind. 1975), *cert. denied,* 425 U.S. 936 (1976); and *In re* D. D. 394 N.Y.S.2d 139, 90 Misc.2d 236 (Surr. Ct. 1977), *aff'd on other grounds,* 408 N.Y.S.2d 104, 64 A.D2d 898 (1978).

[76]*Cf.* M. Siegler, *Critical Illness: The Limits of Autonomy,* 7(5) Hastings Ctr. Rpt. 12, 13 (1977): "Rather than assessing the rationality of a particular choice, one can ask an alternative question, whether [the patient's] decisions were consonant with his nature as a person."

[77]*Cf. In re* Nemser, 51 Misc.2d 616, 273 N.Y.S.2d 624 (Sup. Ct. 1966).

[78]Olmstead v. United States, 277 U.S. 438, 479 (1928) (Brandeis, J. dissenting).

CHAPTER 5

Medical Care for the Child at Risk

On State Supervention of Parental Autonomy

JOSEPH GOLDSTEIN

Of all tyrannies a tyranny sincerely exercised for the good of its victims may be the most oppressive. . . . [T]hose who torment us for our own good will torment us without end for they do so with the approval of their own conscience.[1]

INTRODUCTION

To be a *child* is to be at risk, dependent, and without capacity or authority to decide what is "best" for oneself.

---

[1]Lewis, *The Humanitarian Theory of Punishment*, 6 RES JUDICATAE 224, 228 (1952).
    Copyright © 1977 by Joseph Goldstein.

JOSEPH GOLDSTEIN ● Sterling Professor of Law, Yale University Law School and Professor, Yale University Child Study Center, New Haven, Connecticut 06520.

To be an *adult* is to be a risktaker, independent, and with capacity and authority to decide and to do what is "best" for oneself.

To be an *adult who is a parent* is to be presumed in law to have the capacity, authority, and responsibility to determine and to do what is good for one's children.

The law is designed to assure for each child an opportunity to meet and master the developmental crises on the way to adulthood—to that critical age when he or she is presumed by the state to be qualified to determine what is "best" for oneself.[2] As Jeremy Bentham observed not so long ago in 1840:

> The feebleness of infancy demands a continual protection. Everything must be done for an imperfect being, which as yet does nothing for itself. The complete development of its physical powers takes many years; that of its intellectual faculties is still slower. At a certain age, it has already strength and passions, without experience enough to regulate them. Too sensitive to present impulses, too negligent of the future, such a being must be kept under an authority more immediate than that of the laws. . . .[3]

That "more immediate" authority is parental authority. Thus, society's law, in accord with nature's law, seeks to

---

[2]*See* Goldstine, *On Being Adult and Being An Adult in Secular Law,* 105 DAEDALUS, Fall 1976, at 69, 71–72.

[3]J. BENTHAM, THEORY OF LEGISLATION 248 (Boston 1840). Similarly, Freud observed:

> The biological factor is the long period of time during which the young of the human species is in a condition of helplessness and dependence. Its intra-uterine existence seems to be short in comparison with that of most animals, and it is sent into the world in a less finished state. . . . Moreover, the dangers of the external world have a greater importance for it, so that the value of the object which can alone protect it against them and take the place of its former intra-uterine life is enormously enhanced. This biological factor, then, establishes the earliest situations of danger and creates *the need to be loved* which will accompany the child through the rest of its life.

S. FREUD, INHIBITIONS, SYMPTOMS, AND ANXIETIES 139–40 (1926) (emphasis added).

assure for each child permanent membership in a family with at least one and preferably two caretaking adults.[4] The law, reflecting Bentham's view, has a strong presumption in favor of parental authority free of coercive intrusion by agents of the state.[5] Indeed, it is a function of law to protect family privacy as a means of safeguarding parental autonomy in

[4]*See generally* J. GOLDSTEIN, A. FREUD & A. SOLNIT, BEYOND THE BEST INTERESTS OF THE CHILD (1973) [hereinafter cited as BEYOND THE BEST ITERESTS].

[5]The extent to which parental authority is protected by the Constitution is not of primary concern in this essay. Yet it should not go unrecognized that the Supreme Court has established that the Fourteenth Amendment protects, as a liberty interest, the very nature of family life. *See* Cleveland Bd. of Educ. v. LaFleur, 414 U.S. 632, 639–40 (1974) 413 U.S. 139, 142 (1973) (constitutional right of privacy includes right of marriage, procreation, motherhood, child rearing, and education): Roe v. Wade, 410 U.S. 113, 152–53 (1972) (right of privacy, founded in Fourteenth Amendment's concept of liberty, extends to child rearing and education): Wisconsin v. Yoder, 406 U.S. 205, 230–35 (1972) (parental right to direct religious education of child); Stanley v. Illinois, 405 U.S. 645, 651 (1972) (presumption that unwed father unfit to keep his children violates due process and equal protection); Griswold v. Connecticut, 381 U.S. 479, 485–86 (1965) (constitutional protection for marital privacy); Pierce v. Society of Sisters, 268 U.S. 510, 534–35 (1925) ("liberty" of parents to direct education of their children); Meyer v. Nebraska, 262 U.S. 390, 400–03 (1923) ("liberty" of parents to raise children). Under these cases, that interest extends from the very decision to conceive children and initiate a family to the right to direct a child's upbringing.

The traditional protection of the family relationship from state intrusion is also acknowledged in tort law by a general rule of reciprocal immunity for both parents and their minor children from liability for personal torts committed by them on one another as well as a specific parental exemption for disciplinary efforts, which otherwise would be perceived as intentional torts on these minor children. W. PROSSER, HANDBOOK ON THE LAW OF TORTS § 27, at 136–38 (4th ed. 1971) (citing cases both upholding immunity and rejecting immunity); *see also* J. GOLDSTEIN & J. KATZ, THE FAMILY AND THE LAW 399 408 (1965); W. PROSSER, J. WADE & V. SCHWARTZ, CASES AND MATERIALS ON TORTS 140–42 639–51 (6th ed. 1976). Such immunity is further reenforced by penal statutes like the following from New York:

The use of physical force upon another person which would otherwise constitute an offense is justifiable and not criminal under any of the following circumstances:

1. A parent, guardian, or other person entrusted with the care and supervision of a minor or an incompetent person, and a teacher or other

child rearing.[6] At the same time the law attempts to safeguard each child's entitlement to autonomous parents who care and who feel responsible and who can be held accountable for continually meeting the child's ever-changing physical and psychological needs.

Like all authority, however, parental authority may be abused. Family privacy may become a cover for exploiting the inherent inequality between adult and child.[7] Thus children who, by definition, are both physically and psychologically at risk may sometimes be placed at further risk by the adult "caretakers" who are presumed to be essential to their well-being.

This essay explores the role for law in protecting children from parental exploitation and parents and children within a family from state exploitation in the provision or denial of medical care. The goal is to determine the extent to which the law should supervene, not only the right and obligation of

---

person entrusted with the care and supervision of a minor for a special purpose, may use physical force, but not deadly physical force, upon such minor or incompetent person when and to the extent that he reasonably believes it necessary to maintain discipline or to promote the welfare of such minor or incompetent person.

N.Y. PENAL LAW § 35.10 (McKinney 1967). A similar provision is contained in the Model Penal Code § 3.07(1).

[6]This notion is not unlike what Chafee said of the First Amendment: "[It] and other parts of the law erect a fence inside which men can talk. The lawmakers, legislators and officials stay on the outside of that fence." Z. CHAFEE, THE BLESSINGS OF LIBERTY 108 (1956). Together, privacy and autonomy give content to another concept, "family integrity," which was explicitly recognized by the Court in Stanley v. Illinois, 405 U.S. 645, 651 (1972), and which is to be found in Justice Harlan's dissent in Poc v. Ullman, 367 U.S. 497, 551–52 (1961) ("The home derives its pre-eminence as the seat of family life. And the integrity of that life is something so fundamental that it has been found to draw to its protection the principles of more than one explicitly granted Constitutional right.") See also Griswold v. Connecticut, 381 U.S. 479, 500 (1965) (Harlan, J., concurring) (relying upon his dissent in Poe).

[7]See Erikson, Growth and Crises of the "Healthy Personality," in PERSONALITY IN NATURE, SOCIETY, AND CULTURE 185 (2d ed. C. Kluckholm & H. Murray 1953).

parents to decide what medical attention should or should not be provided for their children, but also the reciprocal right of children to have their parents assume responsibility for making such decisions.[8] This quest incorporates two questions about empowering the state to breach its commitment to family privacy and to parental autonomy: (1) What circumstances, if any, should constitute *probable cause* for the state to intrude on family privacy by investigating parental decisions about a child's health and medical care needs? and (2) What must such an investigation find in order to *justify* the abridgement of parental autonomy by substituting the state's judgment for that of the parents? Although both of these questions are important, this essay focuses on the second question, for it presents the ultimate dilemma of *when* should the state itself become the "parent"?

This question of primary focus arises in two quite distinct forms. The first, on which this essay does not dwell, takes the form of *generally applicable* societal judgments that no parents shall have a choice, for example, with regard to having their children vaccinated against smallpox. Such legislative infringements of parental autonomy are without regard to any specific individual parent's wishes. They are perceived as a "reasonable and proper exercise of police power" in furtherance of compelling state interests, for example, to safeguard society generally from a smallpox epidemic.[9]

The second form of intrusion and the one on which this

---

[8]Not unlike such other cognizable and substantial liberty interests as freedom of speech, freedom of association, and the right to vote, the "familial bond" of the parent-child relationship is a "reciprocal right." Stanley v. Illinois, 405 U.S. 645, 647, 652 (1972). *See, e.g.,* United States Dep't of Agriculture v. Moreno, 413 U.S. 528, 535 n.7 (1973) (association); Virginia State Bd. of Pharmacy v. Virginia Citizens Consumer Council, 425 U.S. 748, 756–57 (1976) (speech).

[9]*See* Jacobson v. Massachusetts, 197 U.S. 11 (1905) (upholding state compulsory vaccination law). Such laws may remain in force even though, with the passage of time, they may, as in the case of vaccination against smallpox, no longer be medically sound.

essay does dwell, is less precisely defined. It concerns case-by-case determinations that turn on whether the state should supervise or supervene individual parental judgments concerning health care for their children. The authority for state intervention is found in often vague and imprecise neglect, abuse, and delinquency statutes, as well as in administrative and judicial decisions that some children under certain circumstances are entitled to obtain or to reject medical care without regard to or against their parents' wishes.[10] In an effort to tease out some tentative guides for fixing limits to intrusions on parental autonomy and family privacy, a series of cases will be examined that involve (a) a choice between life and death for "normally" formed and "malformed" newborn infants; (b) a choice between life and death for a teenager; (c) non-life-threatening choices for young children and teenagers; and (d) two interrelated life-threatening and non-life-threatening choices concerning a transplant from a well child to a dying sibling.

PRESUMPTIONS OF PARENTAL AUTONOMY AND FAMILY PRIVACY

The cases are analyzed in terms of the strong presumptions in our legal system in favor of parental autonomy and family privacy and *against* coercive intervention. The law presumes the capacity and recognizes the authority of adults to parent their children in accord with their own individual beliefs, preferences, and life styles. It does not establish rules for child rearing to accord with some particular religious or scientific ideal. It requires only that parents meet *minimal* standards of child care *negatively* set in neglect, abuse, and abandonment statutes and *affirmatively* set in provisions such as

---

[10]The neglect laws are collected in S. KATZ, M. MCGRATH & R. HOWE, CHILD NEGLECT LAWS IN AMERICA (1976) [hereinafter cited as CHILD NEGLECT LAWS].

those obligating parents to send their children to school, to keep them out of the labor market, and to have them vaccinated against smallpox. In accord with fundamental notions of liberty, the law thus presumes that parents, as adults, are qualified to decide how to meet the needs of their children until these children themselves become adults presumed competent to decide what is in their own and their children's interests.[11]

The right to family privacy and parental autonomy, as well as the reciprocal liberty interest of parent and child in the familial bond between them, need no greater justification than that they comport with each state's fundamental constitutional commitment to individual freedom and human dignity.[12] But the right of parents to raise their children as they think best, free of coercive intervention, comports as well with each child's biological and psychological need for unthreatened and unbroken continuity of care by his parents.[13] No other animal is for so long a time after birth in so helpless a state that its survival depends upon continuous nurture by an adult. Although breaking or weakening the ties to the responsible and responsive adults may have different consequences for children of different ages, there is little doubt that such breaches in the familial bond will be detri-

---

[11]See Goldstein, *supra* note 2, at 72.

[12]See Mnookin, *Child-Custody Adjudication: Judicial Functions in the Face of Indeterminacy*, 39 LAW & CONTEMP. PROB. 226, 266–67 (1975). The Supreme Court has recognized at least two separate parent-child interests that are protected by the Fourteenth Amendment. One is the entitlement of natural parents and their children to each other, an interest which rests on the fact of biological reproduction and arises when the child is born. The other protected interest is in the "familial bonds" which develop over time between parents, whether biological or not, and the children in their long-term care. Stanley v. Illinois, 405 U.S. 645, 651–52 (1972). For a discussion of the impact of a commitment to human dignity on other legal issues, see Goldstein, *For Harold Lasswell: Some Reflections on Human Dignity, Entrapment, Informed Consent, and the Plea Bargain*, 84 YALE L.J. 683 (1975).

[13]See generally BEYOND THE BEST INTERESTS, *supra* note 4, at 9-52.

mental to a child's well-being.[14] But "so long as a family is intact, the young child feels parental authority is lodged in a unified body and as such is a safe and reliable guide for later identification."[15] Court or agency intervention without regard to or over the objection of parents can only serve to undermine the familial bond which is vital to a child's sense of becoming and being an adult in his own right.

Beyond these supplemental biological and psychological justifications for insulating parent–child relationships and safeguarding each child's entitlement to a permanent place in a family of his own, there is a further justification for a policy of minimum state intervention. It is, as Bentham recognized, that the law does not have the capacity to supervise the delicately complex interpersonal bonds between parent and child. As *parens patriae* the state is too crude an instrument to become an adequate substitute for parents. The legal system has neither the resources nor the sensitivity to respond to a growing child's ever-changing needs and demands. It does not have the capacity to deal on an individual basis with the consequences of its decisions or to act with the deliberate speed required by a child's sense of time and essential to his well-being. Even if the law were not so incapacitated, there is no basis for assuming that the judgments of its decision-

---

[14]W. Gaylin, Caring 25–45, 172–75 (1976); Cohen, Granger, Provence & Solnit, *Mental Health Services*, in 2 Issues in the Classification of Children 88 (N. Hobbs ed. 1975); *see generally* 3 A. Freud, The Writings of Anna Freud (1973).

The breaking of bonds by adolescents should not be confused with their forceful breaking by the state:

> With adolescents, the superficial observation of their behavior may convey the idea that what they desire is discontinuation of parental relationships rather than their preservation and stability. Nevertheless, this impression is misleading in this simple form. It is true that their revolt against any parental authority is normal developmentally since it is the adolescent's way toward establishing his own independent adult identity. But for a successful outcome it is important that the breaks and disruptions of attachment should come exclusively from his side and not be imposed on him by any form of abandonment or rejection on the psychological parents' part.

Beyond the Best Interests, *supra* note 4, at 34.

[15]From a communication with Anna Freud.

makers about a particular child's needs would be any better than (or indeed as good as) the judgments of his parents. Only magical thinking will permit the denial of these self-evident, but often ignored, truths about the limits of law.[16]

To recognize how vulnerable the developmental processes are between infancy and adulthood and how essential parents are for continually safeguarding children from never-ending risks is also to recognize that parents may fail. They may place their children at unwarranted risk rather than promote their survival to adulthood. That danger justifies a policy of *minimum* state intervention rather than one of *no* state intervention.

Yet recognition that parents may disserve their children's interests still does not mean that the state necessarily can or will do better. Nor does it justify acceptance of the vague and subjective language of neglect and abuse statutes which give the state unguided discretion to supervene parental decisions with regard to health care for their children. If legislatures are to give full recognition to a child's entitlement to a permanent family and the entitlement of parents, no matter how poor, to raise their children as they think best, they must acknowledge the need for a realistic reappraisal of abuse and neglect statutes—statutes which generally, vaguely and overbroadly, provide that a child who is being denied proper care may be found "neglected."[17] Legislatures must be made to see that the requisite of parental consent to medical care for children becomes meaningless if refusal to consent automatically triggers state inquiry or a finding of neglect. State statutes then must be revised to hold in check, not release, the rescue fantasies of those it empowers to intrude, and thus to safeguard families from state-sponsored interruptions of ongoing family relationships by well-intentioned people who "know" what is "best" and who wish to impose their personal health-care preferences on others.

---

[16]*See* BEYOND THE BEST INTERESTS, *supra* note 4, at 31–34, 49–52.
[17]For the precise wording of the state statutes, see CHILD NEGLECT LAWS, *supra* note 10; Goldstein, *Why Foster Care—For Whom for How Long?*, 30 THE PSYCHOANALYTIC STUDY OF THE CHILD 647 (1976).

It is in this value-laden setting that an examination of cases is made to determine how and to what extent the state should seek to supervise or supervene parents in their decisions to secure or deny medical care for their children.

LIFE-OR-DEATH DECISIONS

State supervention of parental judgment would be justified to provide any proven, nonexperimental, medical procedure when its denial would mean *death* for a child who would otherwise have an opportunity for either a *life worth living* or a *life of relatively normal healthy growth* toward adulthood[18]—to majority when a person is freed of parental control and presumed competent to decide for himself. The state would overcome the presumption of parental autonomy in

[18]While a life of relatively normal healthy growth is assumed to be a life worth living, it is not assumed that all lives worth living from a societal-consensus point of view could be characterized as relatively normal or healthy. For example, a quadraplegic child, in need of a blood transfusion for reasons unrelated to that condition might, for society, be a "life worth living" though not a life of normal healthy growth.

For an example of a decision about whether a life was worth living, see D. KEARNS, LYNDON JOHNSON AND THE AMERICAN DREAM 89–90 (1976):

> During the summer Sam Johnson suffered another major heart attack. He was put in the hospital and kept in an oxygen tent for months. When Lyndon returned to Texas on his father's sixtieth birthday, Sam pleaded with his son to take him out of the lonely hospital and back to his home where he could be with friends and family. At first Lyndon resisted. The doctors said that Sam needed an oxygen tent, and none was available in Stonewall. But Sam Johnson would not listen to logical objections. "Lyndon," his son recalled him saying, "I'm going back to that little house in the hills where the people know when you're sick and care when you die. You have to help me."
>
> Finally, Johnson agreed. "I realized," Johnson said later, "how dangerous it was to let my father go home. But I also believed that a man had a right to live and to die in his own way, in his own time. God knows that hospital depressed me something terrible and I was only visiting. No matter how sweet the nurses and the doctors are, they're not your family. They don't really know anything about you, they don't know anything about all the things that are going on in your head. . . . Yes, I understood why my daddy wanted to leave and I respected his wish. I brought him his clothes, I helped him dress, and I carried him home."
>
> In his own room in the Johnson City house, Sam briefly seemed to improve. Then only two weeks later, on October 23, 1937, he died.

health care matters only if it could establish: (a) that the medical profession is in agreement about what nonexperimental medical treatment is right for the child; (b) that the expected outcome of that treatment is what society agrees to be right for any child, a chance for normal healthy growth toward adulthood or a life worth living; *and* (c) that the expected outcome of denial of that treatment would mean death for the child.

These criteria for intervention were met by Judge Murphy, for the Superior Court of the District of Columbia, in *In Re Pogue*.[19] He authorized blood transfusions for an otherwise healthy newborn infant who would have died had his parents' decision to reject the treatment been honored. At the same time Judge Murphy, recognizing the distinction between being an adult and being a child with regard to medical care choices, declined to order blood transfusions for the infant's mother who, in the face of death, refused to consent to such intervention. Over the objection of the "adult" parents' wishes and without regard, of course, to the infant's

---

[19]*In re* Pogue, Wash. Post, Nov. 14, 1974, § C, at 1, col. 1 (No. M-18-74, Super. Ct., D.C., Nov. 11, 1974). Judge Murphy relied upon a similar case in which a court refused to order a blood transfusion for an adult. *In re* Osborne, 294 A.2d 373 (D.C. Ct. App. 1972) (34-year-old Jehovah's Witness). In a case that did not involve religious beliefs, a Pennsylvania common pleas court refused to order surgery for a 60-year-old woman. The court based its decision upon the woman's right to privacy. *In re* Yetter, 62 Pa. D. & C.2d 619 (C.P. 1973). But in *In re* President of Georgetown College, 331 F.2d 1000 (D.C. Cir.), *cert. denied,* 377 U.S. 978 (1964), the court ordered a blood transfusion for a 25-year-old Jehovah's Witness who was the mother of a 7-month-old child. Judge Skelly Wright explained that he had ordered the transfusion because the woman wanted to live. *Id.* at 1009. In State *ex rel.* Swann v. Pack, 527 S.W.2d 99 (Tenn. 1975), *cert. denied,* 96 S. Ct. 1429 (1976), the court, after holding that the Holiness Church of God in Jesus Name "is a constitutionally protected religious group," *id.* at 107, held that the state could prohibit, as a nuisance, the handling of poisonous snakes. The court observed: "Yes, the state has a right to protect a person from himself and to demand that he protect his own life." *Id.* at 113. Even here, however, the court's order was influenced by its recognition of the parental right to control the religious upbringing of children. Because of that recognition the court did not restrict its order to prohibiting snake handling in the presence of children. Instead, snake handling was prohibited altogether.

"wishes," Judge Murphy, as a substitute parent, decided to protect the child's right as a person to reach the age of majority when he will become entitled to make such life-or-death decisions for himself. The judge implicitly found the infant's parents temporarily incompetent to care for the child, while simultaneously acknowledging the adult status of the mother by declining to use her refusal of blood as a basis for declaring her a danger to herself and thus incompetent, as if a child, to decide for herself.[20]

The scientific "fact" that death, for both the infant and the mother, was inevitable without transfusion—the nonexperimental medical procedure—was not in dispute. Nor was there any societal doubt about the desirability—the "rightness"—of the predicted outcome of the transfusion—an opportunity for normal, healthy growth, a life worth living. The issue was whether the judge and doctors, as adults with an unqualified value preference for life, could use the power of the state to impose their "adult" judgment on adults in law whose own "adult" judgment gave greater weight to another preference. On behalf of the adult the answer was "No"; on behalf of the child the answer was "Yes."[21] Thus coercive intervention by the state was justified where the parents' decision would have deprived a child of proven medical treatment and consequently of an opportunity for healthy growth and development to adulthood.

There would be no justification, however, for coercive intrusion by the state in those life-or-death situations (a) in which there is no proven medical procedure, *or* (b) in which

[20]Not all courts have acceded to the wishes of adults who refused transfusions. *See, e.g.,* United States v. George, 239 F. Supp. 752 (D. Conn. 1965) (order dissolved once patient recovered); John F. Kennedy Memorial Hosp. v. Heston, 58 N.J. 576, 279 A.2d 670 (1970) (transfusion ordered for victim of automobile accident); Collins v. Davis, 44 Misc. 2d 622, 254 N.Y.S.2d 666 (1964) (transfusion ordered for comatose patient after wife refused consent on nonreligious grounds).

[21]*Cf.* Prince v. Massachusetts, 321 U.S. 158, 168–69 (1944) (state's authority over children broader than authority over adults).

parents are confronted with conflicting medical advice about which, if any, treatment procedure to follow, *or* (c) in which, even if the medical experts agree about treatment, there is less than a high probability that the nonexperimental treatment will enable the child to pursue either a life worth living or a life of relatively normal healthy growth toward adulthood. These standards are anchored in such common law notions as that of plain duty given expression in Justice Field's jury charge regarding criminal liability for acts of omission:

> [T]he duty omitted must be a plain duty, by which I mean that it must be one that does not admit of any discussion as to its obligatory force; one upon which different minds must agree, or will generally agree. Where doubt exists as to what conduct should be pursued in a particular case, and intelligent men differ as to the proper action to be had, the law does not impute guilt to anyone, if, from omission to adopt one course instead of another, fatal consequences follow to others.[22]

Outside of a narrow central core of agreement, "a life worth living" and "a life of relatively normal healthy growth" are highly personal terms about which there is no societal consensus. There can thus be no societal consensus about the "rightness" of always deciding for "life," or of always preferring the predicted result of the recommended treatment over the predicted result of refusing such treatment. It is precisely in those cases in which reasonable and responsible persons can and do disagree about whether the "life" after treatment would be "worth living" or "normal," and thus about what is "right," that parents must remain free of coercive state intervention in deciding whether to consent to or reject the medical program proffered for their child.

The high-probability-of-a-life-worth-living or of relatively-normal-healthy-growth standard is, it must be remembered, designed not to facilitate but to inhibit state intervention. This broad standard is meant to reenforce a policy of minimum state intervention. In its breadth and in its evidentiary demands it saddles the state with the burden of over-

---

[22]United States v. Knowles, 26 F. Cas. 800, 801 (N.D. Cal. 1864) (No. 15,540).

coming the presumption of parental autonomy. Intervention would thus be limited to those individual life-or-death cases in which the state could establish that the medical profession agreed upon the rejected medical treatment and that the treatment would provide the dying child with an opportunity for what societal consensus held to be either a life worth living or a life of relatively normal healthy growth. The state, of course, would remain without authority to challenge parental decisions to provide medical treatment in order to *save* their dying child even if the state could establish that there was a societal consensus that the expected outcome of such treatment was not a "life worth living."

Absent medical agreement about what treatment is indicated, or absent a societal consensus about the rightness of the predicted result of treatment, there would be no justification for disqualifying parents from (or for qualifying agents of the state for) making the difficult choice—for giving their personal meaning to "right" or to "worth living" or to "normal healthy growth." No one has a greater right or responsibility and no one can be presumed to be in a better position, and thus better equipped, than a child's parents to decide what course to pursue if the medical experts cannot agree or, assuming their agreement, if there is no general agreement in society that the outcome of treatment is clearly preferred to the outcome of no treatment. Put somewhat more starkly, how can parents in such situations give the wrong answer since there is no way of knowing the right answer? In these circumstances the law's guarantee of freedom of belief becomes meaningful and the right to act on that belief as an autonomous parent becomes operative within the privacy of one's family.[23] Precisely because there is no objectively wrong

---

[23]Although the case of Karen Ann Quinlan involved a 22-year-old woman, Chief Justice Hughes's opinion contains an apt description of the conflicting interests:

> The claimed interests of the State in this case are essentially the preservation and sanctity of human life and defense of the right of the phy-

or right answer, the burden must be on the state to establish *wrong*, not on the parent to establish that what is *right* for them is necessarily *right* for others. Indeed it is in just such cases that the Constitution, which separates church and, to a different degree, science from state, dictates abstention from imposing one group's orthodoxy about health care or truth about the meaning of life or, for that matter, death upon another.[24]

Ultimately, then, it must be left to the parents to decide, for example, whether their congenitally malformed newborn

sician to administer medical treatment according to his best judgment. In this case the doctors say that removing Karen from the respirator will conflict with their professional judgment. The plaintiff answers that Karen's present treatment serves only a maintenance function; that the respirator cannot cure or improve her condition but at best can only prolong her inevitable slow deterioration and death; and that the interests of the patient, as seen by her surrogate, the guardian [Karen's father], must be evaluated by the court as predominant, even in the face of an opinion *contra* by the present attending physicians. Plaintiff's distinction is significant. The nature of Karen's care and the realistic chances of her recovery are quite unlike those of the patients discussed in many of the cases where treatments were ordered. In many of those cases the medical procedure required (usually a transfusion) constituted a minimal bodily invasion and the chances of recovery and return to functioning life were very good. We think that the State's interest *contra* weakens and the individual's right to privacy grows as the degree of bodily invasion increases and the prognosis dims. Ultimately there comes a point at which the individual's rights overcome the State interest.

In re Quinlan, 70 N.J. 10, 40–41, 355 A.2d 647, 663–64 (1976).

Because of her comatose condition, however, Karen could not exercise her right to decline treatment. "The only practical way to prevent destruction of the right," the Chief Justice explained,

is to permit the guardian and family of Karen to render their best judgment . . . as to whether she would exercise it in these circumstances. If their conclusion is in the affirmative this decision should be accepted by a society the overwhelming majority of whose members would, we think, in similar circumstances, exercise such a choice in the same way for themselves or for those closest to them. It is for this reason that we determine that Karen's right of privacy may be asserted in her behalf, in this respect, by her guardian and family under the particular circumstances presented by this record.

Id. at 41–42, 335 A.2d at 654.

[24]For an initial attempt to develop this argument, see Goldstein, *supra* note 2, at 70.

with an ascertainable neurologic deficiency and highly predictable mental retardation, should be provided with treatment which may avoid death, but which offers no chance of
cure—no opportunity, in terms of societal consensus, for a
life worth living or a life of relatively normal healthy growth.
Dr. Raymond Duff has argued persuasively:

> Families know their values, priorities and resources better than
> anyone else. Presumably they, with the doctor, can make the
> better choices as a private affair. Certainly, they, more than
> anyone else, must live with the consequences. Most of these
> families know they cannot place that child for adoption because
> no one else wants the child. If they cannot cope adequately
> with the child and their other responsibilities and survive as a
> family, they may feel that the death option is a forced choice.
> . . . But that is not necessarily bad, and who knows of a better
> way.[25]

For the law to adopt the Duff position would not mean
abandonment of its commitment to defend human life. Special
procedures could be established within hospitals to protect
infants and their parents from possible misdiagnoses, though
not from "erroneous" moral judgment. The function of such
a procedure would be to verify the medical prognosis, not the
ethical base, on which the parental decision relied.[26] If the

---

[25]Kelsey, *Shall These Children Live? A Conversation With Dr. Raymond S. Duff*,
72 REFLECTION, Jan. 1975, at 4, 7 (Yale Divinity School Magazine). For other
expressions of Dr. Duff's views, see Duff & Campbell, *Moral and Ethical
Dilemmas in the Special-Care Nursery*, 289 NEW ENGLAND J. MED. 885 (1973);
Duff & Campbell, *On Deciding the Care of Severely Handicapped or Dying
Persons: With Particular Reference to Infants*, 57 PEDIATRICS 487 (1976).

[26]In *In re Quinlan* the court proposed the establishment of a review procedure
by a hospital committee which it mislabels an "Ethics Committee":

> [U]pon the concurrence of the guardian and family of Karen, *should the
> responsible attending physicians conclude* that there is no reasonable possi-
> bility of Karen's ever emerging from her present comatose condition to
> a cognitive, sapient state and that the life-support apparatus now being
> administered to Karen should be discontinued, they shall consult with
> the hospital "Ethics Committee" or like body of the institution in which
> Karen is then hospitalized. If that consultative body agrees that there is
> no reasonable possibility of Karen's ever emerging from her present
> comatose condition to a cognitive, sapient state, the present life-support
> system may be withdrawn and said action shall be without any civil or
> criminal liability therefor, on the part of any participant, whether guard-
> ian, physician, hospital or others.

prognosis proved to be incorrect and if the parents refused to accept the revised finding, the state would be empowered, as it was in the blood transfusion case, to order the recommended treatment. If the tragic prognosis is warranted, then the law, as Duff argues, should treat the decision as a "private affair"—whether it be for medical means to sustain life or for humane shelter and care not necessarily designed to avoid death.

If parental autonomy is not accorded the recognition argued for in this essay, and if society insists through law that such children, indeed any children, receive medical treatment rejected by their parents, the state should provide the special financial, physical, and psychological resources essential to making real for the child it "saves" the value it prefers. The state should become fully responsible for making "unwanted" children "wanted" ones.[27] Minimally and ideally the state should fully finance their special-care requirements; in the event their parents do not wish to remain responsible for them, the state should find adopting parents who with un-

---

70 N.J. at 54, 355 A.2d at 671 (emphasis added). Contrary to its own reasoning, which recognized that the ethical question concerning continuance or discontinuance of the life-support system must be left to the parents or guardian to resolve, the court concluded that the attending doctors must not only provide their medical prognosis but also determine the ethical question, that the life-support system "should be discontinued," before such action may be taken. Yet, consistent with its reasoning, and despite the label, the court restricted the hospital to a review of the medical, not the ethical, decision. The "Ethics Committee" would, as it should, only determine if the doctors were correct in their prediction that "there is no reasonable possibility of Karen's ever emerging from her present comatose condition to a cognitive, sapient state." The authority of attending physicians and the function of review would be clarified were the hospital committee called a "medical review" rather than an "ethics" committee.

[27]For a discussion of the concept of a "wanted" child, see BEYOND THE BEST INTERESTS, *supra* note 4, at 5–7. The Model Child Placement Statute proposed by the authors states: "A wanted child is one who receives affection and nourishment on a continuing basis from at least one adult and who feels that he or she is and continues to be valued by those who take care of him or her." *Id*. at 98.

broken continuity could meet not only the child's physical needs but also his psychological requirements for affectionate relationships and emotional and intellectual stimulation.[28]

Except for meeting the child's physical needs the task, however large the allocation of financial resources, may well be beyond the limits of law. The law is too crude an instrument to nurture, as only parents can, the delicate physical, psychological, and social tissues of a child's life. Even if it could force, and it may not, unwilling adults to adopt children, the law does not have the capacity to make an "unwanted" child a "wanted" one. If the past and present provide a basis for prediction, an institutional setting (not adoption or long-term foster care with the same family) is the more likely but hardly satisfactory prospect for the after "care" of such children until their majority or death.[29] Institutional arrangements have not provided the affectionate and other psy-

---

[28]Parents are traditionally free, though not necessarily encouraged, to give up their children for adoption. It is interesting that the Uniform Adoption Act of 1953 provided in optional § 17 that adoptive parents could petition to annul if "within two years after the adoption a child develops any serious and permanent physical or mental malady or incapacity as a result of conditions existing prior to the adoption and of which the adopting parents had no knowledge or notice." The Revised Uniform Adoption Act (1969) has no such provision. For the text of the 1953 Act, see 9 UNIFORM LAWS ANNOTATED 5–10 (1973).

[29]For a description of the conditions in one institution, New York's Willowbrook State School for the Mentally Retarded, see Judge Judd's opinion in New York State Ass'n for Retarded Children, Inc. v. Rockefeller, 357 F. Supp. 752, 755–57 (E.D.N.Y. 1973). Referring to the "inhumane" conditions at the school, Judge Judd mentioned the "loss of an eye, the breaking of teeth, the loss of part of an ear bitten off by another resident, and frequent bruises and scalp wounds" as typical complaints. Id. at 756.

For an effort to reverse the course of the past, see Consent Judgment in the Willowbrook Case, No. 72 Civ. 356/357 (E.D.N.Y. Apr. 30, 1975). Similarly, see Wyatt v. Stickney, 344 F. Supp. 387 (M.D. Ala. 1972), which has been described as "dealing with a remote, rural state institution in Alabama housing some five thousand retarded children in conditions of unrelieved horror." Burt, *Developing Constitutional Rights Of, In, and For Children,* 39 LAW & CONTEMP. PROB. 118, 138 (1975).

chological ties such children—no matter how limited their potential for healthy growth and development—demand and deserve.[30] As long as the state offers institutions that provide little more than storage space and "hay, oats, and water"[31] for medical science's achievements, the law must err on the side of its strong presumption in favor of parental autonomy and family integrity. Thus for the state to do other than *either assume* full responsibility for the treatment, care, and nurture of such children *or honor* the parent's decision to consent to or refuse authorization for treatment would be but to pay cruel and oppressive lip service to notions of human dignity and the right to life.

The case of Karen, a teenage patient suffering from an irreversible kidney malfunction, provides another life-or-death example in which the standard of an opportunity for a life worth living or a life of relatively normal healthy growth toward adulthood would preclude state supervention of parental judgments. Karen's case poses the question whether state intervention should be authorized to review the choice of an adolescent who, with her parents' permission and concurrence, decides to choose death over "life." Following an unsuccessful kidney transplant, Karen and her parents refused to consent to the continuation of "intolerable" life-support devices. The decision to proceed as if family privacy and parental autonomy were, or at least should be, protected was described in an article by her doctors:

> [F]ollowing the transplant's failure, thrice-weekly hemodialysis was performed. Karen tolerated dialysis poorly, routinely having chills, nausea, vomiting, severe headaches and weakness. . . .
>
> . . . [A]fter it was clear that the kidney would never function, Karen and her parents expressed the wish to stop medical treatment and let "nature take its course." . . . [S]taff members

---

[30]*See generally* S. Provence & R. Lipton, Infants in Institutions 159–66 (1962).
[31]From a letter from Judge James H. Lincoln, Judge of the Probate Court, Juvenile Division, Wayne County, Michigan, to Joseph Goldstein dated April 5, 1977.

conveyed to the family that such wishes were unheard of and unacceptable, and that a decision to stop treatment could never be an alternative. The family did decide to continue dialysis, medication, and diet therapy. Karen's renal incapacity returned to pretransplant levels and she returned to her socially isolated life, with diet restriction, chronic discomfort, and fatigue.

On May 10, Karen was hospitalized following ten days of high fever. Three days later the transplant was removed. Its pathology resembled that of the original kidneys, and the possibility of a similar reaction forming in subsequent transplants was established.

On May 21, the arteriovenous shunt placed in Karen's arm for hemodialysis was found to be infected, and part of the vein wall was excised and the shunt revised. During this portion of the hospitalization, Karen and the parents grudgingly went along with the medical recommendations, but they continued to ponder the possibility of stopping treatment. . . . On May 24, the shunt clotted closed. Karen, with her parents' agreement, refused shunt revision and any further dialysis.

Karen died on June 2, with both parents at her bedside. . . . Shortly [before] her death she thanked the staff for what she knew had been a hard time for them and she told her parents she hoped they would be happy. We later learned that before her death she had written a will and picked a burial spot near her home and near her favorite horseback riding trail. In the final days she supported her parents as they faltered in their decision; she told her father, "Daddy, I will be happy there (in the ground) if there is no machine and they don't work on me any more."[32]

For Karen and her parents no medical treatment offered the possibility of resuming a relatively normal life or a life worth living. The recommendation of the nursing and medical staff to continue the life-support system was not a scientific, but a moral judgment. The rightness of forcing the consequences of their choice upon Karen rather than honoring her and her parents' decision could not be established. There was then no basis for exercising the power of the state to super-

[32]Schowalter, Ferholt & Mann, *The Adolescent Patient's Decision to Die*, 51 PEDIATRICS 97, 97–98 (1973); a longer excerpt is quoted in J. GOLDSTEIN, A. DERSHOWITZ & R. SCHWARTZ, CRIMINAL LAW 166–69 (1974).

vene the judgment of Karen's parents. Had Karen been an adult, on the law's chronological scale, there is no question, or there ought not to be, that out of respect for her dignity as a human being, the doctors would have had to abide by her request to end the treatment. As a New York court once declared, "[I]t is the individual who is the subject of a medical decision who has the final say and . . . this must necessarily be so in a system of government which gives the greatest possible protection to the individual in the furtherance of his own desires."[33]

For the doctors to have proceeded with dialysis against the wishes of teenage Karen and her parents would have constituted an assault in tort and in crime.[34] Together as a family they must be entitled in law to be free, as they were,

[33]Erickson v. Dilgard, 44 Misc. 2d 27, 28, 252 N.Y.S.2d 705, 706 (Sup. Ct. 1962).

Likewise, Chief Justice Hughes, for the New Jersey Supreme Court, in *In Re* Quinlan, 70 N.J. 10, 38–42 355 A.2d 647, 662–64 (1976), upheld Miss Quinlan's constitutional right as an adult to her privacy, free from state intrusion, in making such life-or-death choices. The court, because of her incompetence, further acknowledged her father's authority, as guardian, to exercise that right on her behalf. It observed:

> We have no doubt, in these unhappy circumstances, that if Karen were herself miraculously lucid for an interval . . . and perceptive of her irreversible condition, she could effectively decide upon discontinuance of the life-support apparatus, even if it meant the prospect of natural death.
> . . . [N]o external compelling interest of the State could compel Karen to endure the unendurable, only to vegetate a few measurable months with no realistic possibility of returning to any semblance of cognitive or sapient life. We perceive no thread of logic distinguishing between such a choice on Karen's part and a similar choice which, under the evidence in this case, could be made by a competent patient terminally ill, riddled by cancer and suffering great pain; such a patient would not be resuscitated or put on a respirator.
> *Id.* at 39, 355 A.2d at 668.

[34]*See, e.g.,* Gonner v. Moran, 126 F.2d 121, 122 (D.C. Cir. 1941) (consent of parent necessary before surgical procedure to graft skin from 15-year-old to his cousin); N.Y. PENAL LAW § 120 (McKinney 1975) (assault if physical injury caused); *cf.* F. HARPER & F. JAMES, THE LAW OF TORTS 634–35 (1956) (extent of damages recoverable by parent against third person for tortious injury to child).

of the coercive force of the state or of the medical authorities. The law of torts and crime is designed, or ought to be, to protect family integrity by providing such safeguards against the supervention of parental judgment by the medical staff or other "agents" of the state.

Had the situation been different, had Karen's parents insisted, over her objection, on continuing the life-support system, would the state have been justified in supervening their judgment? The answer is "No." Had Karen insisted, over her parents' objection, on continuing the life-support system would the state have been justified in supervening their judgment? The answer is "Yes"—if the state provides, as it should, whatever resources are required to assure full immediate and aftercare for the child. But if the state will not provide such support the answer is an uneasy "No." It is, after all, the function and responsibility of parents to evaluate and make judgments about the wishes and requests of their children. It is, after all, the meaning of parental autonomy to make such decisions. Further, neither court nor hearing agency is likely to be as competent as, for example, were Karen's parents to determine her capacity for choice and whether to abide by it. The law should avoid giving the discretion for such subjective judgments to its agents.

But the uneasiness about the "No" answers remains. It stems from a fear that a few parents might not follow a child's express wish to undergo treatment which might seem intolerable to them, though not to the child. It also stems from a growing concern that for some matters, particularly with regard to health care, the general statutory age of adulthood, of emancipation, has been set too high. The question then, and one addressed in the next section, is not whether Karen specifically but whether all persons age 16(?) in such circumstances as Karen found herself ought to have the controlling voice in law rather than their parents or guardians—whether it be for life or not to avoid death. But until legislatures or courts find a formula for determining under what circumstances and at what age below majority children may become their own risktakers for certain health care decisions, ultimate responsibility must remain with parents or, if they be disqualified, with adult guardians, who may (as Karen's parents did) or may not decide to support their child's choice.

EMANCIPATION OF CHILDREN FOR HEALTH CARE PURPOSES

The law, both case and statutory, has begun to emancipate some minors to determine for themselves what health care course to pursue. For example, 16-year-olds have been granted the right to enter or leave mental institutions over the objection of parents who, in the past, had the authority to arrange for their admission or release as voluntary patients.[35] For another example, pregnant minors have been given adult status for purposes of determining whether to obtain an abortion.[36] In the case of "mentally ill" 16-year-olds, these modifications of parental autonomy silently rest on a not totally unwarranted suspicion that mental institutions provide little, if any, medical treatment, and more openly upon a fear of parental abuse, not unlike the exploitation of the system by members of a family wishing to put a difficult spouse, parent, or sibling out of sight. The reasons which seem to underlie renewed challenges to the commitment of adults for mental health care without their consent[37] prompt

---

[35]See, e.g., Bartley v. Kremens, 402 F. Supp. 1039 (E.D. Pa. 1975), prob. juris. noted, 424 U.S. 964 (1976) (class action by children under 19 in mental institutions challenging Pennsylvania voluntary commitment statute); Melville v. Sabbatino, 30 Conn. Supp. 320, 313 A.2d 886 (Super. Ct. 1973) (holding that parents may not continue voluntary confinement in psychiatric ward against wishes of 17-year-old son).

[36]Planned Parenthood v. Danforth, 96 S. Ct. 2831, 2842–44 (1976).

[37]See, e.g., O'Connor v. Donaldson, 422 U.S. 563 (1975); J. KATZ, J. GOLDSTEIN & A. DERSHOWITZ, PSYCHOANALYSIS, PSYCHIATRY AND LAW 503–632 (1967); T. SZASZ, THE MYTH OF MENTAL ILLNESS (1961); Goldstein & Katz, Dangerousness and Mental Illness, Some Observations on the Decision to Release Persons Acquitted By Reason of Insanity, 70 YALE L.J. 225 (1960); Rosenhan, On Being Sane in Insane Places, 179 SCIENCE 250 (1973).

and seem to justify a limited emancipation of children in this area. As for pregnancy, the justification for emancipation appears to stem from a recognition that those who insist on parental consent are concerned less with the child's well-being than with strengthening their general opposition to abortion, which they cloak in the magical notion that law can improve family communications by compelling a young woman in trouble to consult with her parents when such family trust does not exist.[38]

There may, then, be situations which justify abiding by the health care choices of children without regard to the wishes of their parents—situations that justify emancipating children and thus relieving their parents of the right, as well as the responsibility, to determine whether to consider or to accept the treatment preferences of their children. Unlike the life-or-death problems already addressed, the issue here is whether and when children, not the state, should be given the otherwise parental right to determine for themselves what medical course to pursue. The question, which could only arise in situations in which the state would not be authorized, under the standards proposed, to supervene parental autonomy, is: Under what specific circumstances should the law presume children to be as competent as are adults, to be their own risktakers for all or some health care purposes?

Any answers to this question which favor qualifying minors, as adults, for certain health care decisions should provide standards for establishing emancipation status which are as impersonal and as nonjudgmental as is the chronological-age standard for establishing adult status.[39] Whatever the rationale for the emancipation, access to such status for all children in a designated category should be open and auto-

---

[38]For the view of Planned Parenthood of New York City, see N.Y. Times, May 11, 1976, at 32, col. 2.

[39]For a discussion of this point, see Goldstein, *supra* note 2, at 71–72; and Katz, Schroeder & Sidman, *Emancipating Our Children—Coming of Legal Age in America*, 7 FAM. L.Q. 211 (1973).

matic. The right to partial emancipation should not rest on satisfying, on a case-by-case basis, some body of wise persons that the particular child is "mature enough" to choose or that the particular child's choice is "right."[40] To introduce such a subjective process for decision would be not to emancipate the child but rather to transfer to the state the parental control and responsibility for determining when to consult and abide by the child's choice. To require relatively objective criteria for establishing emancipation statutes is not to take a simplistic view of children but rather to recognize how varied and complex all children are and how inadequate courts are for assessing a child's capacity for decision. The law then must limit the state to determining by some relatively objective standard *who* is entitled to decide, not *what* specific decision is to be preferred in a particular case nor whether a specific child has the "wisdom" to make a choice. To resolve the question of emancipation by authorizing a court or hearing agency to decide each case on the basis of which choice is "right" or which child in a given category is "mature enough" is to deny to both—parent as well as child—autonomy to decide and family privacy in which to decide. The question thus becomes: Under what specific circumstances should persons who are children in law be presumed qualified and authorized to make medical treatment choices free of parental control?

The requisites of an acceptable answer would be satisfied by a law in furtherance of the strong societal commitment to

---

[40]Emancipation from 1900 to the early 1960s was almost exclusively judicial and conformed closely to the dominant societal attitudes during that period. . . . The approach to judicial emancipation was on a case by case basis, and the doctrine was often manipulated by the courts to conform with a judge's own values rather than with the best interests of the child. Katz, Schroeder & Sidman, *supra* note 39, at 213. For a position which fails to recognize that one of the functions of parents is to make judgments about their children's competence to choose and that courts are incompetent to make such judgments, see Note, *State Intrusion into Family Affairs: Justifications and Limitations,* 26 STAN. L. REV. 1383 (1974).

safeguard "life" which provided, for example, that children of any age (or above 12?) are emancipated who in a life-or-death situation wish, against their parents' decision, to pursue treatment. Although such a provision is not being proposed it would meet the criteria set forth above only if emancipation carried with it the right of the child to change his mind—to agree with his parents—and to refuse or to withdraw consent for the proffered treatment. That right would have to be recognized, not for purposes of symmetry, but because to do otherwise would constitute a cruel hoax on child and parent. Far better to acknowledge from the outset in such situations that the child is not being emancipated for health care purposes, that the state knows what is right and that its judgment is being imposed on both parent and child without regard to their wishes. Legislatures or courts could more easily satisfy the requisites of an acceptable answer by avoiding the express wishes of the minor as a standard of emancipation and by establishing, as some have done, such "impersonal," "objective" criteria as *a chronological age* fixed below that for an adult (e.g., 16) coupled with a specific medical diagnosis or prognosis (e.g., pregnancy, irreversible kidney malfunction, or mental illness). Pregnancy alone, without regard to a child's age, would be a sufficiently objective standard for emancipation to determine whether or not to obtain an abortion.

This brief consideration is not meant to provide a definitive answer to this difficult question but rather to illustrate how age and diagnoses could and should be used as statutory criteria for the partial emancipation of children from parental authority in some health care decisions, whether or not they involve life-or-death choices. It is to non-life-or-death choices that this essay now turns.

NON-LIFE-OR-DEATH DECISIONS

When death is not a likely consequence of exercising a medical care choice there is no justification for governmental intrusion on family privacy; nor is there justification for overcoming the presumption of either parental autonomy or the autonomy of emancipated children. Where the question involves not a life-or-death choice but a preference for one style of life over another, the law must restrain courts and medicine men from coercively imposing their "kindness"—their preferred life styles—in the form of medical care upon nonconsenting parents and their children. The law, in adopting such a position, cannot presume that parents do not make "mistakes." Nor can it challenge the scientific "facts," prognoses, or diagnoses upon which experts base their recommendations. Rather the law must recognize that it cannot find in medicine (or for that matter in any science) the ethical, political, or social values for evaluating health care choices. Courts must avoid confusing a doctor's personal preference for a certain style of living with the scientific bases upon which the recommendation rests.[41] The presumption of parental capacity to decide is meant to hold in check judges or doctors who may be tempted to use the power of the state to impose their personal preferences, their "adult parental" judgments upon parents whose own adult judgment may give greater weight to another preference.

In implementing this basic commitment to parental autonomy and to family privacy, the law does not take a simplistic view of parents, of the parent–child relationship, or of the family. Rather, it acknowledges not only how complicated man is, but also how limited is its own capacity for making more than gross distinctions about man's needs, natures, and routes of development. The law recognizes and respects the diverse range of man's religious, cultural, scientific, and ethical beliefs and the overlapping and ever-changing modes of their expression within and between generations at all stages of the life cycle. Thus a prime function of law is to prevent one person's truth (here about health, normalcy, the good life) from becoming another person's tyranny. It is in terms

---

[41] *See* Goldstein, *Psychoanalysis and Jurisprudence*, 77 YALE L.J. 1053, 1059 (1968).

of that function that parental decisions in non-life-or-death situations to reject medical care recommendations for their children will be analyzed.

The case of *In re Sampson*[42] illustrates how vaguely worded neglect statutes may be invoked in the name of health care to violate a family's privacy, to undermine parental autonomy, and to foster a community's, if not a judge's, prejudice against the physically deformed. Under the Family Court Act of New York,[43] Judge Hugh Elwyn declared Kevin Sampson, age 15, "a neglected child."[44] He made this finding in order to establish his authority to veto a decision by Kevin's mother not to permit blood transfusions for Kevin during surgery. He ordered her to force Kevin to undergo a series of operations which had been recommended by the Commissioner of Health and by duly qualified surgeons to correct a facial condition called neurofibromatosis. Judge Elwyn observed that Kevin had "a massive deformity of the right side of his face and neck. The outward manifestation of the disease is a large fold or flap of an overgrowth of facial tissue which causes the whole cheek, the corner of his mouth and right ear to drop down giving him an appearance which can only be described as grotesque and repulsive."[45] He went on to psychologize and predict:

> [T]he massive deformity of the entire right side of his face and neck is patently so gross and so disfiguring that it must inevitably exert a most negative effect upon his personality development, his opportunity for education and later employment and upon every phase of his relationship with his peers and others.[46]

---

[42]65 Misc. 2d 658, 317 N.Y.S.2d 641 (Fam. Ct. 1970), *aff'd,* 377 App. Div. 2d 668, 323 N.Y.S.2d 253 (1971), *aff'd,* 29 N.Y.2d 900, 278 N.E.2d 918, 328 N.Y.S.2d 686 (1972).

[43]N.Y. FAM. CT. ACT §§ 1011–1074 (McKinney 1975).

[44]65 Misc. 2d at 676, 317 N.Y.S.2d at 658.

[45]*Id.* at 659, 317 N.Y.S.2d at 643.

[46]*Id.* at 660, 317 N.Y.S.2d at 644.

Judge Elwyn made this assertion with apodictic certainty even though he acknowledged that "the staff psychiatrist of the County Mental Health Center reports that 'there is no evidence of any thinking disorder' and that 'in spite of marked facial disfigurement he failed to show any outstanding personality aberration.' "[47] Nevertheless, the judge added, "this finding hardly justifies a conclusion that he has been or will continue to be wholly unaffected by his misfortune."[48] He also noted that Kevin had been exempted from school, not because he was intellectually incapable, but, it may be assumed, because he appeared to his classmates and teachers as he did to Judge Elwyn himself, "grotesque and repulsive." But the judge's speculations on behalf of the state as *parens patriae* did not lead him to consider that under the protective cloak of family privacy, a loving, caring, accepting, autonomous parent had somehow been able to nurture in Kevin a "healthy personality." Kevin, after all, had developed in spite of state-reenforced prejudice and discrimination against the physically different in school, health agency, and court.

The testimony of the doctors who recommended surgery justified not a finding of neglect but rather a reaffirmation of parental autonomy. The doctors admitted that "the disease poses no immediate threat to [Kevin's] life nor has it as yet seriously affected his general health" and that surgery was very risky and offered no cure.[49] Further, the doctors found in the central nervous system no brain or spinal cord involvement and that delay until Kevin was 21, would decrease, not increase, the risk. The court replied with blind arrogance:

> [T]o postpone the surgery merely to allow the boy to become of age so that he may make the decision himself as suggested

---

[47]*Id.*, 317 N.Y.S.2d at 644.

[48]*Id.*, 317 N.Y.S.2d at 644. According to Judge Elwyn, a psychologist had found Kevin to be extremely dependent. The staff psychiatrist reported that Kevin demonstrated " 'inferiority feeling and low self concept.' " *Id.*, 317 N.Y.S.2d at 644.

[49]*Id.* at 661, 317 N.Y.S.2d at 644.

by the surgeon and urged by both counsel for the mother and
the Law Guardian . . . totally ignores the developmental and
psychological factors stemming from his deformity which the
Court deems to be of the utmost importance in any consideration of the boy's future welfare and begs the whole question.[50]

And without regard to the relationship of Kevin's well-being
to the integrity and support of his family, the court added:
" 'Neither by statute nor decision is the child's consent necessary or material, and we should not permit his refusal to
agree, his failure to cooperate, to ruin his life and any chance
for a normal, happy existence.' "[51]

The judge, who by an act of conjury had qualified himself
as prophet, psychological expert, risktaker, and all-knowing
parent, described but ignored a powerful reason for concluding that state authority should not supervene parental judgments about the rightness for their child of a recommended
medical treatment when death is not in issue. Judge Elwyn
wrote:

It is conceded that "there are important considerations both
ways" and that the views expressed by the dissenting Judges
in *Seiferth* have not been universally accepted. Moreover, it must
also be humbly acknowledged that under the circumstances of
this case "one cannot be certain of being right." Nevertheless,
a decision must be made, and so, after much deliberation, I am
persuaded that if this court is to meet its responsibilities to this
boy it can neither shift the responsibility for the ultimate de-

---

[50]*Id.* at 672, 317 N.Y.S.2d at 655.

[51]*Id.* at 673, 317 N.Y.S.2d at 656 (quoting *In re* Seiferth, 309 N.Y. 80, 37, 127
N.E.2d 820, 824 (1955) (Fuld, J., dissenting)). For a contrary view of the
importance of a child's preference regarding surgery, see *In re* Green, 448
Pa. 338, 292 A.2d 387 (1972). Ricky Green was a 15-year-old boy who, as
the result of polio, had a 94° curvature of the spine. Doctors proposed a
spinal fusion to straighten the spine, but Ricky's mother refused her consent
for blood transfusions during the operation. Saying that the "ultimate question" concerned Ricky's wishes, the Pennsylvania Supreme Court remanded the case for a determination of Ricky's wishes. *Id.* at 350, 292 A.2d
at 392. After talking with Ricky, the court found that he did not want the
operation; his wishes were honored. Green Appeal, 452 Pa. 373, 307 A.2d
279 (1973).

cision onto his shoulders nor can it permit his mother's religious beliefs to stand in the way of attaining through corrective surgery whatever chance he may have for a normal, happy existence, which, to paraphrase Judge Fuld [author of the dissent in *Seiferth*], is difficult of attainment under the most propitious circumstances, but will unquestionably be impossible if the disfigurement is not corrected.[52]

Were his humility real, the judge would not have allowed himself to believe that he, rather than Kevin's mother, was best qualified to determine the meanings of "a normal and happy existence" for her son. In Kevin's eyes either might be proven "wrong" retrospectively. But nothing, not even magic, can qualify a judge to make that prediction with equal or greater accuracy than the parent. Nor is any judge prepared, let alone obligated, as are parents, personally to assume day-to-day responsibility for giving the Kevins the care they may require as a consequence of such a personal value choice about life style.

Laws of neglect must be revised to restore parental autonomy and safeguard family privacy not only because judges cannot be substitute parents and courts cannot be substitute families but also because the power of the state must not be employed to reenforce prejudice and discrimination against those who are cosmetically or otherwise different. When Judge Elwyn referred to Judge Fuld's dissent, it was to a case in which the court refused to find Martin Seiferth, age 14, a neglected child even though his father would not compel Martin to undergo the surgery recommended for the repair of a cleft palate and harelip.[53] Martin's father, despite his own beliefs, would have consented to the surgery had Martin been willing. Their decisions were based not upon "religious" beliefs, but upon a belief that "forces in the universe" would allow Martin to cure himself. Despite evidence far less equivocal than that in Kevin's case, the majority of the court refused to be trapped by rescue fantasies of the health department

[52]65 Misc. 2d at 674, 317 N.Y.S.2d at 657.
[53]*In re* Seiferth, 309 N.Y. 80, 127 N.E.2d 820 (1955).

and its doctors or by strong prejudices which the court was being asked to reenforce in an effort to "save" the child from himself and his parents. The court refused to order surgery, not because it thought it lacked authority, but because it thought Martin's reluctance to have the surgery foretold an unwillingness to participate in the therapy following the operations. Thus it was unwilling, unlike Judges Elwyn and Fuld, to substitute its or a state agency's value preferences about life style and about who and what is beautiful or natural for those of the responsible parents.

If Martin Seiferth, as an adult, chose to undergo the recommended surgery, it would not invalidate the argument that the court should not even have had discretion to do other than to protect him and his parents from state intrusion. In fact, Martin Seiferth chose not to have the surgery. "After attending one of the vocational high schools in the city, where he learned the trade of upholsterer and was elected president of the Student Council, he set up in business on his own and is, despite his disfigurement, active and successful."[54] The county health department that originated the case reacted as if experience offered no lessons about the need for minimum state intervention on parental autonomy and family privacy:

> "[He] had graduated . . . at the head of [his high school] class. It was his intention then to become an interior decorator. . . . [T]he Health Department [is] still of the opinion that the operation should have been performed in order to give this young man a fuller opportunity for the development of his talents."[55]

The law must be designed to protect its citizens from just such official blindness to the forceful imposition of personal wishes or beliefs on those who share neither the wish nor the belief about the value of medical care or "fuller opportunities" for their children.

---

[54]Letter from Mr. William G. Conable, attorney for Seiferth, to Joseph Goldstein (Apr. 20, 1964), *quoted in* J. GOLDSTEIN & J. KATZ, *supra* note 5, at 993.
[55]Letter from Mr. Elmer R. Weil, county attorney of Erie County, to Joseph Goldstein (Apr. 28, 1965), *quoted in id.* at 993–94.

INTERRELATED DECISIONS NOT INVOLVING LIFE OR DEATH FOR ONE CHILD AND INVOLVING LIFE OR DEATH FOR ANOTHER CHILD

Should the state have authority to invade the privacy of a family in order to review the deliberations of parents who have to decide whether to let one of their children die or whether to attempt to supply a life-saving organ for transplant by consenting to "unnecessary" surgery on one of their healthy children?

The answer ought to be "No." But that was not the answer of a Connecticut court in *Hart v. Brown.*[56] In that case doctors advised Mr. and Mrs. Hart that the only real prospect of saving their eight-year-old daughter Katheleen's life from a deadly kidney malfunction was to transplant a kidney from Margaret, her healthy twin sister. The doctors recommended and the Hart parents consented to the "unnecessary" surgery on Margaret to provide Katheleen with an opportunity to pursue a relatively normal life. But the hospital administration and the doctors refused to accept parental consent without a court review.[57] They acted out of a concern for their livelihood, not for the lives or well-being of Margaret or of Katheleen. Understandably, they feared becoming liable for money damages because the law might not accept parental consent as a defense to assault and malpractice, were such suits brought.

The Harts were thus forced to turn to the state to establish either their authority to decide or the rightness of their decision. They initiated a declaratory judgment action. There

---

[56]29 Conn. Supp. 368, 289 A.2d 386 (1972).

[57]Interestingly, the doctors were willing to rely on parental consent, without court review, to remove both of Katheleen's kidneys and thus leave her with "no potential kidney function" and with the "prospect of survival . . . because of her age, at best questionable." *Id.* at 372, 289 A.2d at 388. *Cf. In re* Nemser, 51 Misc. 2d 616, 621–25, 273 N.Y.S.2d 624, 629–32 (1966) (petition for appointment of guardian to amputate foot of 80-year-old woman; judge's complaint about resort to court).

followed hearings and proceedings before Judge Robert Testo which intruded massively on the privacy of the family and set a dangerous precedent for state interference with parental autonomy. There was no *probable cause* to suspect that the parents might be exploiting either of their children, only that the doctors and administrators in refusing to accept the parental choice might be risking the well-being of both children and the family. The court upheld the parental choice, though not their autonomy to decide.

Although Judge Testo's decision avoided tragic consequences for the Harts, he did set a precedent for unwarranted and undesirable intervention by the state. He held:

> To prohibit the natural parents and the guardians ad litem of the minor children the right to give their consent under these circumstances, *where there is supervision by this court* and other persons in examining their judgment, would be most unjust, inequitable and injudicious. Therefore, natural parents of a minor should have the right to give their consent to an isograft kidney transplantation procedure *when their motivation and reasoning are favorably reviewed by a community representation which includes a court of equity.*[58]

Had the Hart parents refused to consent to Margaret's surgery and the transplant of her kidney to Katheleen, equally unwarranted proceedings might have been brought to establish their neglect in order to obtain court authority to impose

[58]29 Conn. Supp. at 378, 289 A.2d at 391 (emphasis added). For another view of the issues presented by such cases, see Lewis, *Kidney Donation by a 7-Year-Old Identical Twin Child: Psychological, Legal, and Ethical Considerations,* 13 J. CHILD PSYCH. 221–43 (1974). *But see In re* Richardson, 284 So. 2d 185 (La. App.), *cert. denied,* 284 So. 2d 338 (La. 1973) (affirming lower court's refusal to approve of kidney transplant from mentally retarded 17-year-old to his 32-year-old sister); *see also* Howard v. Fulton-DeKalb Hosp. Auth., Civ. No. 3-90430 (Super. Ct., Fulton County, Ga., Nov. 29, 1973) (finding invalid mother's consent to transplant from her 15-year-old, moderately retarded daughter, since mother would be recipient of kidney). The court in *Howard,* however, authorized the transplant under a doctrine of "substituted judgment." The case, along with others that pose similar issues, is discussed in Nolan, *Anatomical Transplants Between Family Members—The Problems Facing Court and Counsel,* [1975] FAM. I. REP. (BNA) 4035.

the doctors' recommendation. Doctors can, because of their special training, make diagnoses and prognoses; doctors can indicate the probable consequences for a Margaret or a Katheleen of pursuing one course or another. But absent a societal consensus, nothing in their training, or for that matter in the training of judges, qualifies them to impose upon others their preferred value choices about what the good or better is for such children or for their families. The critical fallacy is to assume as Judge Testo does in his declaratory judgment—as the legislature does in its laws of neglect and abuse—that the training and offices of doctors, legislators, and judges endow them not just with the authority but also with the capacity to determine what risks to take for someone else's child, in circumstances where there is no right or wrong answer or set of answers.

That some will object to and be uneasy about the substantial limits this essay proposes be placed upon the power of the state to supervene parental decisions about health care for their children cannot be denied. But it is the absence of a substantial societal consensus about the legitimacy of state intrusion on parental autonomy, on the entitlement of children to autonomous parents, and on family privacy in situations beyond the proposed limits which is the best evidence for holding in check the use of state power to impose highly personal values on those who do not share them. Further, the limits set by the standard of normal healthy growth toward adulthood or a life worth living, by the life-or-death choice, and by the requirement of proven medical procedures has a built-in flexibility which can respond both to new findings in medicine and to new and changing consensuses in society.

Acknowledgments

I wish to acknowledge the provocative assistance of my colleagues on the Proxy Consent Committee of the Hastings

Institute and the research and editorial assistance of Benjamin Lopata and Jeff Thaler, students at the Yale Law School. I am also indebted to Lon Babby, Robert Burt, Owen Fiss, Sonja Goldstein, Neil Peck, Donn Pickett, and Albert J. Solnit for their criticism.

Part III

The Values at Stake

Consent, Representation, and Proxy Consent

GERALD DWORKIN

INTRODUCTION

The moral and practical issue that is raised by proxy consent is the issue of when one individual may make decisions about, speak for, and represent the interests of another. In the case of a fetus, or a young child, or a mentally retarded person, or an unconscious person, or a person in great mental distress, or a person who has been found "unfit" to perform certain obligations and duties, the individual whose interests are to be secured and rights protected is viewed as not in a position to, not competent to, make certain important decisions. The issue of proxy consent is one of who shall be authorized to make those decisions and what criteria should guide the proxy in making such decisions.

GERALD DWORKIN • Department of Philosophy, University of Illinois at Chicago Circle, Chicago, Illinois 60680.

The issue of proxy consent can arise in many different contexts. We might be concerned with the financial responsibility of a senile individual. We might be concerned with the legal powers of a guardian with respect to his ward. We might be concerned with who will be best able to look after the interests of a minor child. In this volume we are primarily concerned with the issue as it arises in the biomedical context, and in particular, as it arises with respect to children and their parents. Thus we are concerned with third-party authority to make decisions about the use of children in medical treatment and research.

In this chapter I shall examine the concepts of consent and representation, as they have developed in the context of political authority, to see what implications such concepts might have for the notion of proxy consent. The area of political authority seems a fruitful one in which to begin exploration. In both the political and the biomedical realms we have conflicts between the interests of individuals and the interests of some larger group. In both realms we have conflicts between the interests of individuals as they perceive them, and their interests as perceived by others. As a result, in both cases, we find a contrast between moral theories that emphasize individual rights and autonomy, and those theories that emphasize the total good that might be achieved. And in both areas we find questions about eligibility to participate in the process of decision making and about the benefits and costs of the institutions involved. Children and the mentally incompetent are problematic cases in both areas. Finally, and most directly relevant to our concerns here, there are problems about *who* can (may) consent for *whom*. Can my ancestors' consent bind me to obey the state? Can a parent consent for his child to a risky experimental procedure with no direct benefits for the child?

The analogies will not be perfect, for the two areas are similar not identical. But seeing how and when the analogies fail is itself interesting and illuminating.

CONSENT AND REPRESENTATION

Whenever some persons are thought to have political authority over others the concepts of consent and representation play a crucial role in any theory designed to legitimate or explain this situation. With respect to state authority, the question is: What gives some persons the right to command others, to obligate others to obey such commands, and to enforce such commands by the use of coercion? The answer of political philosophers from Socrates to Rawls has been in terms of some notion of consent. Others may have authority over me if and only if I have granted them that authority. Conversely, I am obligated to obey others only if I have agreed to do so. There must be some voluntary undertaking on my part for any obligation to arise. In Hobbes's words, "there [is] no obligation on anyman which ariseth not from some act of his own."

By consenting, we entitle others to act in ways in which they could not had we not consented. State powers derived from consent are just or legitimate not because they are used in just or benevolent ways, not because they are in the best interests of the governed, but simply because citizens have granted the state those powers.

Closely allied to the notion of consent, but not identical with it, is the idea of representation. In any society, other than the impractical one of unanimous direct democracy, there will be a distinction between the citizens and those who are authorized to make and execute the laws. Some persons will have the right and the responsibility to act for others, to be their agent in the pursuit of their needs or wishes or interests. It is clear in general that the consent of the principal who is being represented is not necessary for his being represented. The existence of various kinds of representation for the incompetent shows this fact. And even if the consent of the principal is sufficient to authorize someone to be his representative there remains the crucial question of what the correct role of the representative ought to be. Ought the representative act as the principal would have acted, or as the principal should have acted, or in the interests of the principal, or in pursuit of his welfare?

I shall first examine some of the varieties of consent that have appeared in the philosophical discussion of political authority. Then I shall argue that the problem of "proxy consent" is not an issue of consent in any straightforward way, but instead an issue of representation. I shall then discuss different ideas of what representation is, and different conceptions of the role of the representative, concluding with some normative remarks about "proxy consent" in the biomedical context, and some problems that need further investigation.

VARIETIES OF CONSENT

The clearest case of consent is actual, explicit consent. If I take a pledge to uphold and maintain the laws of the country I explicitly consent to such authority. If I tell my doctor that he may enroll me in a random controlled clinical trial then there is no question of his justification in doing so, although the fact that he has the right to do so does not preclude the possibility that he ought not to do so on some other grounds.

In the political context two difficulties arose with respect to a theory of explicit consent as the foundation of legitimate authority. Some said that such consent never took place—or at least they never consented. The second difficulty was the view that consent was sometimes not sufficient, and sometimes not necessary to explain legitimate authority.

The first difficulty, that such consent was a fiction, has basically two solutions. The first: the consent really did take place, you just had to know how to find it. The second: it was conceded that it never did occur, but then it was never really supposed to have.

The first solution, introduced by Locke, is that of tacit

consent. There is a kind of consent that takes place without the explicit signs that we normally expect as the mark of consent. As Locke puts it:

> Every man that hath any possession or enjoyment of any part of the dominions of any government thereby gives his tacit consent, and is as far forth obliged to the laws of that government during such enjoyment, as any one under it, whether this his possession be of land to him and his heirs forever, or lodging only for a week.[1]

The problems with this notion seemed infinite. How does one withdraw one's tacit consent? To what have you consented when you use the roads of a country? The terms of the original contract? The current set of laws?

Whatever its theoretical difficulties it is important for the discussion of proxy consent to distinguish tacit consent from inferred consent (see below), and these in turn from situations that give rise to obligations as if a person had consented. Tacit consent is no less actual consent for not being explicit. If we think of consent as an act of agreement, a "saying to oneself," then the difference between express and tacit consent is simply the question of whether the individual has made known his consent to others. He may have consented, and the best explanation of his behavior is that he has consented, although he has not expressed it.

Inferred consent, on the other hand, is not actual consent that remains unexpressed. It is simply a judgment about what the agent would have agreed to under certain circumstances. If a surgeon, performing an operation for an ectopic pregnancy, finds an acute appendix and removes it, he will rely on a view about what the patient would have wanted if she had known about the appendix. She did not consent, either explicitly or tacitly, but (it is claimed) she would have. It would be preferable not to call this consent at all, but if we

---

[1] John Locke, *The Second Treatise of Government* (New York: Library of Liberal Arts, 1952), p. 68.

must, then calling it "hypothetical" or "inferred" consent makes the contrast explicit.

The most recent development in political theory is the use of hypothetical consent, rather than actual consent, as the key legitimating factor. Legitimate government is government that deserves consent. It is government that acts within the limits of the authority that rational agents would (under certain ideal conditions) have granted. Actual consent is neither necessary nor sufficient to create obligations to obey governments. For people might consent to obey governments that were unjust and tyrannical, or they might fail to consent to governments that brought benefits to the members of a society that were paid for by some sacrifices by the citizens of the society. Legitimate government is government that deserves consent.

All these should be distinguished from situations in which my behavior gives rise to obligations and expectations *as if* I had consented. My inner denial that I accept the rules of poker will not prevent me from being held to their observance *as if* I had consented. In legal language, I am estopped from using as a defense the fact that I did not consent. This situation has been called quasi-consent.

It is important to see that neither quasi-consent nor hypothetical consent is a species of consent. Neither is a case of consent, but both appeal to consent or something like consent in explaining the obligations and rights they create. To appeal to what a patient (in the ectopic pregnancy case) would have wanted (or to what was in her best interests) is quite different from appealing to her actual consent.

Similarly, proxy consent is not a species of consent. It is precisely when, for various reasons, individuals cannot, do not, or ought not give their consent that we invoke the notion of proxy consent. In addition the term "proxy," having the connotations of the stockholder's proxy, is misleading. Unlike the stockholder who signs his proxy over to management, and hence explicitly consents to their authority, neither children nor the mentally retarded nor the comatose have expressly abandoned their rights to decide.

Although proxy consent is not a type of consent, the idea of consent is relevant in two ways. First, consent is the background against which delegation of authority stands forward. We only need substitutes when there is a real thing that is lacking. It is because the normal appeal to consent fails that we require a proxy. Second, various theories that attempt to justify the substitution of one person's judgment for another rely on views concerning what the individual whose authority has been delegated would have consented to. This standard will not always hold, for in, say, the case of infants the appeal may be to the interests of the child. But even here there may be lurking in the background a definition of interests in terms of what the child would, on reaching the age of competence, approve or consent to.

The functions that consent serves in the political context are similar to those served in the biomedical area. Consent serves as a check on the power of those agents (political or medical) who are making decisions that affect one's interests in significant ways. Consent makes it more likely that welfare will be maximized since costs are borne only by those willing to pay them and are therefore presumably worth it to those individuals. Consent preserves the autonomy of the individual since his right to self-determination, his control of his body and his possessions, can be abrogated only with his agreement.

However, in both the political and medical contexts it is apparent that consent will not always be possible. In the political realm that is so because we are born into a society with no choice about certain fundamental institutions—which provide the framework within which voluntary transactions can be made and enforced. And short of unanimous, direct democracy these institutions are not such that we can consent to each decision they produce. In the biomedical context, consent fails because of the incompetence of some individuals. In both cases appeal is made to the notion of representation, to the idea that under certain conditions some may speak for and make decisions for others.

REPRESENTATION

There are philosophical differences among political philosophers both about the nature of a representative and about what his role ought to be. Griffiths distinguishes four different notions of representation: descriptive, symbolic, ascriptive, and interest.[2]

A descriptive representative is sufficiently like those he represents that he can be taken as a *sample* on the basis of which one can draw inferences about the represented. As Pitkin puts it, "What qualifies a man to represent is his representativeness—not what he does, but what he is, or is like."[3]

Symbolic representation occurs when an individual is taken as a focus for attitudes appropriate to what he is representative of. Thus the queen is the symbol of the English people. Unlike a descriptive representative, a symbolic one need not resemble what he represents in any obvious way.

Someone who has my power of attorney need neither resemble me nor be symbolic of me. Instead he acts in my name and his actions commit me. That is the ascriptive sense of representation.

Finally, someone who represents the oil interests in Congress may not be authorized to do so, nor do his actions commit those interests.

It is worthwhile to note that these competing conceptions of what a representative *is* parallel (with the exception of the notion of symbolic representation) the three explanations

[2]A. Phillips Griffiths, "How Can One Person Represent Another?" *Proceedings of the Aristotelian Society,* supp. vol. 34 (1960): 187–208.
[3]Hanna Pitkin, *Representation* (New York: Atherton, 1969), p. 10.

given by Capron for allowing third-party permission in the law (see Chapter 4). Corresponding to the idea of a descriptive representative is the "identity-of-interest" doctrine. A proxy is allowed to decide for an incompetent because "the interests of the third party and those of the incompetent are so close that in choosing his or her own interests the third party will choose very much as the incompetent would." The empirical assumption being made here—and it may be as false with respect, say, to a trade unionist in Congress as for a parent choosing to volunteer one of his children's kidneys for the benefit of a sibling—is that there are certain characteristics (class, sex, family identity) such that people who share those characteristics are more likely to choose in the same way than others who do not.

Corresponding to the idea that the proxy "is able to express the choices that the incompetent would have made because of individualized, subjective knowledge of the incompetent" is the notion of the ascriptive representative acting as a transmitter of the inferred desires of the principal—the "substituted-judgment" doctrine. The important point here is that there is no assumption that the choice being made is the "correct" or "right" one. Thus in the *Seiferth* case, where a minor refused to undergo surgery for the repair of a cleft palate, a proxy acting as ascriptive representative could not allow such surgery even if he thought that it would be better for the child.[4] To do so would be to act as an interest representative—a proxy who makes an "objectively reasonable choice that will . . . serve the incompetent's interests." This is what Capron calls the "best-interests" doctrine.

In actuality, of course, these doctrines seldom appear in a pure form. As Capron points out, the subjective nature of the substituted-judgment rule is hedged with objective limitations. Even if there is reason to believe a particular incompetent might have wanted to give away his estate, the court will assume that no reasonable person would want to do so.

[4]See the discussion of this case in Chapter 5.

And, conversely, the "best interests" of a child are often defined in terms of the wishes of its parents.

The debate about the nature of representation in the political context reflects a normative conflict over the proper role of the representative. Ought a representative to act as those he represents wish or as the representative perceives their best interests? Is the representative to make use of his independent judgment or to act merely as a transmitter of the wishes of the represented? Is the representative a trustee exercising discretion on behalf of his clients or an agent faithfully carrying out the orders of his master? Is the representative to act *on* behalf of his principal, or *in* behalf?

These two polarities are associated with Edmund Burke and John Stuart Mill. Burke views representatives as trustees who are obligated to vote in the best interests of the nation as a whole, but who are not bound or obligated to those they represent. Indeed, Burke thought representatives need not even be chosen by those they represent.

> If a part of the kingdom is being well governed, its interest secured, then it is represented whether or not it has the franchise; if it is not represented actually, then it can be said to be represented *virtually*. Virtual representation is that in which there is a communion of interests and a sympathy in feelings and desires between those who act in the name of any description of people, and the people in whose name they act, though the trustees are not actually chosen by them.[5]

Mill, on the otherhand, was unequivocal that representatives must be chosen by those whom they represent, and, though somewhat ambivalent on this matter, thought that the representative should act as an agent of those he represents.

> The meaning of representative government is that the whole people, or some numerous portion of them, exercise through deputies periodically elected by themselves the ultimate con-

---

[5]Edmund Burke, "The English Constitutional System," excerpts from Burke in Pitkin, pp. 169–170.

trolling power, which, in every constitution, must reside somewhere.[6]

It is clear from an examination of their works that Burke's
and Mill's differing views of the proper role of the representative reflect very different views of human nature, of the
capacities of the representative and the represented, of the
nature of political issues. Compare, for example, the respec-
tive views of Burke and Mill on the question of whether the
people know their own interests.

> The most poor, illiterate, and uninformed creatures are judges
> of a *practical* oppression. It is a matter of feeling; and as such
> persons generally have felt most of it, and are not of an over-
> lively sensibility, they are the best judges of it. But for *the real
> cause*, or *the appropriate remedy*, they ought never to be called
> into council about the one or the other. They ought to be totally
> shut out; because their reason is weak, because, when once
> roused, their passions are ungoverned; because they want in-
> formation.[7]

> Human beings are only secure from evil at the hands of others
> in proportion as they have the power of being, and are, self-
> protecting; and they only achieve a high degree of success in
> their struggle with Nature in proportion as they are self-de-
> pendent, relying on what they themselves can do, either sep-
> arately or in concert, rather than on what others do for them.[8]

The issue of the "competence" of those who are being
represented is perhaps the central question in the medical
context with respect to proxy consent. But political theorists
also differ concerning the nature of the decisions a representative makes, and this conflict is also reflected in their
differences concerning the proper role of the representative.
As Pitkin puts it:

> The more [a theorist] conceives of political issues as having
> correct, objectively determinable solutions accessible to rational

---

[6]John Stuart Mill, "Considerations on Representative Government," excerpts
from Mill in Pitkin, pp. 180–181.
[7]Burke, p. 172.
[8]Mill, p. 178.

> inquiry, the more he will incline to independence [for the representative]; there is no point in counting noses accurately among the constituents if the question is a technical one calling for expertise. . . . The more political issues strike him as involving irrational commitment or personal preference, choice rather than deliberation, the more necessary it will seem that the representative consult the people's preferences and pursue their choice.[9]

This controversy occurs in the biomedical context as well. Goldstein's discussion in Chapter 5 of the *Sampson* case shows the judge's view of what determines a happy life (the absence of disfigurement) as an objective, rational matter—not to be impeded by an (irrational) person's preference.

PROXY CONSENT

It is important to bear in mind two essential respects in which the political context differs from the biomedical. In the political arena, some speak for others not (usually) because the others are incompetent but because—barring the special case of direct democracy (New England town meetings)—it is not feasible for all to make policy on a regular basis. The closest political analog to the issue of incompetence is the issue of colonial rule, which played a significant role in nineteenth-century political debate. Even Mill thought that colonial peoples were an exception to his view that each person is the best judge of his own interests, and he classified them with children as those in "non-age."

Related to this issue of the importance of incompetence is the second dis-analogy. Representatives are usually assumed to be chosen or authorized by those they represent. Representatives can act on behalf of others because they have been granted the right to do so. In the medical context, however, we have, because of "incompetence," a lack of explicit authorization. The dying patient in a coma, unless he has

9Pitkin, pp. 20–21.

made a "living will" or otherwise expressed his intentions, has not designated a proxy to act on his behalf. The child has not chosen his parents as his representatives with the right to volunteer him for drug experiments. Whatever the merits of the mother's decision to choose abortion for a fetus, her right to do so does not derive from the consent of that fetus.

Thus in the medical context we have both "incompetence" and lack of specific authorization. How does this fact affect the question of what the proper role of the "proxy" ought to be? To begin with, it raises obvious moral issues having to do with the normal right of individuals to autonomy in the sense of self-determination. An agent is being denied the right to make certain decisions concerning his physical and emotional welfare. It is interesting to note that this situation does not always involve coercion or manipulation—the normal paths to deprivation of liberty.

It is the rare case, such as the refusal to allow a severe-burn victim to leave the hospital and die, that explicitly denies liberty. More usual is the denial of opportunity or power, as in the case of a doctor who refuses a minor the operation that will remove one of her kidneys and transfer it to a sibling.

It is clear how abrogation of the right of self-determination involves other values as well. Our self-esteem and sense of worth are bound up with the right to determine what shall be done to and with our bodies and minds. The obvious justification for some system of delegated authority in the case of those who are incompetent to make certain decisions is that they have already "lost" that right—rather than having had it taken away by others. And given that some decisions will have to be made, the only significant issues are who shall make them and what criteria should guide their judgment. Proxy consent does not serve the same purpose as "real" consent—to ensure that a person is only exposed to those medical interventions that he has chosen freely in an informed fashion. If we insisted on actual consent, then no risky procedures intended to benefit the child as patient could ever be performed. Since it seems contrary to the best interests of the child to adopt such a policy, we decide to accept the consent of a proxy, and choose the parents as the proxies.

The reasons for selecting parents reflect a number of different sociological, psychological, and administrative considerations. These include respect for the family as a decision-making unit; the appropriateness of giving the power of consent to those individuals who were responsible for bringing the child into the world, and who have a legal and moral duty to protect it; the belief that, of all the possible proxies, the parents are most likely to have the interests of the child foremost; and the belief that the administrative costs of assigning this function to other parties (an ombudsman) would be too high. Each of these considerations may be legitimately questioned on both empirical (the high incidence of battered children) and moral (the link between procreation and proprietary rights is dubious) grounds. But since it is extremely unlikely that we shall turn to other candidates for proxies, I prefer to concentrate on the question of the criteria that parents ought to use in choosing for their children. As unauthorized representatives, should they act as the child desires or would desire, or make an independent judgment of what is in the child's best interests?

In the medical context, as in the political, the answer is that neither is always the right thing to do. One needs to distinguish the following variables that affect the matter. In each case I shall give examples from both the medical and political realms.

What is the nature of the issue about which the decision is being made? In the political context one might want to pay more attention to the expressed wishes of one's constituents about an economic issue, say minimum-wage legislation, and less attention if the issue was one of infringing important civil liberties. In the medical context a quality-of-life decision for a minor might call for more respect for his expressed wishes than would a life-and-death issue.

Second, what is the nature of the persons who are being represented? A representative might act as an agent for relatively sophisticated voters who care about issues, and more as a trustee for relatively naïve and unconcerned voters. In the medical context a crucial variable is the nature of the incompetence. A comatose adult is one who has attained competence at some point and then lost it. He, therefore, has had the opportunity to choose life plans, formulate desires and intentions, and so on. It will therefore be easier to infer what he would want were he not incompetent. Obviously, the duration of the incompetence also matters. What he would want, and what is in his interests, will differ depending on whether the incompetence is temporary or permanent.

In the case of children (or those who have been mentally incompetent since they were children) we are dealing with those who have never attained competence and therefore have not been able to choose life plans, form various intentions, develop certain desires, and so on. In such a case, if it is expected that competence will be attained at some point, we ought to choose for them, not as they might want, but in terms of maximizing those interests that will make it possible for them to develop life plans of their own. We ought to preserve their share of what Rawls calls "primary goods"; that is, such goods as liberty, health, and opportunity, which any rational person would want to pursue whatever particular life plan he chooses.

What are the interests at stake? A political representative may have to balance the interests and desires of some against those of others. He may have to consider the interests of current generations against the needs or interests of future generations. This question of balancing conflicts of interests occurs in the case of incompetents as well. The recent case of *Lausier* v. *Pescinski* illustrates this fact dramatically.[10] A mother of six contracted glomerulonephritis, underwent a total nephrectomy, and required a kidney transplant. Her brother had been institutionalized for twenty of his thirty-eight years as a "catatonic schizophrenic." Another sister,

---

[10]Lausier v. Pescinski, 67 Wis. 2nd 4, 226 N.W. 2nd 180 (1975).

who was appointed the guardian for the brother, petitioned the court to approve a transplant. The court denied permission, arguing:

> An incompetent particularly should have his own interests protected. Certainly no advantage should be taken of him. In the absence of real consent on his part, and in a situation where no benefit to him has been established, we fail to find any authority for the county court or this court, to approve this operation.[11]

The lone dissenter argued in terms of what the incompetent would have consented to as opposed to what was in his benefit. He concluded that "in all probability" the brother would consent because "for him it would be a short period of discomfort which would not affect his ability either to enjoy life or his longevity."[12] Thus, because the issue was one of a relatively small risk to the incompetent (it was estimated in testimony before the court to be comparable to the risk of driving) and life or death for the potential donee, the dissenting judge was willing to use the doctrine of substituted judgment (what the incompetent would have done) as opposed to the best-interests test.

I would argue that such inferences are wholly without warrant in the absence of any specific evidence about the incompetent's attitude toward his sister, his inclinations to altruism, his attitude toward risk, and so on. The proxy in such a case ought to be required, as the majority held, to act only in terms of the interests, objectively ascertained, of the incompetent.

CONCLUSION

Let me suggest, in conclusion, a set of problems that deserve intensive philosophical investigation because of their

---

[11]67 Wis. 2d at 8, 9 226 N.W. 2d at 182.

[12]67 Wis. 2d at 12, 226 N.W. 2d at 183. For further discussion of this case and of the more general issue of the doctrine of substituted judgment see John R. Robertson, "Organ Donation by Incompetents and the Substituted Judgment Doctrine," *Columbia Law Review* 76 (1976): 48–78.

significance for the issue of proxy consent. The first is that of the interconnections between the concepts of interests and consent. It is normally assumed that people would choose what is in their interests; hence, arguments for inferring what people would choose will often make reference to their (perceived) interests. Conversely, our conception of what is in a person's interest is often a function of what he would choose. Thus it could be argued that the decision not to transfuse blood to a comatose Jehovah's Witness is a decision made in his interest (even though he will die as a result), because his interest is defined in terms of the choices he regards as morally appropriate. How, therefore, can we conceptually characterize these notions to exhibit both their differences and their interrelations?

Second, with respect to competent persons we normally believe that when their choices conflict with their interests (as others perceive them), their choices ought to be respected—in other words, the Milliam antagonism to paternalism.[13] To what extent, then, ought this respect for choice be carried over to incompetents? If the person, when competent, would have made what we regard as a foolish decision, ought we make that decision for him when he is incompetent?

Finally, if we are going to depend on some notion of "hypothetical consent," what the incompetent would have chosen *if*, then what follows the *if*? Would have chosen, if competent? But that cannot always be what is meant. Consider the sterilization of the mentally retarded. There is a reasonable argument that a mentally retarded person would choose to be sterilized, since only by doing so would he be allowed to have a sex life. But, if we are considering how he would have chosen *if not mentally retarded*, then there would be no obstacle to his sexual activity, and no need to make such a choice. Again, should "if he were to recover compe-

---

[13]For some exceptions and objections to this doctrine, see my "Paternalism," reprinted in Gorovitz et al., *Moral Problems in Medicine* (Englewood Cliffs, N.J.: Prentice-Hall, 1976).

tence" follow? But he may never have had it. Should it be a matter of "if he were to attain competence"? But, if we know he never will, why should that be the appropriate condition? The most plausible candidate is "if he were competent but knew he would become incompetent in this particular fashion." In short, we need a careful examination of what is meant by "what the incompetent would choose," as well as a moral theory that indicates that the conditions we posit in such an analysis are the morally appropriate ones. In other words, we need a theory of what it is to respect an incompetent person as a person. Unfortunately, at this point, we lack such a theory for competent persons as well.

Acknowledgments

I would like to thank Ruth Macklin and Leslie Dach for their helpful suggestions on an earlier draft.

CHAPTER 7

Human Independence and Parental Proxy Consent

PETER G. BROWN

INTRODUCTION

This chapter focuses primarily on the principles that should govern a parental decision to grant or withhold consent for therapeutic and nontherapeutic procedures on their children. Although I hope the discussion will be informative concerning future directions for case and statutory law, I take my main audience to be parents faced with these difficult decisions.

I have two purposes in mind: to provide an account of parental responsibility that can serve as a standard against which to measure the moral authority of the parent to give or withhold proxy consent on behalf of his or her child; and

PETER G. BROWN ● Associate Dean, School of Public Affairs, University of Maryland, College Park, Maryland 20742.

to apply this account by examining when parents should consent to and should withhold consent from therapeutic and nontherapeutic interventions on their children. I argue for a standard by which parents may decide when they have a duty to withhold consent for their children in nontherapeutic situations. I also offer reasons on the basis of which parents may decide to compel their children to accept certain treatments.

For purposes of this discussion, I take "therapeutic" to mean those efforts taken to alleviate clinically identifiable physical or mental disorders. It is not meant to include procedures that might be of some very loosely defined benefit to the individual in question.

I will argue for the thesis that *parental responsibility is to care for their children—and in a society emphasizing individual choice and initiative (and probably in other societies as well) this caring entails the development in children of the capability for independence, and within certain broad limits the means for acting independently.* I will call this the independence principle, which as the argument develops I will rename the principle of primary parental responsibility. By "independence" I understand the ability to conceive, evaluate alternatives, and act on a life plan—to pursue, in other words, a self-given system of ends that has at least rough internal consistency.[1] A person has a life plan when he or she is ordering the means at his or her disposal toward a certain set of objectives and these objectives are not in conflict with one another.

A corollary of my thesis will be that *in light of this responsibility it is not morally permissible for parents to consent to actions—experimental, social, and so on—that interfere with actual or prospective independence, and the securing and nurturing of its*

---

[1]See Charles Fried, *An Anatomy of Values: Problems of Personal and Social Choice* (Cambridge: Harvard University Press, 1970), pp. 97–101, for a fuller discussion of the concept of a life plan. I am indebted to David Luban for assisting me in the precise formulation of this principle.

preconditions.[2] This corollary applies to actions initiated by parties other than the parent in question, including the state, another parent, and, under some circumstances, the child him or herself. As will be shown, this corollary rules out parental consent on behalf of the child to certain other types of nontherapeutic interventions.

PARENTAL RESPONSIBILITY AND THE CONSTRUCTION OF INDEPENDENCE

I shall develop my arguments concerning parental responsibility for children by taking as my point of departure Joseph Goldstein's views (in Chapter 5) concerning the inappropriateness of state intervention in family life. The following passage represents the core of Goldstein's position:

> To be an *adult* is to be a risktaker, independent, and with capacity and authority to decide and to do what is "best" for oneself.
> To be an adult *who is a parent* is to be presumed in law to have the capacity, authority, and responsibility to determine and to do what is good for one's children.[3]

If we take independence—as Goldstein urges—as a fixed feature of what is of value in adult life, in thinking about parental

---

[2]Choosing between the present and future independence of a child will obviously be tricky. A choice between present and future anything is complicated by factors such as whether the person in question will be alive at any given future time, whether the same opportunities will be available, and whether the individual can successfully postpone gratification. Since the parent is deciding on behalf of the child, problems of postponing gratification are eliminated, except to the extent to which the parent is pleased by seeing the child gratified. The other two factors would obviously have to be decided on the basis of the characteristics of the individual child, and likely future circumstances.

[3]See the opening to Chapter 5.

responsibility certain factors about what fosters independence should gain our attention.

I shall argue that it follows from this emphasis on adult independence that the education of children, both formal and informal, both public and private, both familial and societal, should aim at an adult capable of setting and acting on his or her own objectives. Moreover, there is a prima facie case for assigning the responsibility to those who care for the child to secure the resources that serve as material and psychological preconditions to the exercise of independence as an adult.

As a norm, adult independence requires an ability to set objectives of one's own, and to recognize and affirm them as one's own. Lack of ability to recognize and affirm objectives would mean that people could not have *their own* life plan. "As a norm" is used advisedly to indicate a standard toward which actions should be aimed. As will become clear later, it can function as a criterion for discriminating in difficult cases where a choice has to be made between the welfare of two or more individuals.

Parental responsibility on this view will then be: so to care for their children that the children will be capable in the future of (1) affirming certain objectives as their own,[4] and (2) accomplishing other independent acts at least some of which are means to the pursuit of the objectives of their life plans.

What makes such independence possible? Here we look to such factors as education, absence of anxiety, basic health, and so on. We are led to consideration of whether the factors that enhance the setting and affirmation of one's objectives are at hand for the individual. In spite of day care centers and other extrafamilial institutions, parents still have the major

---

[4]The capability for affirming certain acts as one's own is not a necessary condition for personhood, since we speak of persons—though perhaps in an extended sense—who are not capable of doing so. At least the ability to execute one's own ends is a precondition for responsibility and hence for a moral life.

responsibility for providing these prerequisites for the development of independence. The provision of such factors is a root element in the composition of parental responsibility.

The concept of independence is at once empty in content and rich in presupposition. It is empty in the sense that it does not tell us how it will be exercised. It does not tell us whether a given individual will prefer Cadillacs or Chevrolets, whether he will vote Democratic or Republican, but only that he will be able to bring the tools of reason to bear on making these and similar judgments. But it is rich in terms of what it presupposes.

It is on this area that I want to focus our attention. I suggest that what is involved in parental responsibility can be captured by employing a distinction between primary goods and other goods made by John Rawls in *A Theory of Justice*.[5] For Rawls, primary goods are those

> things which it is supposed a rational man wants whatever else he wants. Regardless of what an individual's rational plans are in detail, it is assumed that there are various things which he would prefer more of rather than less. With more of these goods men can generally be assured of greater success in carrying out their intentions and advancing their ends, whatever these ends may be. The primary social goods, to give them in broad categories, are rights and liberties, opportunities and powers, income and wealth.[6]

Notice that from the point of view of an adult, primary goods are the things that figure as preconditions for the exercise of choices.[7] Income and wealth, opportunities and

---

[5]John Rawls, *A Theory of Justice* (Cambridge: Harvard University Press, 1971).

[6]Ibid., p. 92. Rawls later adds self-respect to this list—see p. 440.

[7]Rawls places a very great emphasis on the role of the state in being obliged to distribute these goods in such a way that conforms with what he calls the "difference principle." Liberty and opportunity are not subject to this principle, since they are subject to the first principle of justice. The distribution of goods is just in accordance with the difference principle if there is no other distribution that would improve the condition of those worst off.

power, rights and negative liberties are necessary if an adult is to have the capacity to pursue other choices. I make no claim that Rawls's list is directly applicable to children. Probably it is not. I need only make use of the basic distinction between the specific things a particular person may want, and the facilities, dispositions, and capabilities all persons require in order to exercise choice no matter what their particular wants happen to be. Thus the primary goods for children are those things that children require to secure primary goods as adults.

Primary goods for children will surely include education, sound bodies, and an emotional makeup of sufficient stability to render choice and action possible, both as children and, later, as adults. If a child when he becomes an adult will want to enjoy novels, seek employment, or read the directions on a cake mix—we need not know which—he will have to be able to read. We need not know if he will be a blueberry raker, a flutist, or a marathon runner to know that bodily integrity will facilitate any of these choices. We need not speculate whether the person will be hard-driving or easy-going to know that self-confidence and other aspects of emotional stability will be invaluable. Both the independence to set and affirm one's objectives, and other forms of independence depend on access to the primary goods for children.

To anticipate a possible objection: I do not think the distinction between primary and other goods is rendered useless, at least for my purposes, by the fact that any (or most?) lists of primary goods will seem inapplicable to religious fanatics (or to other such bizarre counterexamples). To handle this objection, the principle of parental responsibility I am seeking can be formulated as follows: parental responsibility consists in securing for children those primary goods that are necessary for successful participation in the central institutions of the society in which the child can reasonably be expected to live as an adult, unless those institutions are themselves morally pernicious. (This qualification marks a point of contact between a discussion of parental responsibility and a general account of social legitimacy.) I will call this principle the principle of primary parental responsibility. This name, I hope, will emphasize simultaneously that the principle captures the major elements of parental responsibility, *and* that this responsibility is for securing, where possible, primary goods.

Under this principle, there is the responsibility on the part of the parent to give children the cognitive, emotional, and physiological capabilities to secure primary goods for adults when they are adults. To accomplish this task parents must have at least an implicit theory of childrearing, that is, a view about the best way to help the child achieve independence. Such a view may be picked up by formal acquaintance with theories of development, but more commonly, by a number of informal mechanisms including references to one's own youth, conversations with other parents, popularized childrearing texts, and so on.

What primary goods for children will turn out to be should be greatly informed by the discipline of developmental psychology. They would surely involve the satisfaction of basic material requirements such as adequate nutrition, clothing, and shelter as well as certain psychic needs having to do with the maintenance and development of self-respect: the belief on the part of the child that his goals are generally worthy of execution and attention, and that he is capable of attaining them.

The principle of parental responsibility is designed to clarify, and give support to, concerns about therapeutic and nontherapeutic interventions.

Parental Consent to Nontherapeutic Interventions

Opinions concerning what may be done to children for nontherapeutic reasons vary greatly. Perhaps the most stringent rule is stated by Pappworth in *Human Guinea Pigs:* "the law both here and in America appears to be definite, namely, the parents either singly or together, cannot give valid legal consent to any action that is not for the immediate benefit of the child concerned."[8]

Or consider the less strict suggestions of Curran and Beecher, who hold:

> There should be strong reason in professional judgment for the use of immature children . . . in any clinical investigation where there is no direct benefit intended for the child. However, such involvement should not be ruled out as illegal and unethical in all circumstances . . . involvement should be allowed where the study has firm medical support and justification, promises important new knowledge of benefit to science and to mankind, and where there is no discernible risk involved for the child-subject.[9]

Although Curran and Beecher believe Pappworth's formulation is too stringent, theirs is fully unspecific, in particular in failing to be clear about the types of risks involved. It does suggest, however, that a balancing of costs and benefits is the appropriate standard of making decisions in some cases.

Writers such as Curran and Beecher waver on nontherapeutic interventions with children, I suggest, because they believe they are confronted with a dilemma. On the one hand, such interventions with children raise the specter of exploitation of children for purposes not of their own choosing, or beyond what they ought to choose. On the other hand, firm adherence to a rule such as Pappworth's seems to go too far, as the example to be discussed will illustrate, in that it seems to rule out even minimal inconvenience to children when they could greatly benefit others.

Should we really prevent a child from giving blood to his sibling (in need of a rare type only to be reliably procured from a brother or sister) if such a transfusion would save the sibling? On the contrary, it seems appropriate to urge the child to pursue such a course of action. We can appropriately argue that children, even very young children down to a few

---

[8]M. H. Pappworth, *Human Guinea Pigs* (London: Routledge & Kegan Paul, 1967). Paul Ramsey's position seems similar to Pappworth's.

[9]William J. Curran and Henry K. Beecher, "Experimentation and Children," *Journal of the American Medical Association* 210 (1969): 77–83.

years of age, should be able to engage in such activities with parental consent, not on the specious ground (see below) that such donations would somehow be in their interest, but on the ground that such donations do not interfere with the independence of the child either presently or in the future. This position would thus come closer to that suggested by Curran and Beecher, but would add some content to the concept of risk. Where the child chooses a certain course of action, even one involving risk, and where such action does not have a high probability of interfering with present independence or with the possibility of future independent acts, I see no reason to argue that parents should not consent. Indeed, to foster the independence of the child they would seem obligated to do so. Here the concept of risk can be made specific by reference to the impairment of present or future primary goods.

Perhaps I have dodged a difficult case. What should happen when a child (say twelve years old) does *not* agree to a blood transfusion that would save a sibling's life? It follows from my discussion that the parent should be permitted to coerce the child into undergoing the procedure. When the two individuals are in the same family, the principle of primary parental responsibility suggests that securing primary goods for one child must take precedence over the loss of secondary goods for another. Where long-term access to primary goods is not at stake for either sibling, the child's opposition to the intervention should be decisive—at least with a child over twelve years old, if this age is generally reliable as an indicator of when people can understand the consequences of their acts. Since the discussion is focused on parental responsibility toward their own children, I do not address the even more difficult case of what to do when the children are not in the same family.

My admittedly tentative principle also seems to clarify the case of a kidney transplant from a severely retarded brother to a normal sibling. We need not go through the contorted reasoning of the court in *Strunk* v. *Strunk* (445 S.W. 2d 145 [Ky. 1959]) intended to show that it is in the retarded brother's interest to preserve the life of his sibling. Instead, we need only demonstrate, if it can be reliably predicted, that the donor will never be capable of setting his own life plan. In the extremely rare cases where a retarded sibling's well-being conflicts with a brother's or sister's *primary goods*, the former should give way to the latter.

As noted above, it should be clear that the standard I am proposing depends for its moral appeal on implicit reference to a concept of quality of life. (See Chapter 5.) The standard holds that where alternative measures *are not possible* it is permissible to impair or even sacrifice the life of an incompetent to save a sibling capable of normal development. It proposes a standard to be employed in making these agonizing choices.

It is sometimes argued that the doctrine of substituted judgment (a test that focuses on the inferred wishes of the incompetent) provides the appropriate framework for resolving questions of this sort. (See Chapters 3, 4, and 6.) In "Organ Donations by Incompetents and the Substituted Judgment Doctrine," John A. Robertson formulates this standard thus: "The substituted judgment doctrine would permit transplants from incompetents in situations where the incompetent, if competent, would donate an organ."[10] In the case of children this formulation seems to offer little guidance. Very young children, at least, may be presumed to be incompetent. Does the standard then suggest that we infer what a competent adult would do as a child? How does the standard help in dealing with individuals who are by their nature incompetent?[11]

---

[10]John A. Robertson, "Organ Donations by Incompetents and the Substituted Judgment Doctrine," *Columbia Law Review* 76 (1976): 48.

[11]Ibid., p. 68. This standard is formulated quite differently on p. 73—there the focus is on "what a competent person in the position of the incompetent . . . would do." This notion is very unclear. Is the standard what a competent person would do as competent; or what would be reasonable for a "temporarily" competent person to do who will be returning to incompetence?

The principle of primary parental responsibility seems preferable—for intrafamily purposes at any rate—because it focuses on comparing the life prospects of the two siblings. Making the necessary inferences for employing the substituted-judgment doctrine is tricky at best, whereas the principle of primary parental responsibility makes use of any empirical evidence that is obtainable.

If the principle of primary parental responsibility is correct, the focus of our attention is also shifted away from that proposed by Curran and Beecher. Whether a parent should consent to nontherapeutic interventions affecting his or her child should not turn on a balancing of social gain against individual risk. If the position sketched above is correct, the degree to which the procedures in question go against the express wishes of the child (if it is meaningful to ask him or her)[12] and whether they enhance the child's current and prospective independence should be the major issues of concern.

It should be noted that the principle, at least in my use of it is that parental responsibility is first and foremost toward one's own children. By and large one does not have enforceable authority over the children of others. Parental responsibility is first to secure and enhance the procedural independence of their own children, and then to facilitate access to other present and future primary goods for their own children. On this view, the parent is not obliged to, and would be mistaken to, think of him or herself as Bentham's policy maker trying to maximize overall social utility. (Bentham held that a person involved in setting policy should try to maximize the happiness of those for whom he is responsible.) Goldstein argues correctly, I believe, that respecting family autonomy (having a presumption in favor of letting the parents follow their judgments about what is in the best interest of the family) will—as a rule—be utility maximizing. Be that as it may, it is not the responsibility of the parent to pass on the appro-

---

[12]Here I have in mind only such common-sense tests as whether the child can understand the risks involved.

priateness of the institution of the family—when deciding how to carry out his or her responsibilities within it.

When a child is asked to undergo a procedure for a stranger that would impair the child's access to primary goods, parental responsibility requires a denial of the proxy. For interventions on behalf of strangers or for broad objectives such as the advancement of science that do not involve present, or impair access to future primary goods, the wishes of the child should be regarded. In cases where it is uncertain whether it is meaningful to regard the child's wishes (or those where it is certain that it is meaningless), parental consent would be appropriate unless present or future access to primary goods would suffer.

Parental Consent to Therapeutic Interventions

If parents have a duty to withhold consent from actions that would interfere with present or prospective access to primary goods, they have a correlative obligation to permit and even require those that enhance it. The moral rationale for the latter is familiar: the parent consents on behalf of the child to those actions that the child would consent to if he or she were able. So far so good? Obviously, at this point it is crucial to know what the child would consent to if he or she were able and were an adult. In many cases, the child's wishes will not be knowable, and even if known will appropriately not be taken as definitive. Moreover, the parent's role in influencing what the child wishes cannot be ignored.[13] What particular objectives the child adopts will be significantly affected because they are those of the parent, or because they are not those of the parent—in the case of the rebellious child. In the cases where the parent has determined or is determining the child's wishes, proxy consent is only partly a matter of the parent acting for the child—it is also the parent acting

[13]I am indebted to Susan Brown for suggesting this point.

for the parent: What happens then to the moral logic of the proxy?

To know how to decide in the face of this paradox we should distinguish between primary and secondary parental proxy consent along the following lines: parental consent on behalf of the child to secure primary goods of children, I shall call primary proxy consent. Secondary proxy consent will then designate those actions taken by the parent to secure the child's own wishes or the specific wishes of the parent. As noted above, this distinction has the virtue of replicating and adding content (once an appropriate list of primary goods for children or adults is developed) to the requirement that parents prevent serious harm to their children.

Clearly, parental consent to an appendectomy is of the first type, that is, a case of primary parental proxy. So are interventions to remedy severe reading or speech deficiencies. Psychotherapy undertaken for certain mildly dysfunctional problems, plastic surgery, and training in some religious cults are examples of secondary consent. Where the child's wishes and those of the parent coincide there is little or no issue. Where they do not, I think that different thresholds are generally applicable. Children who fail to consent to procedures necessary for the securing of primary goods should be required to do so. Indeed, failure to choose these procedures itself should count as evidence of lack of rationality, since by definition these are goods an adult person will want no matter what else he or she may want. However, a qualification is necessary concerning parental responsibility to require that children undergo procedures necessary to secure or maintain primary goods. (Where secondary consent is involved the wishes of the child should prevail, since, by definition, secondary consent is consent for the child's own wishes to be fulfilled.) This qualification will apply to children below, but near the age of majority: when the child has taken steps to demonstrate independence of the parent, such as marriage, establishment of separate domicile, or economic self-support, such responsibility no longer rests on the parent, and a corresponding set of rights to consent or withhold consent is conferred on the child.

Those who are adults by either or both standards may renounce primary goods—just as an individual may turn down an inherited fortune, or a Jehovah's Witness refuse a blood transfusion. Parental responsibility ends when the weight of evidence shows that the means for making such momentous decisions have been conferred.

Acknowledgments

The author is especially grateful to Ruth Macklin for careful criticisms of earlier drafts of this chapter.

Children's Rights, Parental Rights, Family Privacy, and Family Autonomy

MARGARET O'BRIEN STEINFELS

Over the past two decades there have been vigorous challenges to the traditional belief that parents can fairly represent their children's interests. A series of contentious public discussions, important legal decisions, and thoroughgoing ethical reexaminations have questioned this traditional consensus and suggested in its stead a policy acknowledging the independent interests of children—interests that can be in conflict with those of their parents. It is further proposed that when in conflict these interests should be adjudicated

MARGARET O'BRIEN STEINFELS • The Hastings Center, Hastings-on-Hudson, New York 10706.

by the state or professional representatives of the child's interest—physicians, judges, social workers, teachers, psychiatrists.

The contentious nature of family life is at least as old as recorded history; Sophocles, the authors of Genesis, and Shakespeare recorded family conflict in exquisite and painful detail. But only in the last decade did anyone imagine that a full-scale public policy could be mounted to manage the sometimes divergent interests of parents and child. In contrast, the child welfare measures developed over the last century to limit child labor, to provide education, to ensure financial support for dependent children, and to prevent neglect and abuse were intended to protect, restore, or maintain the child within the family. The conflict of interest between parents and children often implied by the passage of such measures was never openly acknowledged. That has now changed.

In a variety of forums, claims are now made for children's rights and children's liberation on the grounds of inherent conflict between parents and children. A number of explanations have been advanced for this shift in emphasis. Analogies to the civil rights movement and the women's movement point to the minority and thus oppressed status of children; analyses of family breakdown expose the vulnerability of children when parents separate or divorce; a critique of the feminist struggle for social, economic, and reproductive rights has suggested a hidden conflict of interests between children and their traditional protectors, women.[1] The argument that follows from these explanations supposes important disjunctions in the interests of mother and child, child and family, and concludes that the state has an obligation to

[1]Beatrice Gross and Ronald Gross, eds., *The Children's Rights Movement: Overcoming the Oppression of Young People* (Garden City, N.Y.: Anchor Books, 1977), esp. Sections 2 and 3; Hillary Rodham, "Children under the Law," *Harvard Educational Review* 43 (1973): 487–514; Sheila M. Rothman, *Woman's Proper Place* (New York: Basic Books, 1978), pp. 267–289.

adjudicate the ensuing conflicts, particularly in order to protect the interests of the now defenseless child.

The increase in child protection services, in abuse and neglect statutes, in claims for children's rights in courts and elsewhere have signaled a shift in the long-standing reluctance of the state and society to intervene in the parent–child relationship except in extreme and life-threatening situations. This shift has been marked by a series of Supreme Court decisions establishing that, in some areas, minors like adults have rights protected by the Constitution—rights that neither parents nor the state can override, and that the state must protect.[2]

Although the full measure of constitutional rights has not been extended to minors, the assumption that minors have no protection under the Constitution has been decisively rebutted. These changes in law and social policy inevitably raise the question: Who speaks for the helpless? Proxy consent in medicine and medical research has become suspect like all other areas where parents have traditionally represented their child's interests. Who should give consent? The parent? The child? A third party? When is it necessary? Is proxy consent a viable notion for adolescents, or is it an outworn form of paternalism? What role should the state or professional play in arbitrating these questions?

In examining some of these issues, I want to look at the consequences of these legal and social policy modifications, point out the ethical dilemmas that follow from them, and explore some ways for resolving those dilemmas. First, we need, in summary form, to look at a representative sample of the changes that have occurred in law and social policy. Second, the competing claims of children's rights and parental authority need to be explicated. Third, privacy—the tradi-

[2]*In re* Gault, 87S. Ct. 1428 (1967); Tinker v. Des Moines Independent Community School District, 89 S. Ct. 733 (1969); Carey v. Population Services International, 97 S. Ct. 2010 (1977); Planned Parenthood of Central Missouri v. Danforth, 96 S. Ct. 2831 (1976).

tional defense against state intervention in family affairs—has double-edged consequences that need to be examined. Finally, the overlapping concepts of family autonomy and family responsibility will be explored as one means of resolving some of the key issues in the contest over proxy consent.

CHANGES IN THE LAW AND PUBLIC POLICY

The tensions of the present situation are starkly posed by *Bellotti v. Baird,* a 1979 Supreme Court decision, in which Justice Louis Powell wrote for the plurality:

> Unquestionably, there are many competing theories about the most effective way for parents to fulfill their central role in assisting their children on the way to responsible adulthood. While we do not pretend any special wisdom on this subject, we cannot ignore that central to many of these theories, and deeply rooted in our nation's history and tradition, is the belief that the parental role implies a substantial measure of authority over one's children. . . .
>
> Properly understood, then, the tradition of parental authority is not inconsistent with our tradition of individual liberty; rather, the former is one of the basic presuppositions of the latter. Legal restrictions on minors, especially those supportive of the parental role, may be important to the child's chances for the full growth and maturity that make eventual participation in a free society meaningful and rewarding.[3]

The Court's fulsome praise of parental authority in *Bellotti* accompanied an opinion that finally concluded that parental and judicial oversight of a minor's decision to have an abortion was unconstitutional. The effort to resolve the question of who should consent for a minor's abortion—the minor herself, the parents, or a court—stemmed from an earlier Court decision, *Danforth* (1976), which declared the requirement of parental consent in minor abortions unconstitutional, but left unclear whether all minors were sufficiently mature to con-

[3]Bellotti v. Baird, 99 S. Ct. 3035 (1979).

sent themselves and, if not, who could or should provide proxy consent for them.[4] The Massachusetts statute struck down in *Bellotti* was one effort to solve that problem through legislation. The Supreme Court was clearly aware of the lacunae left in the law, and the justices speculated at some length on appropriate and constitutional means to ensure proper consent by the minor and to encourage parental consultation voluntarily by the minor. They saw the abortion decision as an important one, referring to it as a momentous decision, one that they recognized many minors would make (or not make) in an unexamined and perhaps not totally voluntary manner. Nevertheless, the justices saw the turn to arbitration by local courts as unduly burdensome to the right of a woman, even though a minor, to seek an abortion.

In *Parham*, another 1979 case, contesting the right of parents to commit children to state mental hospitals without a judicial hearing, the Court responded in apparent contradiction to *Danforth* and *Bellotti*:[5] "Most children, even in adolescence, simply are not able to make sound judgments concerning many decisions, including their need for medical care or treatment. Parents can and must make those judgments." In fact, in *Parham*, as in *Danforth* and *Bellotti*, the controlling person, the gatekeeper, becomes the medical professional involved: in abortion decisions, the obstetrician; in psychiatric commitments, the psychiatrist. "What is best for a child is an individual medical decision that must be left to the judgment of physicians in each case."[6]

This gatekeeping function is not nearly so neutral or merely so technical as the phrase would imply. In fact, it empowers the physician to act as guardian of the child's interests insofar as those interests fall within the scope of the physician's medical knowledge. In addition, the child's interests may also be subject to the physician's personal values,

---

[4]Danforth.
[5]Parham v. J. R., 99 S. Ct. 2493 (1979).
[6]Ibid.

covertly expressed as matters of professional opinion. In such circumstances, we would want to ask why the nonmedical interests of the physician should prevail over those of the parents. This difficulty is tacitly acknowledged in Justice Steven's dissent in *Danforth:*

> Even doctors are not omniscient; specialists in performing abortions may incorrectly conclude that the immediate advantages of the procedure outweigh the disadvantages which a parent could evaluate in better perspective. In each individual case factors much more profound than a mere medical judgment may weigh heavily in the scales. The overriding consideration is that the right to make the choice be exercised as wisely as possible.[7]

Beyond this gatekeeping role there is the traditional and well-established authority of physicians to care for the child's interests while under medical care. Thus, even with parental proxy consent, the ability of the parents to protect a child's interests while under medical care may be quite limited. For example, parents, short of court action, may be unable to withdraw their consent when they believe that the physician is no longer protecting the child's interests, medical or otherwise. The following account suggests some of the barriers parents may face.

> Andrew was born at Community Hospital in our town on December 17, 1976, at a gestational age of 24½ weeks and a weight of 800 grams. . . . He was admitted to the Pediatric Hospital Center weighing 600 grams . . . was placed on a respirator against our wishes and without our consent on January 13, and remained dependent on the respirator until he was finally permitted to die on the evening of June 14. . . .
>
> Whose interests were really served by this six months of imposed hospitalization? Certainly not Andrew's. He had the misfortune of being declared "salvageable" (the ICU's word) by people who knew neither how to "salvage" him nor when or how to stop. Certainly not ours. . . . It seems clear to us that

---

[7]Danforth, Steven's dissent; see Paul Ramsey, *Ethics at the Edge of Life* (New Haven: Yale University Press, 1978), pp. 20–23, for a discussion of Steven's dissent.

all the benefits in this case went to Pediatric Hospital and its staff. The medical students got a chance to broaden their education by working with a baby with malfunctions of virtually every system of his body, the specialists took part in some "interesting consults" and gathered some data, and the hospital collected the mind-boggling sum of $102,303.20 from our insurance company.[8]

Nor are medical settings the only place where, in preference to parents, a profession is empowered to define and protect a child's interest. For example, during the 1960s, all fifty states passed legislation requiring that physicians, teachers, and other child care professionals report suspected cases of child abuse. The instatement in some communities of twenty-four-hour "hot lines" and child protection officers was meant to encourage greater reporting by the public. Certainly the lives and well-being of some children were protected by these measures. It is also the case that the lives of some families and their children were unnecessarily intruded on. A minor intrusion on some families might be warranted, if there were well-drawn benefits to those who require and receive protection. But as Rosenfeld and Newberger, two physicians expert in this area of child welfare, point out:

> As the statutory basis for this protection has rapidly evolved in the last two decades, there have developed neither clear-but legal guidelines for family intervention nor a scientific foundation for protective service work. The lack of a rigorous, practical and theoretical framework for law and for clinical practice has created a muddled and perplexing situation for professionals concerned with the health and welfare of children.[9]

According to a recent Carnegie Foundation report, *The Unexpected Minority: Handicapped Children in America*, a similar

---

[8]Robert Stinson and Peggy Stinson, "On the Death of a Baby," *Atlantic Monthly*, August 1979, pp. 64–72.

[9]Alvin A. Rosenfeld and Eli H. Newberger, "Compassion vs. Control: Conceptual and Practical Pitfalls in the Broadened Definition of Child Abuse," in *Critical Perspectives on Child Abuse*, ed. Richard Bourne and Eli H. Newberger (Lexington, Mass.: Lexington Books, 1979), p. 81.

problem occurs with the professionals who deal with handicapped children.[10] Empowered to act as gatekeepers and providers of service, their lack of familiarity and immediate knowledge of a handicapped child may incapacitate them to meet the interest of that child at the same time as their control over resources and services will frustrate and undermine parental efforts to secure appropriate care and treatment.[11]

In a similar vein, children in foster care may find themselves removed from their families to protect their health and well-being. Having acted in the children's interest in removing them from their presumably inadequate parents, foster care agencies keep children in temporary placements that all too often become indefinite stays, neither restoring the child to its own family nor finding a permanent home for adoption.[12]

These examples are drawn to emphasize two points: (1) in turning to professionals as possible alternatives to parental representation of a child's interests, courts and legislators may find as many perplexing issues raised as solved, since professionals may lack the resources, skills, and intimate knowledge of the child necessary to represent and meet his or her interests; and (2) the debate over proxy consent in medical therapy and research is an integral part of a larger debate over fair representation of a child's interests—a debate that may be resolved ultimately without particular reference to the limits and possibilities of the medical setting.

Thus the potent challenge raised to the traditional consensus that the family, whether in harmony or conflict, should be treated as a single unit necessarily bonded together by biological, psychological, and economic ties has led to reforms that may prove as troublesome as the difficulties they were

[10]John Gliedman and William Roth, *The Unexpected Minority: Handicapped Children in America* (New York: Harcourt, Brace, Jovanovich), 1979.

[11]Rosalyn Benjamin Darling, *Families against Society: A Study of Reactions to Children with Birth Defects* (Beverly Hills, Calif.: Sage Publications, 1979).

[12]David Fanshel and Eugene B. Shinn, *Children in Foster Care: A Longitudinal Investigation* (New York: Columbia University Press, 1978).

meant to remedy. In modifying the view that law and social policy should give parents the benefit of the doubt in representing their children's interests, even when that assumption is tested by deviant parental behavior, we ought to look carefully and critically at the consequences.

One place to begin looking is Justice William Douglas's dissenting opinion in *Wisconsin v. Yoder*, a case involving the right of Amish parents to terminate their children's education in public schools at the eighth grade.

> On this important and vital matter of education, I think the children should be entitled to be heard. While the parents, absent dissent, normally speak for the entire family, the education of the child is a matter on which the child will often have decided views. He may want to be a pianist or an astronaut or an oceanographer. To do so he will have to break from the Amish tradition.
>
> It is the future of the student, not the future of the parents, that is imperiled by today's decision. If a parent keeps his child out of school beyond the grade school, then the child will be forever barred from entry into the new and amazing world of diversity that we have today. The child may decide that that is the preferred course, or he may rebel. It is the student's judgment, not his parents', that is essential if we are to give full meaning to what we have said about the Bill of Rights and of the right of students to be masters of their own destiny. If he is harnessed to the Amish way of life his entire life may be stunted and deformed. The child, therefore, should be given an opportunity to be heard before the State gives the exemption which we honor today.[13]

The logic of Douglas's critique and those who share it then follows: it is in the child's interest for the state to establish childrearing boundaries, especially with regard to parental preferences and behavior, with those limits to be set and monitored by public institutions such as schools and hospitals. Where the parents appear to transgress those limits, state intervention or adjudication is required. The social policy that would have followed from Douglas's view, had it been in the

---

[13]Wisconsin v. Yoder, 92 S. Ct. 1326 (1972).

majority, would have required that school officials be allowed to ask every Amish child whether or not he or she wished to go on to high school and then to ensure such attendance in every case where the child said yes. This, in the face of court testimony that the alternate system provided by the Amish, although different, was in many respects as good as that provided by the school district. The disruptions to family, community, and ultimately the children themselves were such a policy implemented are not hard to imagine. The constraints on the lives of the families and children were the children to continue to live in the Amish community while attending public high school could hardly operate in the interest of the child and would ultimately raise the question of whether parents and community had any legal obligation at all to support this choice.

Although the challenge of this new critique stems from a complex web of historical, legal, and political conditions that cannot be fully developed here, it is important to point out that part of this intractable debate over parental authority and children's rights is built into our legal and political system. There is a deep contradiction between the political theory underlying our law with its impulse to protect individuals by an appeal to rights, and the biological and psychological requirements for successfully rearing children to participate as adults in such a polity. In effect, one of the most perplexing questions raised by these changes is whether the efforts to extend the rights of citizens to minors will not inhibit and undermine the kind of parental authority and family autonomy necessary to foster the qualities and virtues adult citizens must possess and be able to exercise in our society.

CHILDREN'S RIGHTS, PARENTS' RIGHTS, AND PARENTAL AUTHORITY

There are, logically speaking, three ways to describe the relationship between parents and children: (1) the parents' desires and authority are dominant and the child has no interests apart from those of the parents; (2) parents have duties and responsibilities to the child that have as their ultimate goal raising that child to fulfill some religiously, socially, or professionaly agreed-on ideal state that may not necessarily represent the direct self-interests of either parent or child; and (3) the child has individual interests and needs that must be given consideration and expression apart from those of parents or other definers of children's interests. Although this typology has representative examples in contemporary American society, it more accurately describes the historical movement from an era of patriarchal family life to our own with its emphasis on individual rights and self-development. And quite clearly, the third view inspires most children's rights advocates who act, in part, as a reaction against the first two views and, in part, as the result of new theories about child development.

The first view sees the parent–child relationship as dominated by parental interests and authority, which may entail fairly rigorous subordination of the child to the family's economic and social interests; favor loyalty to the kinship network over interpersonal relationships; assign adult roles by ascription rather than achievement; and insist on arranged marriages. The full historical picture of this patriarchal system is only now to be filled in and may prove to be less grim and cold than previously believed. Nevertheless, the image of the all-powerful parent lives vividly in our imaginations, fairy tales, and literature: Freud's tribal leader of the primal horde against whom the sons rise up; the transmuted figure of the wicked stepmother in "Cinderella" and "Hansel and Gretel"; the vicious Murdstones in *David Copperfield*. These archetypal figures are the embodiment of what many children's rights advocates battle against—unbridled parental authority, dominance, and injustice in instances ranging from etiquette ("Children should be seen and not heard") to economics (the exploitation of children's labor on farms and in factories).

The second view, which Stone has called the "restricted patriarchal nuclear family," emphasizes the duties and obligations of parents to raise the children they bring into the world for some larger goal, a greater end than simple loyalty and obedience.[14] In addition, they ought to become good citizens, God-fearing men and women, wise leaders, rich men, scholars. The goals of childrearing are to go beyond the relationship itself and are ordered by broader social, religious, or economic norms. The parents are stewards of the child's interests and, in the Puritan households that Stone describes, especially are they stewards of the child's spiritual well-being. This view dispenses with the hobgoblins of the first view that children may be disposed of at the pleasure of their parents. Instead, it focuses on the obligation of the parent to benefit the child by placing the goals of childrearing in a framework larger than that of parental interests alone.

This shift in outlook may subtly alter childrearing styles, but in ways that are historically difficult to sort out. Outwardly the child may still be subject to rigorous parental demands, parental authority (now often including the mother) still may go unchallenged, and harsh punishment may continue to be meted out for disobedience. But inwardly parents see children in a different light. The child has become the subject of intense parental concern and scrutiny. Over time, the cumulative effect of this parental attentiveness has been to increase awareness and knowledge of the child's distinctive needs. Although their motivations differed, there is a great psychological resemblance between Cotton Mather's intense scrutiny of his children's souls and Jean Piaget's meticulous observations of his children's developmental patterns. Surely this resemblance is more than a felicitous analogy, for out of this second type of parent–child relationship flows the third, their common point being precisely that concentrated attentiveness peculiar to Puritan divines, students of child development, and modern parents.

The third view—the child has individual interests and needs to be given independent consideration—thus both

---

[14]Lawrence Stone, *The Family, Sex, and Marriage in England, 1500–1800* (New York: Harper & Row, 1977).

grows out of and is a reaction against the second. For, on the one hand, the nuclear family with its close bonds between mother and child has fostered the tendency to prize and nurture the individual capacities and needs of each child, contributing to the notion that each child is unique. Within the confines of the modern nuclear family this tendency leads to the belief that the child will reveal his or her own needs and interests and that parental duties lie essentially in respecting and developing the child's distinctive qualities. On the other hand, the intense emotional involvement (even overinvolvement) between parents and child that is characteristic of this constellation has itself become the object of criticism and, in my view, has fueled certain of the movements to establish children's rights and to form a children's liberation movement. R. D. Laing embodied the fervor of this outlook when he wrote:

> From the moment of birth, when the Stone Age baby confronts the twentieth century mother, the baby is subjected to these forces of violence, called love, as its mother and father . . . have been. These forces are mostly concerned with destroying most of its potentialities, and on the whole this enterprise is successful.[15]

His words confirm a strong current in our culture generally and a sentiment assumed by many in the children's rights movement: children must be saved from their parents.

Although there are narrow, but telling, differences between the children's rights and children's liberation movements, they share a vision of the child as above all an individual—an individual with his or her own personality, needs, capacities, and desires; an individual with interests independent of and potentially in conflict with parents and other family members. In this view the idea of the family as an interdependent social group is minimized in favor of one that sees the family as an aggregate of individuals bent on self-

[15]R. D. Laing, *The Politics of Experience* (New York: Ballantine Books, 1967), p. 58.

development and self-fulfillment; in short, the family is not seen as a whole with a life and meaning of its own. As we shall see, important public policy questions flow from the assumption that family members must secure their individuality primarily through assertion of individual needs.

Although the genesis of this rights–liberationist movement is to be found in the strong and negative reaction against the hothouse atmosphere of the nuclear family, its theoretical groundings lie elsewhere. They derive generally from the Enlightenment critique of traditional values and specifically from the work of Freud and Piaget—two very different yet important theoretical strands of the developmental perspective.

In particular, Piaget's minute descriptions of intellectual growth in the child and adolescent and his careful assessment of that growth as part of their developing attitudes toward rules and authority has encouraged an effort, on the part of some advocates, to develop reliable cognitive and psychological measures of maturity. Such a test might indicate the capacity of some young people to exercise greater control over, for example, their own medical care by establishing their capacity to consent to medical care. Although no such measure has actually been refined, Piaget's proposition that there is a link between the capacity for formal reasoning and moral autonomy has stimulated the search.

> After the age of 10 on the average, i.e., from the second half of the cooperative stage and during the whole of the stage when rules are codified, consciousness of rules undergoes a complete transformation. Autonomy follows upon heteronomy: the rule of a game appears to the child no longer as an external law, sacred insofar as it has been laid down by adults, but as the outcome of a free decision and worthy of respect in the measure that it has enlisted mutual consent.
>
> The psychological and educational interest of all this stands out very clearly. We are now definitely in the presence of a social reality that has rational and moral organization and is yet peculiar to childhood. Also we can actually put our finger upon the conjunction of cooperation and autonomy. . . . But the peculiar function of cooperation is to lead the child to the practice

of reciprocity, hence of moral universality and generosity in his relations with his playmates.[16]

Piaget's observations give empirical grounding to the view that the present age of majority, eighteen in most states, does not accurately reflect the capacity of many young people to speak and to act in their own interests. Thus, although Piaget's theories and observations are not easily converted into measures of maturity and from thence into policy recommendations regarding consent to medical therapies, they have clearly given backing to the challenge of rights–liberation advocates: parents alone should not be permitted to speak or consent on their children's behalf when it is possible that children can speak for themselves.

What specifically is advocated then in the name of children's rights? First, children need food, shelter, education, and psychological and physical nurturance, and they should have the right to claim these things from the state, absent a parental ability to provide them. Such an argument forms the basis for limits on proxy consent and a justification for child neglect statutes, foster care programs, programs such as Aid to Dependent Children, survivor's benefits under social security, and special education programs for handicapped children. The new dimension of the argument claims liberties for children that go beyond merely protective mechanisms that are exercised by the state to demand autonomous rights to be exercised by the child him or herself. Thus the Supreme Court has recognized certain rights to freedom of speech (*Tinker*) and to autonomous decision making about reproduction (*Carey, Danforth*), and has barred parental or state intervention in the exercise of those rights.[17] Thus to traditional "welfare" rights, civil libertarians have attempted to extend rights derived from the Bill of Rights and the Constitution and guaranteed to all adult citizens. Theirs is not an invention of rights, but an extension of well-established rights to a new "minority."

[16]Jean Piaget, *The Moral Development of the Child* (New York: Free Press, 1969), pp. 65, 70–71.
[17]Rodham.

More radical advocates—the liberationists—would invest children with new rights that go far beyond those we have been discussing. They depart substantially from welfare advocates and civil libertarians in proposing a set of rights that embody significant cultural innovations in the way children would be raised, and they embody those innovations in drastic social, economic and legal changes. A fairly complete and representative list was drawn up by psychologist Richard Farson in the form of "Birthrights."

1. The Right to Self-Determination. Children should have the right to decide the matters that affect them most directly. . . .

2. The Right to Alternative Home Environments. Self-determining children should be able to choose from among a variety of arrangements: residences operated by children, child-exchange programs, twenty-four-hour child-care centers, and various kinds of schools and employment opportunities. . . .

3. The Right to Responsive Design. Society must accommodate itself to children's size and to their need for safe space. . . .

4. The Right to Information. A child must have the right to all information ordinarily available to adults—including, and perhaps especially, information that makes adults uncomfortable.

5. The Right to Educate Oneself. Children should be free to design their own education, choosing from among many options the kinds of learning experiences they want, including the option not to attend any kind of school. . . .

6. The Right to Freedom from Physical Punishment. Children should live free of physical threat from those who are larger and more powerful than they. . . .

7. The Right to Sexual Freedom. Children should have the right to conduct their sexual lives with no more restriction than adults. . . .

8. The Right to Economic Power. Children should have the right to work, to acquire and manage money, to receive equal pay for equal work. . . .

9. The Right to Political Power. Children should have the vote and be included in the decision-making process. . . .

10. The Right to Justice. Children must have the guarantee of a fair trial with due process of law, an advocate to protect

their rights against the parents as well as the system, and a
uniform standard of detention.[18] . . .

Farson's formulation is neither the best or worst of such
efforts to catalog a comprehensive set of rights for children
in the liberationist mode. In contrast to the efforts of civil
libertarians, who limit their arguments to areas of judicial and
legislative competence and work to change the law, the liberationists regard the whole society as responsible for the
oppression of children, and it is the reform of the whole
society that is required by their "Bills."

But in confounding the language of the law with the
language of cultural criticism, they obscure the true nature
of the reforms they seek. Many people might agree that children have "The Right to Responsive Design," if it is adequate
play areas, scaled-down school furniture, and safe homes and
schools that are required. But should public transportation
systems be required to install child-sized steps and seats as
they have been required to install special lifts and seats for
the handicapped? And in what sense ought a child have the
right to self-education? A good school system tries to meet
the capabilities and limits of individual children, but no one
alone, child or adult, can truly educate him- or herself. We
must all depend on the knowledge of others, at least, for an
introduction to an unknown subject or for acquiring new information. What reason have we to assume that children pick
up arithmetic, grammar, or spelling solely by their own efforts? Either such "Bills" are purposely imprecise in an effort
to provoke reaction and thought or they are not serious. For
as they stand, they seem neither to reflect the limited capacities of children nor to reflect our world with its limited economic and social resources. In reality, law and public policy

[18]Richard Farson, "Birthrights," in Gross and Gross, pp. 325–328. For other
versions of such "Bills," see in the same volume: John Holt, "Why Not a
Bill of Rights for Children?" pp. 319–325; Youth Liberation of Ann Arbor,
"Youth Liberation Program," pp. 329–333; and the more moderate, "UN
Declaration of the Rights of the Child," pp. 333–339.

have been more guarded and realistic in the rights and liberties extended to children.

Although the claims made in court by children's rights advocates seem more modest than Farson's proposal and the actual rights granted by the courts even more limited, both views present the same kinds of tension: How far can rights be extended in the interests of protecting children from parents without fatally undermining the authority, responsibility, and affection of those who are, in most cases, their surest and best protectors? Whatever the shortcomings—and there are many—in our present family arrangements, there is no group or institution that is more likely to know a child's real interests and to be prepared to meet them than a child's own family. Thus, although it is important to provide legal protections for those children who suffer from life-threatening parental inadequacies, neglect, and abuse, it is equally important to recognize the serious inadequacies, neglect, and abuse of the state itself, and the professionals whom it hires, when they are called on to protect and speak for the helpless.[19]

Children's rights cannot be the basis on which to develop public policy concerning children and families. Instead, children's rights is a luxury that rests on the solid and often unacknowledged dependence we have, as a society, on the willingness and ability of most parents to raise the kinds of children capable of assuming the rights and responsibilities of maturity. Exercising and possessing rights cannot be the soil on which children grow, but only the flower that may signal their ripening maturity. Consequently, it is no surprise that the limited extension of rights to children has been granted to those most likely to have the maturity and competence to express them, namely, adolescents.

[19]Michael Wald, "State Intervention on Behalf of 'Neglected' Children: A Search for Realistic Standards," *Stanford Law Review* 27 (1975): 985–1040; see throughout Wald's discussion of family autonomy with regard to neglect charges. Also see Fanshel and Shinn.

Thus over the last several years there has been a steady revision downward from 21 to 18 of the age of majority in specific areas such as voting, drinking, and, to some extent, finance and credit and in specific areas of biomedicine like reproduction and experimentation.[20] What is now contested is whether the present lower limit should be generally lowered again, say to 16 or 14, as it has been in the specific area of reproduction.[21]

In summary, far broader claims for children's rights have been made than have been granted or embodied in the law. Nevertheless, there is a tension between those who argue that we have much further to go and those who ask if we have not already gone too far. Although certain practices and certain rights are clearly protected by law, they are not well established in the everyday behavior of parents and children, nor are the sociocultural and economic supports for the protection of such rights and those children who choose to exercise them presently in place. That does not mean, pace the rhetoric of some advocates, that parental rights and authority are a scourge in themselves. Ultimately the judicious exercise of parental rights and authority fosters the development of children in order that they can maturely exercise their own rights and meet their own responsibilities.

---

[20]Angela Roddey Holder, *Legal Issues in Pediatrics and Adolescent Medicine* (New York: Wiley, 1977).

[21]For a vigorous counterargument in favor of extending children's rights on the basis of a power–rights model, see David J. Rothman and Sheila M. Rothman, "The Conflict over Children's Rights," *Hastings Center Report*, June 1980, pp. 7–10. In some states, experience with a lowered drinking age has actually led to a reversal in this downward trend. In 1973 New Jersey lowered the drinking age from 21 to 18. An increase in traffic accidents and the easy availability of liquor to high school students led the state legislature in 1979 to raise the age to 19. A similar move was made by eight of 19 states that had previously lowered the age limit (*New York Times*, November 20, 1979).

PARENTAL RIGHTS AND AUTHORITY

The overwhelming weight of history, law, and moral thought has been on the side of parental rights, authority, and responsibility. And even with the limited constitutional rights now extended to children, it remains true that "the scope of effective parental power in a particular household probably is restrained more by the imagination of the parents and the efficiency of the available sanction than by the law."[22] Even John Stuart Mill, the philosopher of liberal individualism, retreated from applying his principles to minors:

> Over himself, over his own body and mind, the individual is sovereign.
>   It is, perhaps, hardly necessary to say that this doctrine is meant to apply only to human beings in the maturity of their faculties. We are not speaking of children, or of young persons below the age which the law may fix as that of manhood or womanhood. Those who are still in a state to require being taken care of by others, must be protected against their own actions as well as against external injury.[23]

In a later passage Mill specifies more exactly what is meant by the mature exercise of faculties: "Liberty, as a principle, has no application to any state of things anterior to the time when mankind have become capable of being improved by free and equal discussion."[24]

The affinity of history and Mill to our everyday experience, whether as parents or as observers of parents and children, cannot be dismissed lightly and ought, at least, to raise questions about the assumption that the exercise of parental authority precludes meeting the best interests of the child.

---

[22]Andrew Jay Kleinfeld, "The Balance of Power among Infants, Their Parents and the State," in *The Legal Rights of Children*, ed. Robert H. Brenner (New York: Arno Press, 1974).

[23]John Stuart Mill, "On Liberty," *Essential Works of John Stuart Mill* (New York: Bantam Books, 1961), p. 263.

[24]Ibid., p. 264.

Thus Bluestein argues:

> We start with the assumption that child rearers have certain duties to care for, educate, and socialize their children. The successful discharge of these duties requires the child's active cooperation or at least non-interference with the rearers' endeavors. Therefore, the child has duties to facilitate and not to interfere with the rearers' reasonable efforts to discharge their duties.[25]

Underlying the common argument is the recognition that the child's long-term interest will only be met if parents fulfill their duties and responsibilities and that therefore the child's cooperative efforts to meet parental requirements are in the child's long-term best interests even if, as in the case of eating spinach, or in more serious matters like school attendance and sexual activity, they seem to be against a child's immediate desires.

Further implicit critiques are raised in this vein when the query is made: "Who will do the job of parenting if parents don't do it, and how will it be done?" For example, can the state meet the long-term best interests of the child and the needs of a liberal polity in the area where it already exercises great influence—the public education system? No. As Guttmann argues:

> So long as secular standards of education are as constricting as some forms of private, religious education, a liberal state cannot rightly mandate an exclusively secular education for children. . . . If no educational system devised (or even conceived) has the capacity for teaching children to make strictly rational choices as adults, the presumption of a liberal society must be that parents retain the nonpaternalistic freedom to influence —perhaps even to determine—what are (in the strict sense of the word) prejudices of their children, until they become capable of their own judgment.[26]

---

[25]Jeffrey Bluestein, "Child Rearing and Family Interests," in *Having Children*, ed. Onora O'Neill and William Ruddick (New York: Oxford University Press, 1979), p. 120; see also Chapter 7, this volume.

[26]Amy Gutmann, "Children, Paternalism and Education: A Liberal Argument," *Philosophy and Public Affairs* 9:4 (Summer, 1980), pp. 338–358.

This argument can be taken further, and has been. In an essay provocatively subtitled "Abandoning Youth to Their Rights," Hafen argues that the liberal state could not survive under a regime of children's rights:

> The individual tradition is at the heart of American culture. Yet the fulfillment of individualism's promise of personal liberty depends, paradoxically, upon the maintenance of a set of corollary traditions that require what may seem to be the opposite of personal liberty: submission to authority, acceptance of responsibility, and the discharge of duty. The family tradition is among the most essential corollaries to the individual tradition, because it is in families that both children and parents experience the need for and the value of authority, responsibility, and duty in their most pristine forms.[27]

These philosphical and legal arguments do not derive their effectiveness solely from an uncommon degree of common sense, but certainly their appeal to observable facts lends them great persuasive power. First, the great physical and psychological needs of infancy and childhood make some constellation of interested and attentive adults, usually the parents, biological or adoptive, a necessity for the care and nurture of children. Second, what alternative do we have? No state, whether collectivist like the Soviet Union and China, or individualistic like the United States or the West European nations, has yet managed to develop an institutional means that succeeded over the long term in raising children as well as could their own parents. Short-lived experiments, whether in nature or by design, either have not succeeded or have not sustained themselves long enough to become a resource even for a very small number of children.

Where out of necessity the state or professionals acting at its behest have had to act in place of parents in cases of

---

[27]Bruce C. Hafen, "Children's Liberation and the New Egalitarianism: Some Reservations about Abandoning Youth to Their 'Rights,' " *Brigham Young University Law Review* (1976): 605, 656.

abandonment and neglect, evidence suggests that children are as easily abused and neglected by their putative defenders as by their parents. Notable examples of supplementary family care—day centers, nannies, kin networks, or the collective nurseries of the kibbutzim—all depend on allowing parents still to play a central role in their children's lives and to help form the policies that govern their physical care and social surroundings.

If parental authority is necessary, then, for the provision of the child's physical, social, and emotional well-being and the protection of the child's interests, is there any need at all for children's rights? Clearly the law must provide some protective measures where parental neglect or failure to act in a child's interests presents life-threatening situations. However, I agree with Joseph Goldstein in his Chapter 5 that the state and its professional surrogates are a problematic alternative to parental care and that the line drawn to protect children ought to be drawn at a point that tolerates a great degree of parental discretion.[28] Nevertheless, there will be children who need protection and who should receive it.

But this view points to another tension between children's rights and parental authority that needs further scrutiny; it is the tension that arises not from the misuse of parental authority, but from the uncritical promotion and exercise of children's rights. Where law and social policy join with a general cultural permissiveness in treating children, and adolescents, as if they were capable of autonomous decision making when, in fact, many are not, we are, in effect, forcing the helpless to speak for themselves. Indeed, we are abandoning children to their rights. It is here, I believe, that the greatest ambiguity lies in judging the consequences of extending rights to children.

[28]See Chapter 5, this volume. See also, for Goldstein's general theory, *Beyond the Best Interests of the Child* (New York: Free Press, 1979). The latter was written with Anna Freud and Albert J. Solnit.

FAMILY PRIVACY

The protection of the family and parent–child bonds from incursions by the state has not depended solely or even primarily on arguments about parental authority or rights. Another important factor, certainly in the United States, has been constitutional protection of privacy. The views expressed in the Fifth Amendment, and greatly expanded beyond that, are deeply embedded in expectations about the inviolability of our domestic and family lives. The degree of privacy we regard as necessary for a tolerable family life in our society is a relatively modern phenomenon. In past centuries most people had relatively little privacy in either their domestic or business affairs; public and private life in some periods were practically indistinguishable. Beds were as ready centers of business as affairs of the heart; dining tables as often the center of political discourse and judicial findings as of the family feast.[29]

The historical and economic conditions that have brought us to a state of domestic and family privacy are too complex to describe here, but private quarters, protected from the eyes and ears of strangers are certainly now regarded as necessities of a decent family life. In fact, one of our society's characteristic fears is embodied in stories told of children in Nazi Germany, the Soviet Union, and, more recently, Cambodia who report to teachers and other public officials their parents' opinions and activities—a sign of the intolerance of totalitarian societies for private life and the sacrosanct boundaries of the family circle. Every American schoolchild learns early in his or her school career that one of the great transgressions

[29]For the general background of this theory, see Philippe Aries, *Centuries of Childhood: A Social History of Family Life*, trans. Robert Baldick (New York: Vintage Books, 1963). For a look at the public nature of family life in colonial America, see John Demos, *A Little Commonwealth: Family Life in Plymouth Colony* (New York: Oxford University Press, 1970). And for more detail, see *The Diary of Samuel Sewall, 1674–1729*, ed. M. Halsey Thomas (New York: Farrar, Straus & Giroux, 1973).

of the English army in colonial America was the unwarranted searches of private homes; hence the Fifth Amendment.

Recent court and legislative actions have moved to protect and reinforce that tradition of privacy, both in individual claims to liberty from state interference as well as from technological invasions of privacy by wiretaps, tape recordings, and unauthorized access to confidential medical and educational records. Complaints against unauthorized access to information center on the invasion of privacy involved in people's inability to control information about themselves, information that they would not want to become public knowledge or that they would wish to restrict to trusted friends or relatives. For "privacy is not simply an absence of information about us in the minds of others; rather it is the control we have over information about ourselves."[30]

This sense of control has many applications to family privacy. There is the privacy implied by the marital bond: spouses cannot be compelled to testify against one another in court proceedings. More recently, the Supreme Court, under the rubric of privacy, has acted to protect sexual activities and the use of contraceptives both within and outside of marital relationships.[31] Privacy is respected in childrearing practices: within limits parents make choices about schools, about medical and dental care, about discipline, about chores, and a plethora of everyday family activities. More important, they may pass on to and inculcate in their children a wide array of values, opinions, and attitudes about religion, the government, food, other people, science, and toothbrushing. Finally, privacy is implicitly extended to children by restricting authority over them to their parents (or appointed guardian), that is, children cannot be arbitrarily subject to the authority of any and all adults. In psychological terms, parents feel a great compulsion to correct their child's errant behavior in

---

[30]Charles Fried, *The Anatomy of Values* (Cambridge: Harvard University Press), p. 140.
[31]Griswold v. State of Connecticut, 85 S. Ct. 1678 (1965).

public, whereas they feel great reluctance, like most adults, to correct the behavior of children not their own.

In discussing the necessary conditions of adult friendships, Fried captures the potential threat to spouses, parents, and children if adults' lives should be subject to constant and uninvited public scrutiny.

> If we thought that our every word and deed were public, fear of disapproval or more tangible retaliation might keep us from doing or saying things which we would do or say if we could be sure of keeping them to ourselves or within a circle of those who we know approve or tolerate our tastes.[32]

We assume that the secret lives of adults are important, but children as well need freedom from total scrutiny in order to develop as persons, at first in distinction from their parents, then from other adults, and finally sometimes from their playmates and schoolmates.

Similarly, parents cannot be subject to the constant scrutiny and correction of outsiders if they are to carry out their childrearing responsibilities with any degree of confidence. Recent critiques of the relationship between family and society have subtly played on this theme of privacy and extended it beyond mere physical scrutiny and invasion to include the more diffuse influences of various professionals (like educators, psychiatrists, and social workers) and of various childrearing theories. In what he labels "the proletarianization of parenthood," Lasch argues that

> We . . . have paid too little attention to the way in which public policy, sometimes conceived quite deliberately not as a defense of the family at all but as an invasion of it, contributed to the deterioration of domestic life. The family did not simply evolve in response to social and economic influences; it was deliberately transformed by the intervention of planners and policymakers.[33]

---

[32]Fried, p. 141.

[33]Christopher Lasch, *Haven in a Heartless World: The Family Besieged* (New York: Basic Books, 1977), p. 13.

Lasch's criticisms may push the invasion-of-privacy metaphor too far, yet they make a telling point. What we mean to protect by family privacy is not simply the physical space in which the family dwells, but the historical, cultural, and psychological space in which it lives and grows. Without privacy the family could not express and practice its particular and unique values and ideas; without privacy parents could not foster in themselves or their children those basic human qualities of trust and affection that facilitate the ability to engage in deep and important social relationships both within the family and outside of it.[34]

THE DILEMMA OF PRIVACY

Any discussion of privacy must acknowledge the troublesome and paradoxical nature of its effects; such is particularly the case with family privacy. For one of the consequences of sequestering its particular, unique, and idiosyncratic values and ideas behind the veil of privacy is to bar or to restrict their appearance in public places—a situation nourished by our belief that certain values should not be the object of public conflict. Although we regularly celebrate the heterogeneity of our population and the pluralism of our values, in fact, as a society we have little tolerance for the conflict that this heterogeneity and pluralism might bring if they were fully expressed in public life. For one way in which we manage both to have a diversity of values in our society and yet not incessantly quarrel about them is to extrude from public life certain values, behaviors, and ideas that we label private.

Religion is the most traditional and notable example of this practice, but as our society is increasingly secularized, many moral and civic values too are relegates to the private

---

[34]Joseph Bensman and Robert Lilienfeld, *Between Public and Private: The Lost Boundaries of the Self* (New York: Free Press, 1979), p. 110.

sphere. For example, a whole range of what are now referred
to as self-regarding behaviors, such as the use of intoxicants,
sexual relationships, sexual orientation, and marital status
have been in earlier periods of our history the subject of stiff
legal regulation reinforced by strong community pressures.
To a considerable degree the movement to decriminalize and
deregulate individual behaviors has been accompanied by
their desocialization; that is, the social implications of these
"private behaviors" are no longer regarded as appropriate
topics for public debate and policy, although the consequences may require public attention—for example, insurance
reimbursement for detoxification programs.

This extrusion of values from the public sphere has important consequences with regard to the family and public
policy—a situation we shall examine when we turn to the
question of family autonomy. For although we tolerate a wide
variety of family constellations and family preferences in childrearing, and, in principle, support the diversity of values
kept alive by differing family histories and traditions, we do
not live easily with the expression of those values in public
life. When, for example, the Amish of Wisconsin refuse to
send their children to the public high school because "the
high school tends to emphasize intellectual and scientific ac-
complishments, self-distinction, competitiveness, worldly
success, and social life with other students," no thought is
given to the possibility of modifying the curriculum so that
Amish children might benefit from the school along with the
non-Amish. Instead, the Amish are confirmed in their belief
that they must "take care of their own." What they cher-
ish—"informal learning through doing; a life of 'goodness,'
rather than a life of intellect; wisdom rather than technical
knowledge; community welfare, rather than competition; and
separation from, rather than integration with, contemporary
worldly society"[35]—is not seen as a contribution to the public
good.

[35]Bluestein, pp. 282–283.

Clearly our devotion to family privacy supports diversity in family life—at home—whereas it bars its expression in public life and public policy. The continuing controversy over parental notification requirements for a minor's abortion is a case in point. As a reaction to the Supreme Court decision in *Danforth* prohibiting parental consent for abortion, many states have attempted to provide for parental involvement by requiring that parents be notified of a minor's intent to have an abortion. Thus far, no state has had such legislation stand Supreme Court scrutiny. Although such notification may create difficulties for the minor and the physician willing to perform the abortion, it cannot ultimately prevent the abortion. It does allow discussion, argument, and expression of family values on the subject; values that may not, in fact, be at variance with those of an adolescent daughter. Opposition to notification requirements has centered on assertions about the minor woman's rights to decide for herself and ignored the potential support, emotional and financial, that might flow from a full and frank discussion with parents. In a culture that stigmatizes adolescent pregnancy and motherhood, we may well question the ability of a young and immature adolescent to decide for herself, especially in medical settings that strongly favor abortion and provide little prenatal support or counseling about adoption as an alternative to abortion.

An analogous point was made in a federal district court decision in Michigan concerning notification of parents about prescription of contraceptive pills for minors. In that case, *Doe* v. *Irwin*, Judge Fox argued:

> Defendants [state family planning clinic] admit that the procedures used at the Center are not aimed at determining emotional maturity of the children who seek the Center's services.. . .
>
> A state-run clinic, predisposed to prescribe contraceptives and having only minimal contact with the child, cannot and should not attempt to displace the parents' rights in such matters.
>
> . . . [T]he Center is interacting with the children of the plaintiffs in a manner which keeps the parents in total ignorance

of what is occurring. In the present case the Center is, whether
or not it is done intentionally, influencing the children of the
plaintiffs—an influence these parents find insidious and indi-
vious. . . . [T]he parents here are not put on notice as to what
these influences are and, therefore, cannot begin to exercise
their parental rights to counteract such influences in the manner
they see fit.[36]

FAMILY AUTONOMY

The word "autonomy" refers to the self-government (*au-
tonomos*) of the Greek city-states. In one of those curious twists
of language and history, "autonomy" has lost its political and
social connections, and is now coupled with the notion of the
individual person's capacity for self-rule and independence,
usually prefaced in our language with the adjective "personal" or "individual." Thus the expression "family autonomy" has a contradictory ring to it; to speak of family autonomy is to bring together two words that seem uneasy in each
other's company. But clearly "family privacy" implies some
notion of autonomy or self-rule since there otherwise would
be little concern about the consequences of state intervention
in the family. Because families have some capacity for autonomy, privacy is possible and even required. At second glance
then, the conjunction of "family" and "autonomy" is at least
not contradictory; but is it anything more than a synonym for
family privacy?

Let us think of family autonomy as the sphere of self-
regulating behavior operating among family members, and
based on an internally consistent set of rules, conscious and
unconscious, verbal and behavioral. It is too simple to equate
this rule making, as some might, with parental authority,

---

[36]Doe v. Irwin, 44 F. Supp. 1247 (1977). Also see Theodora Ooms, ed., *Teenage
Pregnancies* (Philadelphia: Temple University Press, 1981).

although notions of control and channeling are certainly part of the picture. But who does the controlling and channeling?

In an infant's first days and months, parents certainly have effective control over most aspects of a child's life—but it is control that early on will be modified by the infant's own reactions and behavior. Recent research only confirms the experience of many parents that "behavior control" is by no means exclusively in the hands of the adults of the family. Infants have compelling powers to control behavior and elicit responses in adults that can as effectively establish the modus vivendi of family life as any parental theory about infant care and childrearing. Parents are not helpless pawns in this social construction of reality, but neither are they so commanding as the uninitiated seem to believe.[37]

Whether we speak of the social construction of reality, family dynamics, or other such descriptive concepts from the behavioral or social sciences, any notion of childrearing clearly implies a notion of parentrearing as well. In short, "family autonomy" is not a covert expression for parental authority, but a label for the process by which children and parents act and react within the context of a particular set of outlooks governed by a distinct set of rules and expectations.

The most spectacular examples of these distinctive qualities often appear historically or publicly as family dynasties, whose intellectual, political, or economic power may extend over several generations. The Adams family, which gave us presidents, diplomats, writers, intellectuals, and critics, is probably our own best national example. Other notable examples of only one or two generations where parents and children or several siblings embody a unique constellation of

[37]Jerome Kagan, *The Growth of the Child: Reflections on Human Development* (New York: W. W. Norton, 1978); Marshall Klaus and John Kennell, "Care of the Mother," in *Care of the High-Risk Neonate,* ed. Marshall Klaus and Avroy Fanaroff (Philadelphia: W. B. Saunders, 1973). The phrase "social construction of reality" is from a book of that title by Peter L. Berger and Thomas Luchmann (Garden City, N.Y.: Anchor Books, 1967).

values include the James family, the Kennedys, the Reuther brothers, the Fondas. Citing these "public families" for ease of reference should not obscure the essential point about family autonomy; every family is a small and self-governing body expressing a distinct and unique way of being.

The values embodied in any family may come from religion, race, ethnicity, class, special intellectual, artistic, or manual skills, characterological or temperamental qualities, geographic setting, and occupational preferences. The unique combination of these and other factors in a family draws on and constitutes the family's history, culture, and present social organization. A given generation may embrace those values and the rules that flow from them, adapt them to larger social and economic conditions, or come to deplore them and rebel against them. Accepted or rejected, these values are central to the story of the family, and to the identity of its members; and they form the boundaries within which children will develop, mature, and themselves come to reshape the values and rules their parents pass on to them. Family autonomy is integral to that process.

When parents and children cross the domestic threshold and step into public space—hospital, school, courtroom—certain limits are placed on the expression of family autonomy; on its preferences, values, and rules. In most states, children must start school by the age of six; in many places there are no provisions for those ready to begin at four or five, and truancy laws will catch up with those who wait until eight or nine. The musically or artistically gifted child will find meager support for his or her potential in school, whereas the verbal child will be an instant success; physically or mentally handicapped children will have a hard struggle to find a place at all. The Wisconsin Amish found little to their liking in the local high school curriculum; and the youthful genius with an IQ of 150 or the natural-born auto mechanic will probably feel the same. Both puritans and hedonists are going to be troubled by sex education courses as they are now taught; as the pious Jew or Christian is annually dismayed by the sanitized celebrations of the Hannukah/Christmas season.

On the medical scene, limits on family autonomy escalate to more devastating issues. Contraceptives and abortion routinely available to adolescents without parental counsel may deeply trouble both child and parent; expeditious but inappropriate use of certain contraceptives may pose future threats to a child's fertility. Parents of a child with end-stage renal disease will be dismayed at the legal barriers to a donation by a sibling with a well-matched kidney. The technological imperatives of a pediatric intensive care unit may overwhelm a family's capacity to care for and comfort a sick or dying child.

These examples of the trivial and the tragic do not automatically prove that family autonomy is unreasonably limited in public places; they do suggest its extensiveness and hint at the legitimations that are offered for limits on its scope. Any given example will, for reasons of efficiency, public tranquillity, or individual rights, prove defensible, perhaps even be legally required. Indeed, most families welcome medical services, education, and therapies that support and help their children. Furthermore, society rightly takes an interest in providing those services in order to develop the potential of its future citizens. But, amid these arguments for limits on family autonomy and the concomitant legitimations for state and professional interventions in childrearing, critical questions ought to be asked: Who is doing the public childrearing? Whose values operate? What values and preferences are embodied in the rules we adopt as public policy?

A full answer to those questions would require a multivolume inquiry into the nature of professions, the values they espouse, and the bureaucratic expression of those values in public policy and in institutions. But briefly, the professions (teachers, judges, physicians, social workers) and the bureaucracies that service them and maintain institutions (schools, courtrooms, adoption agencies, hospitals) have become central figures in formulating policies, providing ser-

vices, and advocating change on behalf of children.[38] Parents
have very little control over these professions or institutions;
children have none.

As a result, in the domain of public childrearing, family
autonomy, family responsibility, and family values are restricted while professional, bureaucratic, and institutional
definitions and values are extended. If the chief virtue in
policy making of these latter values is that they favor the
abstract, the general, and the norm, then their chief vice is
that they ignore what is individual and distinctive—precisely
those qualities most needed to meet a child's best interests
and most likely to be known and appreciated by the child's
family.

A defense of family autonomy is not then simply a preference for the maintenance of parental authority, although
it is that, too. More important issues are at stake—that of the
capacity for parenting itself and the willingness to discern and
meet the particular best interests of *this* child, *my* child. Whatever conscious and unconscious motives men and women
may have for bearing and rearing children, their willingness
to assume responsibility for what will be a long-term and
sometimes onerous task rests on the assumption that they
will have control over and responsibility for their child's best
interests. The precise details of a child's individual well-being
will be defined by all those factors I enumerated earlier. The
intimate knowledge parents have of their children, in fact,
makes them uniquely qualified to meet the particular best
interests of each child, as well as those general needs that
must be met for all children. In addition, as children mature,
they subtly and not so subtly become partial definers of their

[38]Kenneth Kenniston, *All Our Children: The American Family under Pressure*
(New York: Harcourt, Brace, Jovanovich, 1977). This book, a product of the
Carnegie Council on Children, seems resigned to these facts and refers to
the parents' role vis-à-vis professionals as "The Weakened Executive," pp.
16–23.

own best interests—a process that gradually augments and corrects the parents' definition.

One of the responsibilities parents feel most keenly is the transmission to the next generation of a set of values that express their sense of what it means to be human, what is to be valued in human interactions. In no society has that ever been a totally harmonious process and in our own it is possibly less harmonious than in most. With us, however, the danger is not that children will be overwhelmed by the dictates and values of their parents, but that an excessive and uncritical emphasis on children's rights and liberation in public policy, in the law, and in the culture in general will undermine the capacity and confidence of parents to pass on their distinctive view of life and in so doing to meet the particular best interests of individual children.

CONCLUSION: FAMILY AUTONOMY IN THE MEDICAL SETTING

Law, social policy, and general cultural attitudes are increasingly limiting family autonomy. Our traditional paternalistic view of children and adolescents has given way to advocacy for increased individual rights and greater personal autonomy. In deference to the strong antipaternalistic views now current, we encourage and rely on minors to act on their own behalf, often without due attention to the social and moral contexts in which they live.

Throughout this chapter I have drawn examples from medicine to illustrate this argument and have pointed out a variety of subtle and not so subtle ways that health care policy and professionals may act to limit family autonomy. Because physicians have always maintained a rather paternalistic stance toward their patients, adult and child, and because of legal constraints placed on the medical care of children, the response to demands for children's rights has been guarded.

Thus, whereas medical professionals may show little enthusiasm for family autonomy as I have defined it, they are also unlikely to become ardent advocates for children's rights in medical decision making. As a result, medical settings, more than other settings, could potentially develop a more complex view of the matter—one that in some circumstances might more clearly support and enhance family autonomy. A brief examination of four areas in medicine will illustrate my point: trauma due to abuse, critical-care medicine for acutely ill children, gynecologic care for adolescents, and medical research.

Increased consciousness of child abuse in tandem with legislation requiring health care personnel to report suspected cases to the authorities initially had the effect of turning up more abused children. More recently, greater clinical and research attention has been given to the abusive parent. A recent volume edited by two physicians, *Critical Perspectives on Child Abuse*, examines both sides of the issues; that is, both the need to protect the child from further injury or death, and the need to protect a viable parent–child relationship from unnecessary or ultimately destructive disruption. Although the authors are pessimistic about finally resolving the problem within the limited purview of medicine or social welfare, what emerges is a far more sophisticated view than usual of the ingredients for a potential solution:

> We physicians face a dilemma with respect to cases of child abuse. We have an ethical obligation to intervene in situations where a child's life may be in danger. Yet the technologic tools of intervention can be incompetent or destructive. Fortunately, there is evidence that specific, vigorous activity directed at the causes of an individual family's particular crisis can make a difference in the safety of a child in jeopardy.
>
> Physicians and medical institutions can work toward making public agencies' activities with regard to children more adequate to the task of sustaining families.[39]

---

[39]Eli H. Newberger, "The Myth of the Battered Child Syndrome," in Rosenfeld and Newberger, p. 18.

In critical-care medicine, decision making usually centers on questions of treatment: to treat, not to treat, and to withdraw treatment. Certain childhood cancers, life-threatening genetic anomalies, extreme prematurity, asphyxiation in the newborn period, and serious trauma following accidents all represent situations where medical prognosis is uncertain. Rapid advances in medical knowledge and technology mean that medical criteria for treatment are ambiguous in the extreme. Parents and physicians may well disagree about treatment. Where physicians have little medical ground on which to stand, why should the physician's decision to treat or not treat prevail over the views of the parents, since other than medical criteria are clearly at work?[40]

The Stinson case cited earlier suggests that parents may more easily see the suffering of a child and the hopelessness of its condition than the physician bent on an all-out technological effort to prolong life. In their article the Stinsons raise directly the question of who ought to have been their child's advocate. Who most clearly saw his best interests?

> We recognize that there are very real legal and ethical problems in the area of consent for medical treatment when children are involved. We were told repeatedly that "someone must be the child's advocate." But how is it possible to be sure in a case like Andrew's just what that means? Who can determine whether or at what point the child's true advocate is the person proclaiming his right to life or the person proclaiming his right to death? We felt that we as the child's parents were more likely to have feelings of concern for his suffering than the necessarily detached medical staff busy with scores of other cases and "interesting" projects.
>
> However, the "someone" who became our child's self-appointed advocate was the attending physician of the ICU. It was argued that we were not the baby's advocates but merely the parents' advocates. By that logic, why are Drs. Farrell, Craft, and Carvalho not recognized as the doctors' advocates? For it is useless to pretend that there was ever such a thing as an objective advocate of Andrew's rights. Is any neonatologist,

---

[40]Robert M. Veatch, "The Technical Criteria Fallacy," *Hastings Center Report*, August 1977, pp. 15–16.

who has, in addition to his ethical commitments as a human being, a professional interest in a baby's problems, a pride in his expertise and in the statistics of success in his unit, and concerns about protecting his reputation in the eyes of his associates, really the right person to be trusted as the baby's sole advocate?[41]

Other infants, whom physicians may have little inclination to treat—those with serious genetic anomalies or brain damage—may have parents who think treatment is warranted, and whose views ought to be respected insofar as medical means are feasible. Darling, in interviews with the parents of retarded children, found that parents often had difficulty in securing even routine medical care for their children: "One mother noted that whenever her severely handicapped son (now ten years of age) was ill, she had to fight to get treatment for him against the advice of physicians who believed he should be allowed to die."[42]

Yet, in some medical settings, other standards are in effect—ones far more attentive to the family. Duff, a pediatrician, counsels:

Professionals must work together as allies with children and families in a collegial atmosphere of respectful, supportive interdependence. . . .

. . . Generally, the choices should be made in accordance with the values of the child, his family, the physician of record, and others on the team in that order of importance.[43]

More ambiguous problems arise in the case of burdensome treatments that are unlikely to be curative. The prohibition against blood transfusions among Jehovah's Witnesses has regularly been overturned in the case of children. Physicians seek court orders that are routinely granted. Indeed, where these measures will save the life of the child such

[41]Stinson and Stinson, p. 68.

[42]Rosalyn Benjamin Darling, "Parents, Physicians, and Spina Bifida," *Hastings Center Report*, August 1977, p. 11.

[43]Raymond S. Duff, "Guidelines for Deciding Care of Critically Ill or Dying Patients," *Pediatrics* 64 (1979): 17–23.

intervention is warranted. Recent discussions in the pediatric literature have raised questions about this policy in treating certain childhood cancers. One medical group has reported a small number of cancer cases where the medical prognosis for survival was bleak. They asked themselves whether they ought to seek a court order. Was the potential rupture in the relationship between parents and child, and between the family and the physicians, worth the very small chance of prolonging the life of a terminally ill child? In those limited circumstances, they argued, it was more important to forgo court action and to acknowledge the family's religious values.[44]

The case of "Karen" offers another example of medical attentiveness to family values. Karen was a sixteen-year-old victim of kidney failure. An extended course of treatment that included first dialysis and then transplantation of one of her father's kidneys left Karen feeling ill, depressed, and ultimately unwilling to continue treatment. Karen and her parents agreed not to allow replacement of an infected shunt, thus making dialysis impossible. Angered by her decision, the medical staff first considered seeking a court order, but finally refrained after they came to accept the decision and the fact that Karen and her parents foresaw only a life of suffering and pain for her on dialysis, to which death was preferable. Although Karen's age and maturity made her the primary decision maker, it is clear that her family's support of that decision influenced the medical staff.[45]

These examples from critical-care medicine suggest the ways in which medical care settings can take family values into consideration, supporting family autonomy without violating either the rights of the child or the authority of the parents.

---

[44]Laurence Frankel, Catherine Damme, and Jan Van Eys, "Childhood Cancer and the Jehovah's Witness Faith," *Pediatrics* 60 (1977): 916–21. Terence Ackerman, "The Limits of Beneficence: Jehovah's Witnesses and Childhood Cancer," *Hastings Center Report*, August 1980, pp. 13–18.

[45]John E. Schowalter, "The Adolescent Patient's Decision to Die," *Pediatrics* 51 (1973): 97–103.

Gynecologic care for adolescents, contraceptive devices, and abortion represent a more troubled and conflict-ridden area. The conflict stems from two sources. First, becoming sexually active is a decisive reminder to parents that their children are in the process of leaving home and leaving the family. Traditionally such moves, whatever degree of sexual involvement obtained, were carried on especially by women with potential spouses. Such is less the case now than in previous generations; sexual involvement is no longer a sign that a child is about to leave home, leave the family, or get married. The ambivalence and conflict create enormous stress for parents and adolescents alike. Second, the attempt to provide a medical solution by way of contraceptives and abortion to a social, economic, and intergenerational conflict has focused the hostilities on the issue of parental consent for contraception and abortion. The courts predictably turned this issue into a rights issue, favoring—in these cases—the privacy rights of adolescents. The ambiguity and conflict that surround the sexual activity of an unmarried adolescent at home remain unresolved. The autonomy granted the adolescent in making sex "safe" limits the family's autonomy not simply in matters of domestic life, but in the expression of values and attitudes about dating, courting, marriage, and childrearing.

Ultimately these are not matters that courts or medical personnel can resolve. Yet, in favoring the child over the parents or in excluding the parents from a role in the decision-making process, legal and medical policy has shifted the balance of power in ways that acknowledge adolescents' rights without necessarily meeting their best interests—a situation likely to prevail especially with younger adolescents. Recent efforts to provide for parental notification, especially for abortion, have attempted to redress the imbalance, and from the point of view of making room for family autonomy, such measures make sense. Their success in fostering family autonomy will depend, of course, on the ability and willingness of clinic and health care personnel to facilitate the discussion rather than exacerbate it by keeping it a conflict between children's rights and parental authority.[46]

One final model for protecting family autonomy was developed by the National Commission for the Protection of Human Subjects in its recommendations concerning research on children.[47] The present model for research on children simply requires the consent of parents (along with the usual requirements for IRB approval). The child's consent is not required. The commission suggested that seeking the parents' permission and the child's assent for research would provide greater protections as well as acknowledging the capacity for older children and adolescents to understand and acquiesce in research. In addition, it implicitly makes a place for the notion that although the generations may have different outlooks on an issue—in this case, research—it is possible to show respect and to encourage discussion by treating both parents and children as central figures in securing cooperation with researchers.

[46]Ooms.

[47]Lucy Rau Ferguson, "The Competence and Freedom of Children to Make Choices Regarding Participation in Biomedical and Behavioral Research," DHEW Publication No. (OS) 77-0005; and *Report and Recommendations*, DHEW Publication No. (OS) 77-0004, p. 5.

Return to the Best Interests of the Child

RUTH MACKLIN

THE VALUES AT STAKE

Few areas in the intersection of medicine, ethics, and law are fraught with as much uncertainty, as many inconsistencies, and as much controversy as that of the role of parents, minor children, and the state in decisions concerning medical treatment and research. Behind current practices in this area lies a history of custom and tradition in which parents were virtually the sole deciders, acting on behalf of their children's interests until the children reached the age of majority. That this parental power was not seen as absolute, however, is evident from the introduction of laws and policies designed to protect children from abuse and neglect at the hands of their own parents. Yet the assumption has remained that in

---

RUTH MACKLIN • Department of Community Health, Albert Einstein College of Medicine, Bronx, New York 10461.

spite of occasional or even frequent cases of child abuse or neglect, parents generally act in their children's best interest, and families ought to remain free from state supervention of parents' decisions about medical treatment for their own children.

A number of developments have contributed to confounding this once simple picture. One is the rise of the children's rights and children's liberation movements,[1] leading to a call for increased decision-making autonomy for adolescents and even younger children. A related development is the idea that children need advocates of some sort outside the family unit, advocates who will speak on their behalf when parents decide or act wrongly. At the same time, judicial decisions and statutes enacted in various states have lowered the age of consent for a number of medically related procedures, most notably those that involve sexuality: obtaining contraceptive devices, receiving treatment for venereal disease, and procuring abortions.[2] This situation has led to foolish inconsistencies of the sort noted by Gaylin in Chapter 1: a seventeen-year-old in New York State is not permitted to give her informed consent for donating a urine sample for the purpose of medical research, yet her eleven-year-old sister may seek an abortion and grant consent for that purpose without parental permission. Similarly, a fourteen-year-old may go to a private doctor or to a clinic and obtain treatment for venereal disease, but that same adolescent may not, without parental permission, serve as a research subject in a question-and-answer survey about the sexual practices of teenagers.

Still another recent development is an increased societal concern with a variety of issues central to bioethics: the right to refuse treatment for oneself or one's child; the need to arrive at a clear meaning of the "best-interests" doctrine; a focus on *quality* of life, in addition to older concerns about

---

[1]For the difference between these two movements, see Chapter 8.
[2]See Chapter 3.

sanctity of life; and a growing scrutiny of research practices, with the aim of protecting the rights and dignity of human subjects.

The foregoing chapters have dealt with these issues. Sometimes explicitly, but more often implicitly, they have drawn on the precepts and moral principles that underlie such issues as the right of parents to refuse life-preserving or life-prolonging treatment for their child, the appropriateness of minors as self-deciders in research and treatment contexts, and the role of the state in supervening parental decisions. In spite of the many difficulties that plague efforts on the part of parents and the state to act in accordance with the best interests of the child, I believe that doctrine remains the only sound moral basis for decisions concerning biomedical procedures for minors.

THE COMPETENCE OF MINORS AND FAMILY AUTONOMY

It is worth recalling just how these various topics are linked. The problem of minors' competence to make decisions regarding their own medical treatment or to participate as subjects of biomedical research raises one central question: Are children below the age of eighteen (sixteen in some states) psychologically competent to grant or refuse consent, despite their status as *legally* incompetent? Even if many can be considered psychologically competent, are there nevertheless good practical and social reasons for retaining a fixed chronological age, and moreover, an age that remains close to the legal majority set for other purposes? To sharpen the focus on the relation between competence and consent, we might compare the problems of third-party permission for minors with like problems of other (legally) incompetent populations: the mentally retarded, the emotionally disturbed, and the elderly who have become senile. Even if it were possible to arrive at a sound, objective criterion for psychological competence (a task most writers have despaired at even attempting), we may decide that the standard of decision-making autonomy should be different for children than for marginally competent adults. One reason might be the fact that the family unit of parents and minor children has a special status, one that ought perhaps not be jeopardized by granting children within that unit the legal right to act independently of or in opposition to their parents' judgment about what is best for them.

Although this reason may not be the only one for deciding to use different criteria to determine competence and consent for children on the one hand and for marginally competent adults on the other, it does link our first central question with the second main topic: state supervention of parental autonomy. Wherever the legal age of competence is set, cases will arise in which parents make treatment or refusal-of-treatment decisions for their children that others will deem wrong, misguided, or against the best interest of those children. Thus the question arises whether parents have the unqualified right to make those decisions, or whether legal mechanisms should be invoked on behalf of the child to override their decisions.

Also related to the question of the competence of minors is the problem of what to do when legally competent minors and their parents disagree on a matter involving treatment or participation in biomedical research. The lower the legal age of consent for minors, the more cases will occur in which parent or child brings suit against the other. All parties to the dispute live under the same roof, and furthermore, the children are still financially and psychologically dependent on their parents. Who will act as arbiter in such cases? What role should the state play? Will child be set against parent—legally as well as emotionally—in an unprecedented erosion of family unity?

Thus, although the issues surrounding the competence of children to make their own decisions about biomedical treatment and research can be addressed separately from the issues of family privacy and autonomy, both sets of concerns come together in the cluster of ethical, legal, and psychological topics explored in this book. Recognizing that to do so is somewhat artificial, I want to distinguish sharply two questions that pervade the preceding chapters. The first is, Who decides?; the second is a question about the rightness or wrongness of substantive decisions made by parents, children, or courts.

DECISION MAKING ON BEHALF OF CHILDREN: TWO VALUE QUESTIONS

"Who decides?" questions appear to be largely procedural in nature, whereas questions about the moral rightness of decisions are clearly substantive. That a question is procedural rather than substantive does not mean, however, that people do not hold strong opinions about it. Consider, for example, a particular procedure that has been adopted, in which a court order can override parents' treatment decisions regarding their minor child. A commitment to such values as family autonomy, family privacy, and family integrity is one basis for favoring a particular procedural arrangement over another. Thus the question of whether parents ought to have final say in matters concerning medical treatment of their own children, regardless of the substantive content of the parental decision, is surely a value question; but it is an entirely different question from that of the rightness or wrongness of the decision itself.

We need to examine carefully the relationships that may hold between these two different value questions, because it is easy to confuse a number of possible positions. I believe that questions about the rightness or wrongness of a decision about medical treatment, whoever makes that decision (parents, the child, a judge), are always *meaningful* questions no matter how much difficulty or uncertainty may attend the answer. Some writers, however, seem prepared to reject the meaningfulness or appropriateness of such questions once the procedural question—the "Who decides?" question—is settled. I think that position can fairly be attributed to Goldstein in Chapter 5. Although Goldstein is not wholly explicit on this matter, and his remarks are not altogether consistent, the following passage states his position clearly:

> Absent medical agreement about what treatment is indicated, or absent a societal consensus about the rightness of the predicted result of treatment, there would be no justification for disqualifying parents from (or for qualifying agents of the state for) making the difficult choice—for giving their personal meaning to "right" or to "worth living" or to "normal healthy growth." No one has a greater right or responsibility and no one can be presumed to be in a better position, and thus better equipped, than a child's parents to decide what course to pursue if the medical experts cannot agree or, assuming their agreement, if there is no general agreement in society that the outcome of treatment is clearly preferred to the outcome of no treatment. Put somewhat more starkly, how can parents in such situations give the wrong answer since there is no way of knowing the right answer? . . . Precisely because there is no objectively wrong or right answer, the burden must be on the state to establish *wrong*, not on the parent to establish that what is *right* for them is necessarily *right* for others.

Under the limiting conditions he sets out in the first sentence of this passage, Goldstein is explicit in stating his belief that "there is no objectively wrong or right answer." That belief about the subjectivity of values, at least in this domain, leads him to reject state supervention of parental decisions.

THE OBJECTIVITY OF MORAL VALUES

It appears from Goldstein's passage that the only thing that could count for him as an "objectively wrong or right answer" to these problematic value questions is society's general agreement "that the outcome of treatment is clearly preferred to the outcome of no treatment." Although general agreement in society would certainly be an *objective* way of determining rightness or wrongness, it could hardly be considered an appropriate criterion. General agreement in ancient Greek society that slavery was an acceptable and desirable social arrangement does not validate the claim that slavery was morally right in ancient Greece. It simply confirms the truth of the judgment that the Greeks generally approved of slavery, that they *believed* slavery was right. Similarly, widespread agreement in Nazi Germany that the country (and the world) would be a better place without any Jews does not morally legitimate the holocaust. It is a simple but often overlooked point that universal agreement about moral matters is, at best, *evidence* for the truth of moral judgments; all it succeeds in demonstrating is that everyone *believes* such judgments to be right or wrong, not that they *are* right or wrong.

If society's agreement about the rightness or wrongness of moral judgments, acts, or practices cannot serve as a criterion for their rightness or wrongness, what can? The vast number of writings by philosophers and others over the past several centuries have not brought us much closer to a solution to the problem of finding an appropriate criterion for the objectivity of moral judgments, or to a sound rebuttal of the notion that values are irreducibly subjective. Some philosophers, recognizing the inadequacy of Goldstein's candidate for objectivity—namely, general agreement in society—have nevertheless refused to abandon their quest for an appropriate criterion for making objective moral judgments (utilitarians, Kantians, and intuitionists have all taken different approaches to this task). Others, however, similarly persuaded that society's agreement that something is right or wrong does not thereby make it right or wrong, have adopted the stance of ethical relativism or ethical subjectivism. For ethical subjectivists—those who maintain that all values are valid only for the individual who holds them ("What's right for me is right for me; what's right for you is right for you")—the "Who decides?" question in medical and other moral contexts assumes great importance. If there is no objectively right or wrong answer to questions about accepting or refusing medical treatments, then the question of who is the appropriate decision maker becomes the only important question to settle.

PARENTAL RIGHTS AND RESPONSIBILITIES

Another troubling feature of Goldstein's statement is his conflation of the rights and responsibilities of parents with the issue of how "well equipped" they are to decide on the best course of action for their children. Parents may be granted the right to decide, and they may bear the responsibility for decisions about medical treatment or treatment refusals for their children. But it is a separate question whether they are "best equipped" to make such decisions. The parents of Chad Green, believing in the efficacy of nutritional therapy and laetrile to combat the form of leukemia their little boy suffered from, abandoned chemotherapy, which is known to have an eighty-percent rate of cure for children in the same age range and having leukemia of the same type as Chad. I do not think that the simple fact that the Greens were Chad's parents rendered them "well equipped" to refuse the standard medical treatment for their child, whatever may be the appropriate criteria for judging when people are well equipped to decide. But whatever their equipment, and leaving open the question of whether or not there is a right or wrong decision in such cases, one might still argue that Chad's parents had the right and the responsibility to make that decision.

For entirely different reasons, I think Phillip Becker's parents were far from well equipped to decide to refuse lifesaving heart surgery for him at age thirteen, surgery that could easily correct his heart defect but would not, of course, improve his mental retardation—the ground on which his parents chose to refuse the proposed surgery.[3] Among other

---

[3]For discussions of this case see George F. Will, "The Case of Phillip Becker," *Newsweek*, 14 April 1980, p. 112; and George J. Annas, "Denying the Rights of the Retarded: The Phillip Becker Case," *Hastings Center Report*, December 1979, pp. 18–20.

things, Phillip Becker had been in a home for handicapped children since birth, and was visited by his parents only infrequently. Goldstein's notion that no one can be presumed to be in a better position than parents to make treatment decisions for their children, and therefore that no one is better equipped to make those decisions, is surely flawed. Yet it remains an open question whether the right to decide nevertheless resides with parents, so long as they are not incompetent, as judged by independent criteria.

A final example in support of this point is that of the parents who granted consent for their retarded children to become research subjects in the Willowbrook hepatitis study. The researchers in that study, which involved deliberately infecting with hepatitis virus children whose parents consented to their participation, defended the experiment by pointing out that virtually all children enrolled in Willowbrook (an institution most of whose inmates were retarded children) contracted hepatitis anyway, and that serving as research subjects afforded these children better living conditions—better hygiene, more attention from staff, less crowding—than others in the institution. There was a long waiting list for Willowbrook, and parents who agreed to enroll their children in the hepatitis study were assured of early admittance. I submit that the fact that these parents were made a "coercive offer" rendered them singularly *ill* equipped to make such a decision for their children, especially in light of their probable anger, frustration, and discomfort in having had to bear and rear a retarded child.

MORAL PRINCIPLES AND DISPUTED VALUES

How valid is the assumption that many (but not all) cases of parental decision making on behalf of minor children have a right and a wrong answer? That assumption is, no doubt, as unacceptable to some readers as it is to Joseph Goldstein. Nevertheless, I suspect there is more agreement—even if it stems only from intuitive beliefs and deeply held moral feelings—on the content of the substantive decisions regarding consent to treatment of or research on children than there is on the procedural, or "Who decides?" question. My own firm belief is that a good many of these cases have *no* right or wrong answer. They reside in the realm of disputed values—a realm populated not by mere tastes, as in preferences for one ice cream flavor or type of cuisine or style of music or art over another. In the moral sphere, this realm is one where different ethical values with roots in different moral traditions collide. When utilitarians and Kantians (or Rawlsians) disagree, they do so not on the basis of mere tastes—that they just happen to like Kant or Rawls or Mill better than his rivals. Instead, adherents of one moral stance or another are convinced, on the basis of the soundness of the arguments, of the compelling features of the central moral principles, or of some crucial aspects of the well-documented facts of the situation, that one moral alternative is morally superior to its competitors.

In some cases, the principles at the heart of different moral traditions all seem compelling. Whether we call it an expression of moral sentiments, an acceptance of moral principles, or an appeal to moral intuitions, most of us incline toward at least one of these ethical viewpoints, and more often than not in our pluralistic society, we adopt more than one. When two or more different moral theories underlie a society's beliefs and practices, the basic precepts of those theories are bound to come into conflict at least sometimes. The issue of "proxy consent," like others in bioethics, appeals to several such traditions at once, and thus raises ethical dilemmas whose resolutions require settling deeper theoretical problems in moral philosophy. When individual rights—of autonomy, privacy, or liberty—clash with what is good for a group or for society as a whole, which values should prevail? How much should cultural tradition, the strongly held religious beliefs of a minority, or other idiosyncratic factors influence broad public policy?

When fundamental principles in the Western ethical and political tradition come into conflict, it produces inconsistent court decisions and a variety of incompatible moral beliefs and attitudes among policy makers as well as among private citizens. Many people experience an irresolvable ambivalence, leading them to acknowledge simultaneously the compelling features of each moral approach. It is not surprising, then, that moral conflicts occur within individuals, as well as among them, when issues like state supervention of parental authority become central ethical and legal concerns.

The most difficult issue of all arises when we ask: What is the source of the objectively right and wrong answers to these questions about parents' decisions on behalf of their minor children? That is a question at the foundations of ethics; it cannot possibly be examined in this book. But it is worth noting one candidate for that objective source: the position advanced by Brown in Chapter 7. In spite of the numerous difficulties of making precise applications of a principle such as Brown's—that parental responsibility entails the development in children of the capability for independence—there are nevertheless objective features of this principle. Those features are spelled out in Brown's account of Rawls's "primary goods." According to Brown, "primary goods for children will surely include education, sound bodies, and an emotional makeup of sufficient stability to render choice and action possible, both as children and, later, as adults." Although this position does not yield a clear or unequivocal mandate regarding specific parental decisions, it does provide some rough guidelines for assessing the rightness or wrongness of parental decisions regarding biomedical procedures. Clearly, Brown's view stands in opposition to that of Goldstein, who denies that any such objectivity is possible.

A cluster of conflicting values lies at the heart of the controversy over state supervention of parental decisions concerning biomedical treatment or research. One source of conflict is the disagreement about whether there is an objectively ascertainable right decision in some or many cases. A second major source of conflict emerges in several of the preceding chapters: the value of preserving family autonomy and privacy against state intrusion versus the value of protecting children, when they cannot speak for themselves, against potentially harmful decisions made by their own parents. This latter source of conflict may well be one of those rock-bottom oppositions of value for which no rational resolution is forthcoming. In that case, it would fall into the realm of disputed values, where reasonable people disagree in their most deeply held moral commitments. It is possible, however, that a partial resolution could be achieved by arriving at a clear and uncontroversial interpretation of the proper sense of "representation."[4] But before looking at the relations among representation, interests, and consent, let us return to an earlier question: How are the "Who decides?" question and the question about the rightness or wrongness of decisions in this realm connected to one another?

RIGHT AND WRONG PARENTAL DECISIONS

To begin, let us allow that it is at least a *meaningful* question to ask what is the right decision in cases where parents must grant consent for treatment or research on their minor children. To say that a question is meaningful is not, of course, to hold that the answer is clear, or uncontroversial, or easy to arrive at. It is simply to hold that contrary to Goldstein's view as analyzed above, granting parents the procedural right and responsibility to decide for their children does not automatically confer substantive rightness on anything they may decide. The possibilities before us are shown in Figure 1.

I have included in this figure two groups of cases in which the state does not intervene at all, either to override or to provide legal endorsement of a parental decision. Although C and D do not bear directly on our inquiry here, some paradigm cases falling in these categories are worth considering since they support the point that there is a right and a wrong decision in a large range of cases.

[4]See Chapter 7.

	STATE SUPERVENES PARENTAL DECISION	STATE DOES NOT INTERVENE
Parents grant Consent to pursue Biomedical procedures on child	A	C
Parents refuse Consent to conduct Biomedical procedures on child	B	D

Figure 1

As an example of a wrong parental decision under C, I suggest the viral hepatitis research at Willowbrook. This illustration is drawn from an experimental rather than a therapeutic context; moreover, the controversy continues even though the events have long since passed. I agree with those who have argued that the research design was morally objectionable, and that both the researchers who conducted the study and the parents who consented on behalf of their children made an objectively, morally wrong decision.[5] I maintain this conclusion even in the face of the impressive results of that project and its follow-up studies, which would probably demonstrate that the research was morally right when judged from a utilitarian perspective. This is not the place to offer all the reasons in support of any particular ethical judgment, but

[5]For further details and discussion, see the "Willowbrook" articles and letters in *Moral Problems in Medicine*, ed. Samuel Gorovitz, Andrew L. Jameton, Ruth Macklin, John M. O'Connor, Eugene V. Perrin, Beverly Page St. Clair, and Susan Sherwin (Englewood Cliffs, N.J.: Prentice-Hall, 1976), pp. 123–142.

the principle I would use in defending my position is something like the Kantian precept that mandates respect for persons, under which both children and the mentally retarded must, as individuals, deserve respect. That principle is in conflict here with the utilitarian precept holding that actions or practices are right insofar as they tend to promote the greatest happiness of the greatest number of people. It is probably true that the Willowbrook hepatitis research resulted in significant and positive benefits, both in the knowledge gained and in its eventual application (development of a vaccine for hepatitis). Nevertheless, this case is one where values besides that of promoting the welfare of the whole must be brought into the moral arena. The judgment that parental decisions to enroll their children in the Willowbrook research project were morally wrong can be defended only by appealing to the rights, the welfare, and the interests of the children who served as experimental subjects. Despite the claims of the researchers that these children actually benefited from serving as research subjects, the chief moral defense of the study must be made on utilitarian grounds. Although such grounds should not always be ruled out in moral arguments—indeed, maximizing desirable consequences is often the only good ground for performing an action—they need to be tempered by considerations of human rights and by taking into account the legitimate interests of the persons involved. Thus, in spite of the fact that no state intervention occurred in the Willowbrook research project, it stands as a paradigm of wrongful decision making on the part of both parents and researchers.

The vast majority of cases in C are surely those in which parents make morally right decisions that further the health and well-being of their children. As for D, the case of Karen, the sixteen-year-old who expressed her wish to withdraw from hemodialysis, is a paradigm of a right parental decision. In a classic case of life versus quality of life, the adolescent and her parents agreed on the choice. In spite of their initial opposition to this decision, which was a painful one for everyone concerned, the medical and nursing personnel eventually concurred without attempting to get a court order. Although I said earlier that quality-of-life cases are chief among those having no clearly right or wrong answer, I think the parents' decision in Karen's case could be judged objectively right, largely because Karen was (psychologically) competent to make the decision herself, just as a legally competent adult would be. The adolescent girl could judge her present quality of life better than anyone else. And there was no chance that that quality could ever improve. Since Karen was a minor, her parents were required to grant consent for cessation of treatment.

It is interesting to speculate on what might have occurred if the parents had refused to grant consent for cessation. Goldstein engages in just such speculation and concludes, not surprisingly, that the state would not have been justified in supervening the parents' judgment. This conclusion could readily be supported by the principle that the wishes of a mature minor should be respected in such cases, although that cannot be the ground on which Goldstein rejects state supervention. That much is clear from the second hypothetical question he poses: "Had Karen insisted, over her parents' objection, on continuing the life-support system would the state have been justified in supervening their judgment?" Goldstein's reply to his own hypothetical question raises the horrifying prospect of the law's allowance of parental tyranny over their children in life-and-death matters: "The answer is 'Yes'—if the state provides, as it should, whatever resources are required to assure full immediate and aftercare for the child. But if the state will not provide such support the answer is an uneasy 'No.' " Goldstein goes on to assert that it is "the function and responsibility of parents to evaluate and make judgments about the wishes and requests of their children." One can readily agree with this benign observation. But does it follow that parents are invariably correct, however their evaluation turns out and whatever the content of their judgments? Goldstein continues: "It is, after all, the meaning of parental autonomy to make such decisions." If such is, indeed, the proper interpretation of "parental autonomy," then it is a notion that may have belonged in Roman law, where the *paterfamilias* had absolute authority over other family members, but that ought to be abandoned *for moral reasons* in the law of the United States of America in the late twentieth century.

To argue further, as Goldstein does, that neither court nor hearing agency is likely to be as competent as were Karen's parents to determine her capacity for choice and whether to abide by it is, first of all, to utter a non sequitur, and second, to carry the notion of an adolescent's "incompetence" to a preposterous extreme. Need anyone—parents, court, or hearing agency—determine the "capacity for choice" of one who asserts a wish to continue living? It may well be necessary to determine the capacity for choice of anyone who elects to die. But choosing to die (by ceasing life-prolonging treatment, in this case) and choosing to go on living, even if one's quality of life is exceedingly poor, are not symmetrical choices with regard to the need to determine the *capacity* for choice. The decision to die requires some explanation, and perhaps also a justification. A person's choice to continue living, however, requires no explanation or justification, and surely no determination of that person's "capacity" so to choose. It is paradigmatic of a moral wrong to leave a sixteen-year-old—hardly a "borderline" age of psychological competence—the victim of a parental judgment on whether to abide by her choice to go on living. That is a consequence, however, of Goldstein's principle of the law's respect for parental autonomy.

Treatment Refusals

The class of cases that concern us most, and that are most numerous, are those falling in B. In this category are a range of treatment refusals, some of which are especially problematic, and some of which I hold are entirely straightforward, having clear-cut moral answers. The latter are those involving blood transfusions for children of Jehovah's Witnesses. The former are cases in which the value of continued life must be weighed against the quality of that life, a balancing act made especially difficult in cancer patients undergoing chemotherapy or radiation treatments. Unlike the cases with children of Jehovah's Witnesses, there is probably no objectively right or wrong decision in these life-versus-quality-of-life cases, whether the patient is terminally ill or not. But although competent adults ought to be allowed to refuse life-prolonging treatment for themselves if they judge the quality of that life to be so diminished that it is not worth preserving, the situation is more problematic with children. The prognosis is a crucial factor when children have a debilitating or life-threatening illness. Although this position remains highly controversial, I hold that it is morally permissible for parents to refuse life-prolonging treatment for their terminally ill child when the therapy is so painful or distressing that the child's quality of life is utterly miserable. State supervention would not be warranted in such cases simply to gain a few more weeks or months of deteriorating life for a child suffering both from a disease and its treatment. The key factor, however, is the prognosis. Although Chad Green had an illness that is often fatal, his "chances," according to reliable medical data, were around eight out of ten for complete recovery if chemotherapy had continued and if the leukemia had remained in remission for eighteen months. A charitable interpretation of the boy's parents would not construe them as fanatics seeking a quack therapy; instead, out of concern for their child's misery, they wanted to abandon further conventional therapy in a desperate search for unproven remedies. Had the prospects for Chad's recovery from leukemia been *much* less (how much less I am unwilling to say), the parents should have retained the right to refuse and state supervention would have been unwarranted.

The following seem to me paradigm cases of morally wrong treatment-refusal decisions made by parents, cases in which I believe the state ought to intervene on behalf of the child's continued life or health: (1) the case of Chad Green; (2) the case of Phillip Becker; (3) all cases in which Jehovah's Witnesses refuse blood transfusions for their child; and (4) the case described below.

> Jim Powley, a fourteen-year-old, was on a summer vacation with his parents, two older brothers, and a younger sister. They were driving to a cabin they had rented in the country. On the way they were involved in a head-on automobile accident, killing the father and two older brothers. Jim Powley's leg was pinned in the wreckage, breaking the femur in two places and crushing some of the thigh muscle and hip. His mother and sister were cut severely but escaped permanent injury.
>
> Jim spent several months hospitalized while the leg began to heal. For the past month he had been at home with his mother providing the nursing care. The orthopedist was now recommending corrective surgery.
>
> Mrs. Powley had not recovered from the trauma of losing her husband and two children. She had developed a pattern of praying every morning and evening for Jim's recovery and had visited him daily during the months he was hospitalized. When the orthopedist asked Mrs. Powley for permission to perform the operation, he explained that the risk was minimal. With the operation Jim would have an excellent chance of complete recovery of the function of the leg, perhaps walking with a slight limp. Without it, there was a 90 percent chance he would lose the use of his leg for life. The greatest risk was from the general anesthesia which, according to the physician, had a risk of about one death in two thousand cases. After reflection, Mrs. Powley said that even though the risk was small, the thought of endangering his life was horrifying. She refused permission to operate, saying, "God's will be done." Jim said he agreed with his mother.[6]

State Supervention of Parental Decisions to Pursue Treatment

We come finally to cases falling in A. These are bound to be somewhat idiosyncratic: parents seek a medical proce-

[6]Robert M. Veatch, *Case Studies in Medical Ethics* (Cambridge: Harvard University Press, 1977), pp. 315–316.

dure for their child and the state intervenes. The rarity of such cases is attributable, in part, to the fact that someone has to act to bring such cases to court. If parents and physicians agree on a course of medical treatment, who is likely to seek legal intervention to prevent such an action? A class of cases that comes readily to mind is that involving sterilization of the mentally retarded.[7] More commonly in the past than now, parents have sought sterilization for their retarded daughters, almost always obtaining the willing compliance of an obstetrician. Although most court cases suing for damages have occurred after those sterilizations had been performed, it is not hard to imagine a case in which an advocate of the retarded might seek a court order to prevent a proposed sterilization. Many states now have legislation designed to protect the mentally retarded from involuntary sterilizations. The situation is somewhat complicated for our purposes by the fact that retarded persons over the age of eighteen are usually deemed legally incompetent, and it is often difficult to obtain a "voluntary" sterilization procedure.

Goldstein discusses a relatively uncommon yet highly pertinent class of cases. These are the unusual circumstances, made possible by advances in modern medicine, in which decisions not involving life or death for one child are made in an effort to save the life of a sibling. Goldstein poses the question as follows:

> Should the state have authority to invade the privacy of a family in order to review the deliberations of parents who have to decide whether to let one of their children die or whether to attempt to supply a life-saving organ for transplant by consenting to "unnecessary" surgery on one of their healthy children?

Goldstein's answer, by now predictable, is negative. The case he goes on to describe did involve a court review, but the

---

[7]For a detailed discussion of this issue, including a history of legal trends, see *Mental Retardation and Sterilization: A Problem of Competency and Paternalism*, eds. Ruth Macklin and Willard Gaylin (New York: Plenum Press, 1981).

reasons the court review was sought were not truly *moral* reasons. They were reasons of self-interest and self-protection on the part of the hospital administration and the doctors, who feared lawsuits on grounds of assault and malpractice. Initially, however, doctors had advised the parents that the only real prospect of saving their one daughter from death as a result of kidney disease was to transplant a kidney from her healthy twin sister. Thus the doctors recommended and the parents consented to "unnecessary" surgery; but fears born of an oppressive legal system of medical malpractice prompted the request for a court review.

My aim in mentioning this case is not to defend the intrusion of the state on the same grounds that its intervention was sought. Instead, the point is to describe still another kind of circumstance which, although rare, might legitimate a court review on *moral* grounds. Is it morally justifiable for parents to decide to invade the body of a normal, healthy child—one who could not speak for herself—in order to save the life of their diseased child? The parental power to authorize such intervention is awesome. Should parents be granted that right? Such cases are among the most difficult to resolve. To reassert an earlier point, it is not at all clear that parents are "best equipped" to make this decision. The terminal illness and impending death of a child is one of the most tragic circumstances to befall a family. Desperate parents might seek any conceivable means to preserve and prolong that life, even a means that requires placing another of their children at risk.

It is surely true that this situation, like many others in the moral arena, gives rise to conflicting judgments among sensitive, reflective people. Parents are not especially well equipped to make decisions in cases regarding their own children. Their emotions, their intense involvement, and their desperation may well make them less than fully rational. They may, nevertheless, be the *appropriate* decision makers, especially where there is no clearly right or wrong course of action. But on the assumption that there is a right and a wrong decision in many of these cases, as in the paradigms proposed above, the problematic question still remains: Should parents have the (moral) right to make such decisions, regardless of the fact that they may sometimes decide wrongly? Or ought the law be invoked to decide, in the hope that in their impartial administration of justice, judges will be more likely to make the morally right decision? Goldstein does not divide the issues in this way, since he reverses the questions. Because, on his view, parents have the right and the responsibility to decide, there can be no "wrong" decisions on their part (subject to the conditions he specifies). I think it is important to separate these questions, thus allowing for the twofold possibility that the law may intervene to supersede a parental decision, or it may allow that decision to stand because the parents have the right and the authority to make it. But that right and authority do *not* thereby render their substantive decisions morally correct.

REPRESENTATION AND "PROXY" CONSENT

Dworkin, in Chapter 6, sketches several interpretations of the concept of representation by way of analogy with political contexts. He argues, correctly, that so-called "proxy" consent is not a species of consent at all. The relevant notion is that of representation, "the idea that under certain conditions some may speak for and make decisions for others." Federal regulations governing the protection of human subjects of biomedical research refer, in their passages on informed consent, to the consent of potential research subjects, or "their legally authorized representative." The problem before us is to determine which of the relevant senses of "representation" that Dworkin spells out is the correct one in the context of parental consent for treatment of or research on their children. If we could settle that much, it might take us at least part way to resolving the question of when state supervention of parental decisions is warranted.

The three main candidates Dworkin identifies as relevant

senses of "representation" parallel three legal explanations of the practice of third-party permission described by Capron in Chapter 4. These roles of the representative decision maker are: (1) substitute judgment ("the person giving permission is able to express the choices which the incompetent would in fact have made because of individualized, subjective knowledge of the incompetent"); (2) best interest ("the person giving permission will make an objectively reasonable choice which comes close to being what the incompetent, as a reasonable person, would want or which will at the least serve the incompetent's interests"); and (3) identity of interests ("the interests of the third party and those of the incompetent are so close that in choosing his or her own interests the third party will protect the interests of the incompetent").

Identity of Interests

This legal doctrine is the most likely basis for Goldstein's wholesale endorsement of parental authority to decide for their children. According to this view, the independent determination of a child's interest need not occur or even be possible. In its extreme form, it asserts that the interests of parents and their minor children are identical; whatever the parents *decide* is in their children's interest *is* in the latter's interest. Despite this untenable extreme, there is a sensible core to the identity-of-interests position, presented convincingly by Steinfels in her discussion of family privacy and family autonomy in Chapter 8. The sensible aspect rests on several assumptions, chief among which is that because children gain a great many of their values from their parents beginning very early in life, it is reasonable to expect them (while still young, at least) to have internalized those values and thus for their interests to coincide with those of their parents. Note, however, that this assumption presupposes that children can be said to have interests of their own—interests that may or may not be identical with those of their parents or of the family unit as a whole. It is an empirical matter whether the interests of parents and children coincide in any given instance, so long as there is a meaningful notion of children's interests independent of those of their parents.

A second sound assumption underlying the identity-of-interests view is that children's interests are better served when the family remains a harmonious, autonomous unit, free from the strife and turmoil likely to ensue when the state intervenes. Parents can probably better perform their nurturing and childrearing tasks when the family is intact and when its values remain strong. But this assumption, too, presupposes that children have interests that can be identified independently from those of their parents. The difficulty with the identity-of-interests view, however, is that it can too easily degenerate into an extreme position—as embodied, for example, in treatment refusals by Jehovah's Witness parents. If those parents, in accordance with their own beliefs, judge that their child is better off dead as a result of not having received a lifesaving blood transfusion than alive but with a soul condemned to eternal damnation, then the identity-of-interests doctrine would have to deem the interests of parents and child identical.

Freedom of religious belief and action is a deeply cherished value in our society, but not so inviolable that it can sanction any action whatever in the name of those First Amendment rights. Members of a religious cult demanding the sacrifice of the firstborn child would not be allowed to practice that ritual in our society. Mormons have been prohibited by law from engaging in polygamy, a practice that has much less drastic consequences for its victims than death. The law has allowed competent Jehovah's Witness adults to refuse lifesaving blood transfusions for themselves. But the law has not permitted Jehovah's Witness parents to refuse transfusions necessary to save the life of their minor children. If the identity-of-interests doctrine were to prevail in this sphere, it would be hard to rebut the contention that the interest of children of Jehovah's Witnesses is precisely what their parents deem it to be. Happily for the many children whose lives have been saved by court orders, their interests have been construed as separate and distinct from those of their parents.

Best Interest

The best-interests doctrine requires little comment, since it has been the prevailing legal rule in this domain, and its precepts and shortcomings are well-known. The views Goldstein espouses in Chapter 5 are well documented and fully elaborated in his book *Beyond the Best Interests of the Child*.[8] One can have little quarrel with the claim that a great many efforts to serve the best interests of children have been flawed through mistakes, ignorance, rigidity, and poor judgment on the part of those who applied and administered the law.[9] Furthermore, the situations children actually find themselves in as a result of efforts on the part of others to serve their best interests often turn out worse than those chosen by their parents in the first place. Many criticisms of the way the best-interests doctrine has been interpreted, applied, and administered are utterly well founded. Where, however, is the evidence that keeping the state out of family affairs altogether leads to better results? It is at least reasonable to hold that the fewer battered children (spouses, too, for that matter) the better. Which alternative or outcome is to be preferred has an irreducible value component, one that cannot be resolved merely by looking at data about outcomes or generalizations from clinical cases. One must attach a value to these alternative outcomes; the question of just what value should be assigned to which outcomes provokes a deeper ethical debate. In the extreme cases at hand, preserving the life or limb of

[8]Joseph Goldstein, Anna Freud, and Albert J. Solnit, *Beyond the Best Interests of the Child* (New York: Free Press, 1979).
[9]See, in addition to Goldstein, the similar position argued by Steinfels in Chapter 8, as well as the references she cites.

a child is pitted against family autonomy, family privacy, or the position that the child's best interest has no meaning apart from what is determined by his or her parents. In the more moderate cases, matters of life and death are not at stake, but matters of disfigurement, crippling, and poor lifelong health may well be.[10] Although the best-interests doctrine is no doubt flawed, the proposed alternatives do not necessarily seem superior.

Substitute Judgment

I have left the substitute-judgment position for last, since this remaining candidate for deciding who represents the child's interests links the topics discussed so far with our other major line of inquiry: the competence of children as self-deciders. The substitute-judgment doctrine rests on the precept that the representative has "individualized, subjective knowledge of the incompetent." Now the "incompetent," in the case of adolescent and even younger children, is incompetent by virtue of the law's need for a fixed, chronological age.[11] It is not a *psychological* judgment that a minor under eighteen or sixteen is incompetent. That judgment, in the case of adolescent and even younger children, is a purely legal one, unlike with other special populations such as the senile or the mentally ill where it is a mixed—that is, both legal and psychological—concept.

Of what, precisely, is the representative supposed to have individualized, subjective knowledge in regard to the incompetent? In Capron's words, "the person giving permission is able to express the choices that the incompetent would in fact have made." In situations where the incompetent person was once competent, such as one who has become mentally ill or senile, the subjective knowledge a close

[10]See Goldstein's discussion of "Non-Life-or-Death Decisions."
[11]For exceptions to the use of a fixed, chronological age, and for current trends in the law, see Chapter 3.

relative has of that person's hypothetical choices is drawn from familiarity with the now incompetent person's formerly competent self. It may even be based on values or wishes the incompetent person has expressed recently in moments of lucidity or rationality. But this notion of inferred consent breaks down when the incompetent person is an infant or a young child who has not yet acquired a value system or a set of wishes or preferences. Thus the substitute-judgment doctrine cannot meaningfully be applied in cases where the incompetent person was never (or has not yet been) capable of making judgments or expressing wishes of his own. One of the other two senses of "representation" must then be operative.

As children grow older, however, it is reasonable to think of them as acquiring a value system and a set of preferences of their own that will develop into their adult beliefs and values. For children who have attained this state of "developing competence," their parents' individualized subjective knowledge of them is supposed to be used in rendering the substitute judgment. But as Dworkin points out, in the case of the substitute-judgment doctrine "there is no assumption that the choice being made is the 'correct' or 'right' one." If parents are to occupy this role of representing their child's interests in cases of biomedical treatment or research, they do nothing other than rubber-stamp the child's expressed wishes in the matter. Substitute judgment, then, is tantamount to treating the child as a competent self-decider. If the law does not recognize minors as competent to decide, that can be remedied by parents who adhere strictly to their own children's wishes, faithfully transmitting those wishes through consent procedures. Substitute judgment, then, would yield exactly the same substantive decisions as would recognizing children as legally competent.

But how many parents would go along with their child's decision if they believed that decision to be foolish or self-destructive? More important, however, is the normative question: How *should* the parents of, say, an adolescent who firmly expresses his or her wishes respond when their beliefs about the right course of action clash? Brown's principle of primary parental responsibility speaks clearly to this point:

> parental responsibility consists in securing for their children the capability of achieving those primary goods that are necessary for successful participation in the central institutions of the society in which the child can reasonably be expected to live as an adult (unless those institutions are themselves morally pernicious).

Brown explicitly rejects the substitute-judgment doctrine on the ground that it offers little guidance, at least in the case of very young children. He also states the clear priority of the principle of primary parental responsibility over any other doctrine of how parents should act in representing their children's interests:

> Where the child's wishes and those of the parent coincide, there is little or no issue. Where they do not, I think that different thresholds are generally applicable. Children who fail to consent to procedures necessary for the securing of primary goods should be required to do so.

Brown introduces a qualification, however, in cases where children are below but near the age of majority and have taken steps to demonstrate independence of the parent (marriage, establishing a separate domicile, or economic self-support).

Dworkin, too, holds that

> we ought to choose for [children], not as they might want, but in terms of maximizing those interests that will make it possible for them to develop life plans of their own. We ought to preserve their share of what Rawls calls "primary goods"; that is, such goods as liberty, health, and opportunity, which any rational person would want to pursue whatever particular life plan he chooses.

The Competence of Minors as Self-Deciders

Gaylin, in Chapter 2, offers the boldest and most detailed prescription for treating minors as competent to decide for themselves about biomedical procedures. After outlining six categories of conditions that generally limit people's capability to make autonomous decisions (limits of consciousness, intelligence, rationality, perception, experience, and age), Gaylin presents a grid with several dimensions along which the competence of minors may be determined. His account has the virtue of placing the concept of competence on as objective a footing as possible, according to what is now known about child development and the capacity of adolescents for sound judgment where their own interests are concerned. At the same time, Gaylin examines these objective considerations against a series of elements that spell out what is at stake in the particular biomedical interventions: the degree of risk, the degree of gain, the amount of social benefit or cost, and the nature of the decision itself. He thus constructs a concept of variable competence, one that is relativized to the multiple factors he describes. The application of this grid to cases that come before the law would no doubt yield a different set of judgments from those that Capron, by successive modifications of case law and statutes, arrives at in Chapter 3. But whereas case law must proceed slowly and incrementally, based on precedents and time-honored legal principles, a proposal such as Gaylin's is grounded in a mixture of theoretical and practical knowledge about children and in an assessment of changing social values, along with the desire to fashion some consistency of approach across different areas of biomedical treatment and research. Gaylin's account thus occupies a rational, objective middle ground between the unacceptable extremes of nearly total parental domination over their minor children until they reach a uniform age of majority fixed by law, and the radical perspective of children's liberation described (but not endorsed) by Steinfels.

A peculiar blend of facts and values underlies each of the various principles espoused by the authors of this book. These fact–value mixtures embrace different beliefs about the following: the capacity of children to make wise decisions for themselves (psychological competence); the desirability of allowing children, even if (psychologically) competent, to have ultimate decision-making authority that may conflict with what their parents would decide for them; the sense in which there is a "best interest" for children, independent of what their parents say it is; precisely what representative role, among the three discussed above, parents ought to play in granting or refusing consent for their children; and the weight that should be accorded family autonomy and family privacy in the face of other values that directly conflict with them.

JUSTIFIED PATERNALISM: CHILDREN, PARENTS, AND THE STATE

Only the most extreme proponents of children's liberation would maintain that if children were permitted to make autonomous decisions to accept or reject biomedical procedures, whatever decisions they might make would be substantively correct, that is, in their own best interest. It follows, then, that to lower the age of consent would be to open the door to a greater number of cases of state intervention, simply because various agents, speaking on behalf of the child, would surely come forward. Leaving aside the role parents would play under such circumstances, I wish to consider the question of the legitimacy of the state overriding a minor's decision. It seems to me that even those of us who would be willing to see the laws governing the age of consent liberalized somewhat or at least made more flexible—for example, along the lines Gaylin proposes—would nevertheless remain eager to have the state retain its protective stance toward minors' interests. Moreover, there is no inconsistency in that position. It is perfectly consistent to be prepared to grant more autonomy generally to minors (adolescents in particular) while still supporting a paternalistic role for the state in protecting children against foolish, self-destructive choices. If we are reluctant to allow the law this same paternalistic interference into the lives of competent adults, it is probably because where children's welfare is at stake there is a legitimate place for "justified paternalism." Contrary to those who hold that the phrase "justified paternalism" is self-contradictory, I maintain that the term "paternalism" can be seen as a value-neutral, descriptive term, and that *some* paternalistic interferences with an individual's liberty can be justified.

Paternalism has gotten an especially bad press in recent years, particularly from liberals, libertarians, advocates of special populations (the mentally retarded and the mentally ill)—in sum, proponents of individual rights. Some public policy manifestations of this reaction against paternalism are the deinstitutionalization movement of the last two decades; legislation barring involuntary sterilization of the mentally retarded even in cases where evidence suggests it is in their best interests; judicial decisions that support mental patients' refusal of antipsychotic medication; and even the upholding of patients' rights to refuse lifesaving and life-prolonging medical treatment. Yet if there ever was a paradigm of justified paternalism, it remains in the very domain from which such actions derive their name: treating children in a "fatherly" (and "motherly") manner.

Debates are bound to continue over at just what age of children, and in just what circumstances, justifiable paternalism turns into unwarranted tyranny of parents over their offspring. But the difficulty of drawing sharp lines, and the impossibility of arriving at a set of necessary and sufficient conditions, should not confuse us into thinking that there is no sound basis for paternalism with regard to children. A useful philosophical method to use here is that of paradigms—the identification of clear cases of a problematic concept under investigation. Unlike the alternative approach of searching for hard and fast criteria for applying a concept, the paradigms method proceeds by identifying the relevant features of the paradigms and seeing how closely new instances approximate those key features. Although this method leaves an inevitable gray area of disputed instances, that situation always exists in practice, even if law or psychiatric theory purports to provide criteria for applying difficult concepts.

What the method of paradigms lacks in precision it gains in being an honest, readily applicable approach to the sorts of decisions that arise in law, public policy, and moral choice.

The undisputed paradigm of justifiable paternalism is the proper treatment of infants and very young children. I concur with Gaylin's statement in Chapter 2:

> But there is one place where paternalism cannot be abandoned, and that is in the relationship of parent to child. Here an abandonment of parental authority would be an act of immorality, as well as a failure in nurturing. The good parent does not just nurture to a point of maturation; he is expected to inhibit self-destructive impulses; he is expected to substitute his superior judgment for the short vision of the child; he is expected to use education, persuasion, seduction, and even force and coercion when necessary in the service of producing a healthy and independent adult.

The goals of parenting that Gaylin specifies are similar to those cited by Brown under his main thesis: "Parental responsibility is to care for their children—and . . . this caring entails the development in children of the capability for independence . . ." Explicitly included as elements in such independence are "education, absence of anxiety, and basic health."

Now if it is the duty and responsibility of parents to act toward their children in the way Gaylin and Brown urge, then certain consequences follow both for the question of children as self-deciders regarding biomedical procedures and also for the question of state intervention. One thing that clearly follows is that children may be mistaken about what is in their own interest. If a child exhibits "short vision" in rejecting a medical treatment that would aid in furthering his later independence or his ability to secure primary goods, then it is a parent's duty to override that poor judgment and to consent to the therapy on the child's behalf. If we allow that a child can be mistaken in rejecting a medical treatment, or even in refusing to serve as a research subject (as in Gaylin's telling example in Chapter 2), and that parental responsibility lies in correcting such mistakes, then a child cannot be considered the ultimate judge of his or her own interest. In serving as representatives of their children's interests, parents must be assumed to be wiser by virtue of greater knowledge and experience, and thus better able to make good decisions.

But if children can be wrong in these ways about what is in their own interest—where "interest" is construed in terms of long-range goals, as Gaylin and Brown suggest— why cannot parents themselves similarly be wrong about what is in their children's interests? To be wiser and more experienced is to be more likely to make good decisions; it does not confer infallibility.

NON-LIFE-OR-DEATH TREATMENT DECISIONS

Doubts will surely linger, however, about the objectivity of the rightness and wrongness of parental decisions. Those who adhere to a view such as Goldstein's believe that virtually all values—including moral values—are subjective. I have acknowledged that there are many hard cases, cases of disputed values in which there is no clearly right or wrong answer, or at least no available method for determining it. That may well be the status of a range of such cases as *Seiferth* and *Sampson*. In *Sampson*, fifteen-year-old Kevin Sampson had a large, disfiguring growth on his face (neurofibromatosis). The boy's mother refused to allow any necessary blood transfusions during surgery. After testimony by doctors who recommended the operation, although they admitted that the disease was not life-threatening and that surgery was risky and did not offer a certain cure, the judge declared Kevin a neglected child and ordered a series of operations recommended by the commissioner of health and a number of surgeons.

For non-life-or-death cases, Goldstein advances a principle that is consistent with the one he uses for life-or-death decisions but more extreme in its absolute rejection of state intervention:

> When death is not a likely consequence of exercising a medical care choice there is no justification for governmental intrusion on family privacy; nor is there justification for overcoming the presumption of either parental autonomy or the autonomy of emancipated children.

Goldstein supports this principle with the assertion that such choices rest on a "personal preference for a certain style of living"; that Kevin's mother was best qualified to determine the meaning of a "normal and happy existence" for her son; and that "the power of the state must not be employed to reenforce prejudice and discrimination against those who are cosmetically or otherwise different." In sum, Goldstein views the values at stake as mere matters of taste, of personal preference, and of lifestyle choices. He rejects the likelihood that this adolescent, afflicted with what was described as a "grotesque" facial deformity, had suffered psychological disturbance or impaired personality development, and thus accuses the judge who raised those prospects of arrogance, of performing an act of conjury, and of declaring himself "prophet, psychological expert, and all-knowing parent." Goldstein himself, however, apparently accords considerable weight to the testimony of a staff psychiatrist who claimed that Kevin showed no evidence of any thinking disorder, and that in spite of marked facial disfigurement the boy failed to show any outstanding personality aberration.

One need not possess psychiatric expertise in order to judge that these factors are hardly appropriate criteria for assessing the case at hand. The problem for this unfortunate adolescent is one of emotional stability and psychological development, of poor body image and a diminished sense of self—not of psychosis ("thinking disorder") or character disorder ("outstanding personality aberration"). In fact, Goldstein points out in a footnote that a psychologist had found Kevin extremely dependent, and the same staff psychiatrist said that the boy demonstrated "inferiority feeling and low self concept." How much evidence needs to be brought forward before a judgment can be removed from the realm of taste to that of moral import? Goldstein acknowledges a psychologist's finding that Kevin was "extremely dependent," a trait that, when possessed by a fifteen-year-old, is already in conflict with Brown's goal of parenting: eventual independence for the child. Further evidence "revealed that the child's deformity prompted social isolation and compelled his withdrawal from school, leaving him virtually illiterate in his teens."[12] One need not amass vast evidence or appeal to obscure findings to assert confidently that in our society illiteracy is clearly against a person's best interest. To be virtually illiterate as a teen-ager, along with the burden of facial disfigurement, is an almost certain guarantee of personal misery. We must weigh these factors against the probable accuracy of Goldstein's judgment that

> under the protective cloak of family privacy, a loving, caring, accepting, autonomous parent had somehow been able to nurture in Kevin a "healthy personality." Kevin, after all, had developed in spite of state-reenforced prejudice and discrimination against the physically different in school, health agency, and court.

Numerous psychological, conceptual, and ethical issues are intertwined in this case and others like it. What should count as "gross disfigurement"? Are such judgments merely matters of aesthetic taste or subjective "lifestyle" choice? Should ethical judgments about the right thing to do rely on psychological facts or psychiatric evidence, such as the degree to which gross disfigurement is psychologically damaging? What constitutes psychological *damage*? And on what basis should conflicting "expert" judgments be adjudicated? Some "facts" are heavily value-laden; some values are matters of individual taste, such as preferences for hair length and cloth-

[12]Stuart J. Baskin, "State Intrusion into Family Affairs," *Stanford Law Review* 26 (1974): 1398, n. 74.

ing styles; other values are embedded in deeply held moral precepts of humaneness and human dignity. There may indeed be wide disagreement over what constitutes a "normal, healthy life." But it is nevertheless true that children should be given a fair chance in life, whenever possible. In order to get that fair chance, they need to look sufficiently normal, which in turn influences their prospects for acquiring autonomy, developing independence, and achieving a reasonable degree of success in school and later life. Equally important for most people is the opportunity to have adequate, fulfilling sexual relationships. Are these merely "lifestyle preferences"? In fact, there are good psychological and sociological grounds for holding that deformities and disfigurements may be sufficiently harmful to the quality of a person's life to warrant overriding the judgment of parents who are blind to or care little about what is at stake.

It is worth pointing out, however, that Kevin Sampson's mother refused surgery for her son *not* on any of these lifestyle preferences or aesthetic choices, but because of a religious opposition to blood transfusions. Goldstein's argument, therefore, appears to be an instance of the type of informal logical fallacy known as *ignoratio elenchi*, the fallacy of irrelevance: it draws a conclusion from an argument that is entirely irrelevant to the premises at hand. Had Kevin's mother defended her refusal of surgery for her son on an aesthetic argument (the Elephant Man was a truly beautiful person), or on Kevin's prospects for success in spite of disfigurement (Immanuel Kant was a hunchback; Attila the Hun was four feet tall), Goldstein's argument would have been relevant (although still mistaken). But Mrs. Sampson was apparently a Jehovah's Witness, and so to be relevant an argument defending her decision must address the right of parents to reject recommended non-life-or-death surgery for their children on grounds of religious freedom. This argument, admittedly, is a harder one to rebut than one that rests on a concept of "relatively normal life," but the judge's contentions and the medical testimony would still be relevant to the case.

RETURN TO THE BEST INTERESTS OF THE CHILD

Which sense of "representative" ought to apply to decisions made on behalf of children for biomedical procedures? It cannot be the sense associated with the substitute-judgment doctrine. For one thing, if children can make wrong decisions on their own behalf, parents who override those decisions in granting or refusing consent are not acting as "substitute judges" in the way that doctrine implies. They are not deciding as the incompetent "would decide, if competent," since there is no way of knowing what children will, in fact, choose when old enough to be considered competent. Furthermore, being competent is no guarantee, as we have seen, of making wise or correct decisions; therefore, parents will and *should* make decisions they at least *believe* correct when empowered to do so on behalf of their own children.

Nor is the identity-of-interest doctrine satisfactory. If a child's interest is not simply what the child says it is, why should it be simply what the parent says it is? If children can be mistaken about what is in their interests, there must be something to be mistaken about. Although the probability that parents will make sound judgments about their child's interests is considerably higher than that the child will, they too are fallible.

The only remaining candidate, then, is the best-interests doctrine. The notion of representation one finds most relevant probably rests on antecedent beliefs and values about what are the morally right outcomes in these issues. I suggested earlier that Goldstein must be adhering to the identity-of-interest sense of parental representation, since that is the doctrine most likely to yield the outcome he seeks (that is, no state supervention). Similarly, when I opt for the best-interests doctrine (in spite of its acknowledged shortcomings), it is because I think many decisions parents make on behalf of their children do have substantively right or wrong content. When parents decide wrongly, the state should supervene those decisions in seeking to promote the child's best interest.

I have tried, by offering several paradigms, to present some clear examples of right and wrong parental decisions. Underlying those paradigms are normative principles, such as those put forward by Brown and Gaylin, that specify objective factors for determining whether or not a child's best interest is being served. Like any other legal or moral principles, those underlying the best-interests doctrine should not be applied dogmatically. Evidence should always be sought to back up a judgment in a particular case. Data about cases that are similar in relevant respects should be incorporated in a careful decision-making process. Even when honest, conscientious people make every effort to take these factors into account, mistakes will occur and children will end up suffering.

In adopting the best-interests perspective one should be especially alert to the tensions pulling in the other direction, which stem from the competing values of respect for family autonomy and family privacy. When these latter values come into conflict with the objectively determined best interest of a child, which should prevail?

To me the answer is clear. It is the best interest of the child that should prevail. Among other things, it is empirically unlikely that state supervention of a family decision will destroy the family unit or make permanent inroads into its autonomy. One invasion of family privacy must be weighed against perhaps a lifetime of health, well-being, or bodily integrity for the child on whose behalf the state seeks to intervene. And in some cases the lifetime may be a matter of hours or days—if, for example, Jehovah's Witness parents are allowed to have rights of final refusal. It is important to weigh any potential damage to the family unit against the potential damage to the child. It is possible to accord a great deal of respect to family autonomy, and to hold a deep commitment to family integrity, and at the same time to recognize that close and loving family units are in no great danger of being destroyed by an occasional outside intervention aimed at serving the best interests of a child.

Index

303